TEACHING YEAR FIVE

Primary teacher

GW00506096

Edited by Lucy Hall

Published by Scholastic Ltd.
Villiers House
Clarendon Avenue
Leamington Spa
Warwickshire CV32 5PR
Text © 1999 Nick Phillips; David Waugh; Peter Clarke; Terry Jennings; Paul Noble;
Margaret Mackintosh; Dorothy Tipton; Gillian Robinson; Pauline Boorman; Richard Ager;
Lynn Newton; Douglas Newton; Geoffrey Teece
© 1999 Scholastic Ltd.
1 2 3 4 5 6 7 8 9 0   9 0 1 2 3 4 5 6 7 8

Authors

Nick Phillips, David Waugh, Peter Clarke, Terry Jennings, Paul Noble,
Margaret Mackintosh, Dorothy Tipton, Gillian Robinson, Pauline Boorman, Richard Ager,
Lynn Newton, Douglas Newton, Geoffrey Teece

Series Editor
Lucy Hall

Editor
Helen Skelton

Series Designer
Lynne Joesbury

Designer
David Hurley

Illustrations
Ray and Corinne Burrows

Cover photograph
Fiona Pragoff

Designed using Adobe Pagemaker

British Library Cataloguing-in-Publication Data
A catalogue record for this book is available from the British Library

ISBN 0 590 53823 3

Contents

Preface

Primary school teachers don't say, as secondary teachers would, 'I teach history'. They say 'I teach year 4s' or 'I teach a reception class'. Why, then, have all the books for primary teachers been wholly subject-orientated? It seems that primary teachers are supposed to buy about 13 different books and read through them all to extract the relevant bits.

It was about 20 years ago that the thought occurred to me that it would make teachers' lives much easier if all the information about teaching their year group was provided in *one* book. Since then I have been waiting for someone to do it. But no-one did. So, finally, fourteen different authors, Scholastic and I have put together the seven *Primary Teacher Yearbooks*.

I should like to thank all the authors. They faced a difficult task in tailoring their writing to a common format and structuring their guidance, about what to teach and what to expect from children, so that it correlated with the seven different stages of the primary school. They have all been extremely patient.

Particular thanks are due to Paul Noble, who not only wrote 13 chapters in the series, but was also deeply involved in the development of the project from the very beginning. His practical, knowledgeable advice and cheerful imperturbability kept the whole project stuck together.

We all hope that you will find your Yearbook useful and that it meets your needs – whichever class you teach.

Lucy Hall, Series Editor

Your Class

Getting started

Planning your classroom

There is no single answer to effective classroom organization. It is, though, essential that the teaching areas available to you are thoughtfully planned and organized in an appropriate way for Year 5 children.

Your classroom is a workshop. It has to allow for a variety of activities, be conducive to learning, and be sufficiently flexible to meet a wide range of needs. Before you begin in the classroom, follow these steps:

- make sure you know what the school expects from you – check all relevant documentation and discuss your ideas with another member of staff;
- spend time planning – consider the space available, keep notes of your ideas, list the furniture and equipment;
- draw an outline plan of the room, including the main fixtures – mark on it where the power points, sink, radiators and wall boards are;
- photocopy the plan several times and file the master in a safe place!

On each plan, start to develop your ideas until you have a practical design with which you feel comfortable. When planning in this way, consider:

- where the 'gathering' area will be;
- whether you will need a role-play area;
- where the class library should be;
- how large any practical area should be;
- which is the best place for the computer(s).

While you might appreciate having a number of areas in your room, the general teaching space should be of a sufficient size. Consider:

- arrangements for the Literacy and Numeracy Hours;
- how many groups you should have;
- how large these groups might be;
- how they can best be arranged in the room;
- how the children will be organized – friendship groups/mixed-ability or ability groups for different activities;
- whether you will have a desk;
- whether all the children can see the board.

Much of this will reflect your teaching style and the strategies you intend to employ in the classroom.

Organize and store your resources with care. Only the materials and equipment that the children will be using regularly need to be immediately available. Put other items away until they are required. Piles or corners of unwanted, unused materials will be confusing for the class, take up valuable space and detract from displays and the appearance of your classroom. Label the areas, storage trays, racks and cupboards.

Establish a Year 5 classroom which encourages independence and responsibility. Develop a sense of ownership and pride so that the children feel that it is their space. These are important principles and the foundations for the future.

Display

Displays should work for children, not children for displays. With this as your guiding principle, plan for appropriate areas in your room. You do not need to rely solely on fixed wall boards as you should be able to use the backs of furniture and other movable items. These will often create effective centres of interest and areas for interactive displays.

Encourage children to contribute to displays. This may include bringing artefacts in from home,

mounting their own work and deciding upon how items should be displayed. Year 5s should be taking an increasing responsibility. You could designate an area in the classroom which they organize to display evidence of achievements.

Roughly planning a display on paper beforehand can be helpful. If you are unsure about heights, spacing or range, ask a colleague to comment.

When preparing a display:
- avoid written work on lined paper;
- rarely display unmounted work;
- take care with the backing paper or fabric you choose or provide for the children to select from;
- make sure the display has a title and that children's work is named.

Draw attention to your displays. Use them to promote good quality and individual children's self-esteem as well as achievements. Take care that your classroom includes a range of children's work on display, including, if possible something from each member of the class, and that you are not providing free publicity for the sunflower (or any other) industry!

The children

Children need security. It is your responsibility to establish a sound organization in your classroom with routines that they understand. Together, draw up a positive behaviour policy for all class members, with a recognized reward and punishment scheme. Year 5 children should be able to participate fully and thoughtfully in this sort of exercise. Explain to the children:
- how the classroom is organized and why;
- how they will be operating in the room;
- why they are sitting where they are;
- where all the resources are kept;
- how equipment should be used and maintained;
- what to do when they first enter the classroom in the morning;
- how they should attract your attention when they need help;
- where finished work should be put.

Invite their input on these practical matters and listen carefully to their suggestions, incorporating them where possible. A classroom that is thoughtfully planned, with appropriate resources and a structure that supports and challenges the children, will help you to work together.

Social and emotional development

Children of this age will normally be confident and well established in the school. They will look towards their Year 6 contemporaries for a lead but, at the same time, may 'lord it' over younger age groups. It is possible that, as the year progresses, friction will develop between groups in Years 5 and 6. This will be a school issue but something you should be aware of. By Year 5, children's experience of 'growing up' will have been very different. You should always look behind their immediate behaviour for possible reasons that cause it. Unfortunately, the sexual abuse of children is not uncommon. Sexually precocious children or children who are withdrawn or exhibit uncharacteristic behaviour will need urgent help and support. You may be the first adult they try to confide in. While you cannot be expected to right all wrongs, it is your responsibility to be vigilant and to pass on your concerns immediately.

Concentration, motivation and responsibility

Levels of concentration and motivation will vary for a variety of reasons which include general maturity, past experiences of success and failure and specific needs. Look carefully at the time available to you during the week and timetable your days to allow for reasonable periods but with plenty of changes during the day. Consider these points:
- have at least three periods of physical education each week on different days, include drama on a different day from PE;
- for the majority of the week, use the morning sessions for your language- and mathematics-based activities when concentration will be better;
- introduce a quiet period of reading after lunch to encourage the children to settle back into a 'working mode';
- during any extended periods that you may have, change around the groups, the activities and your focus.

Keep the children actively involved, with periods of stimulation and opportunities for reflection. Maintain a balance, plan carefully and use your antennae to control each session.

Year 5 children need to be given independence and responsibilities. This is not only as preparation for their future, but also as preparation for taking over the Year 6 mantle at the end of the year. You should look for opportunities to demonstrate your trust in them.

Responsibilities might include:
- helping with the younger children at lunch time;
- representing the school at public events in the community;
- working with community groups.

Other responsibilities will include matters relating to homework, acting as leaders when involved in group activities and monitors' duties in the classroom. Encourage the development of this discipline so that the children leave you as independent and responsible members of the school community.

Respect for property

Children will come to school with a variety of experiences and values. The values that you and the school attempt to instil and develop may not reflect their lives at home. This presents the child with a dilemma and will be confusing.

As with so many aspects of being a teacher, you need to demonstrate the 'how' and 'why' by your example. Develop a climate in your classroom where the children respect school equipment, where their own belongings are safe and where children are confident to confide in you. If you

can win the children over by being genuinely interested so that they sense that you are batting for them, your expressed disappointment at any breakdown in the established code will be more effective than the subsequent punishment.

Friendships

The relationships that exist and develop between the children will have a significant influence on the ethos and attitude of the class. You will need to decide if the children are to sit in 'friendship groups' or whether you will set their places. Avoid single-sex groupings where possible. Find out which friendships are positive for learning and which are not. Teachers who have had the class before will be able to help and parents will normally tell you if there is a particular problem you need to be aware of. It is a balancing act: ensuring that you have children together who will motivate each other and are not antagonistic while, at the same time, avoiding pairings or groupings that are too friendly and where the social exchanges interfere with their learning. One strategy to consider is to have flexible groupings for different activities. A degree of social interaction in an art group can be quite acceptable while a tricky mathematical problem or written composition may require periods of isolation.

Changes at home

The birth of a new brother or sister, while being an exciting family event, can have an effect on the behaviour, attitude and performance of children. Changes at home may result in less attention, and feelings of insecurity. You will need to be aware of these. Give children opportunities to talk to you about how they feel and help them to understand that they will remain just as important once all the initial euphoria has subsided.

Other changes in circumstances, such as parents' separation or divorce, a parent in prison or the death of a relative, will have a dramatic effect. A change in character will be the first symptom: for example, the outgoing, confident child who becomes withdrawn; the friendly, popular pupil who is suddenly falling out with friends; the happy child who is moody and difficult in class.

Your relationship with the child is crucial. If you do notice a change in behaviour or attitude, seek the child out at an appropriate time. Gently encourage him/her to talk to you. Explain what you have noticed and provide reassurance that you are concerned and want to help. At the same time, ask around. Check if a letter has come in to the school office. Talk to the headteacher and, if you do have an opportunity to see the parents in the playground, let them know that you are concerned. After discussing the matter with the headteacher, you may decide that you need to

make a more formal contact with the parents by telephone or by writing to them, inviting them to come and see you.

The important point is that you need to appreciate what the problem is, so that you can guide and support the child and modify your response accordingly.

Health education
Substance abuse

Children of this age will be well aware of substance abuse, mainly through their exposure to news items, television and contact with other age groups. They may very well be tempted.

Understand the signs and symptoms and educate the children about substance abuse. The school nurse and local police liaison officer will normally be pleased to be involved and offer training as well as spending time working with the children.

If you ever detect a change in a child's behaviour or personality that might be attributed to substance abuse, inform the headteacher immediately.

Sex education

The policy on sex education is the responsibility of the school's governors. They will decide whether it is to form part of the school's curriculum. Find out what your governors' policy says. If you do not feel comfortable with any elements allocated to the Year 5 curriculum, discuss the matter with the headteacher. You are able to 'opt out' if you so wish.

Before you embark on any sex education, inform the parents. You may find it helpful to organize a special meeting with parents where you can outline what will be included and share any material, such as videos, that you will be using with the children.

Parents will need to know when the lessons will be taking place, whether any other members of staff or the school nurse will be involved and how they can support their children's learning.

This is not an easy subject and many children will find it embarrassing. It can affect their behaviour during the lessons, so you need to maintain a professional and factual manner at all times.

By Year 5 some girls may have reached puberty. Make it easy for parents or carers to discuss this with you confidentially so that you can tell them about the arrangements in school and reassure the child. Remember to inform other members of staff with whom the children have contact, especially those who take PE.

Citizenship and moral development
Racial prejudice/multicultural issues

Your school will have a written statement about guaranteeing equal opportunities to all who work in the school. As one of your responsibilities, you have to encourage this principle and monitor what actually happens.

You are in an influential position. Your behaviour and attitude will affect the tolerance and opinions of your children. Any form of harassment will demand an immediate and effective response from you. This will involve dealing with the children in an appropriate way, reporting to the headteacher and informing the parents concerned. Reports may also need to be submitted to the local authority.

Racial harassment can take many different forms, including:
- name calling; ridiculing children because of the colour of their skin or their language;
- the threat of physical violence;
- racist abuse, insults, jokes, verbal threats;
- refusal to co-operate with children or adults in school because of the colour of their skin, race, religion or language.

Encourage the children in your class to talk to you about any racist behaviour. As part of the curriculum, children need opportunities to learn and develop informed attitudes. Promote tolerance, but do not be tolerant of any racist behaviour. If an incident occurs, make sure that you establish the facts correctly. Demonstrate to the children concerned that you have taken the matter seriously by recording details of the incident. Discuss the allegations and your concern and disappointment with the perpetrator before administering any appropriate reprimand or punishment. It is essential that the abused child receives a genuine apology and an assurance that there will be no further occurrences. Be proud of a classroom where equality of opportunity, mutual respect and co-operation allow all your children to flourish.

Bullying

This is an emotive topic. Your school will have well-rehearsed procedures and practices that staff and children should be aware of. Familiarize yourself with the policy so that you know the appropriate steps to take.

Do not wait for a problem before discussing the subject with the children. Establish with the class from an early stage what is understood by the term 'bullying' (and that physical violence is not necessarily involved), what is unacceptable and how they should respond if they are a victim or an observer. Impress upon the children how important it is to be tolerant of each other's differences and how these should be respected. Encourage the children to be a 'telling' class and emphasize that this is responsible behaviour that protects everybody's well-being.

If you witness or are made aware of an incident:
- talk to both parties independently to establish their perception of events;
- reassure victims that any threats of reprisal against them will not be tolerated and remind them of the school's supervision arrangements so they know who to approach and when;
- talk to any other children who may have witnessed what happened;
- discuss the case with your headteacher or a colleague who knows the children;
- keep a log of your interviews so that you have a comprehensive record;
- bring both parties together to discuss the situation if you feel it to be appropriate;
- you or the headteacher should then inform the parents of the children concerned of the incident and of the action you will be taking.

You may need to meet with the parents and explain again what has happened. Both sets of parents will be angry for different reasons and probably defensive. Unfortunately the school may be equally 'blamed', so do keep comprehensive notes and have another member of staff with you at any potentially difficult interview.

Gender

Your conduct and attitude will influence how the children regard and value each other. Gender is not an organizing principle or a classroom management strategy that you should consider. With the exception of the more sensitive elements of sex education, never segregate the boys from the girls. Names in the register should be recorded alphabetically and the class should line up and move around the school as a class and not as two groups. Do not use sex segregation to motivate or control

children. Your role is to promote equality by changing the stereotypical ideas about boys and girls that children may have when they come to school.

To achieve this, you will need to take great care with your planning, as well as the classroom management and organization, to ensure that both boys and girls receive a broad-based education with opportunities to follow up specific interests and activities that may not conform with tradition. Promote sporting activities that can be enjoyed by both sexes. Your PSE programme should deal with gender issues and help to make the children more generally aware and even less confined to particular roles.

Addressing this issue needs to be part of a whole-school policy and should include a considered approach, not only to the curriculum but to assemblies, planning, classroom practices, PE and playtimes. Efforts being made in your classroom or in the school towards equal opportunities will be influenced by external groups. This makes your role even more important.

Stranger danger

At Year 5, it is probable that the majority of children will be making their own way to and from school without an adult to accompany them. This can leave them vulnerable to possible abduction or even assault. As part of your PSE programme, remind the class of the 'stranger danger' message. Invite the police liaison officer to talk to the children during the year. Warn the class of any reported sightings that may be a potential threat to them, but at the same time avoid overstating the case. Being aware is an important part of their development and growing independence.

Children with special needs

Disruptive children

A disruptive child in your class can have a significant influence on the educational experiences and learning of all the children. The child can also cause you a good deal of emotional stress and anxiety and, by this age, may have a well-honed repertoire of attention-getting tactics.

Before you take over the class, find out from the previous teacher, the school's special needs co-ordinator (SENCO) and the headteacher if you have any children with behavioural difficulties. You will need to know:

- who the children are;
- what their particular problem is;
- what triggers their disruptive behaviour;
- the strategies that have been established in response to the behaviour;
- what support is available.

Decide how you will respond *before* an incident occurs. Take care about groupings, seating arrangements and, after any initial input from you to the class, make a point of checking with any potentially disruptive children that they are quite clear about the task.

Your class charter of 'golden rules' or positive behaviour policy must be enforced. Include all children in regular discussions and build up a sense of class community. Try giving particular responsibilities to children who have or may be causing difficulties. Build a relationship with them. Try to find out what kind of approach they respond to best – sometimes a humorous (but

not sarcastic) response works. Praise often does (but it is sometimes difficult to find anything to praise!). Do not humiliate them in front of their peers, keep calm, demonstrate your disapproval, disappointment and talk through any incidents with the child at an appropriate time.

Able children

The identification of able children should normally be part of a whole-school process. It is not always easy. Do not take a parent's opinion as confirmation! Exceptional ability may be identified in a specific area or across a range of curriculum subjects. Careful observation, together with regular discussion with children about their learning, hard evidence from assessments, test scores and reports should help establish if there is exceptional ability.

By Year 5, able children can be mentally outstripping not only their contemporaries but, occasionally, their teacher, too. Accept this without resentment, enjoy and make the most of their gifts to enrich everyone's learning, but remember that, in emotional and physical development, the child is no farther ahead than the rest of the class. It is your responsibility to provide able children with an appropriate curriculum and opportunities. These need to be challenging and related to the general class work. Some LEAs have developed special materials or opportunities for these children and you should investigate to see if there is anything in your area. It is important that able children remain part of the class socially, while at the same time they are allowed and encouraged to work at an appropriate level. You should be careful that your attitude to these children does not isolate them from their peers.

Always discuss your thoughts with the headteacher and other members of staff. Take care about how the matter is shared with parents, as this is potentially a subject that could motivate a number of parents to put unreasonable pressure on the school and limited resources.

Mobile children

Children of travelling or other mobile families have the same entitlement at school as children of the settled population. Schools have a responsibility to provide for mobile children, however short their stay may be.

Roadside travellers are usually highly mobile and often educationally disadvantaged and, by Year 5, the gaps in their education may be becoming increasingly apparent. The whole process of their introduction to the class needs to be handled with great sensitivity. The headteacher will have made contact with the proper authorities and support will be available to you and to the children. If you are to have travellers' children in your class:

● make sure you have basic information about them, such as their names, how old they are, where they are staying, if there is any friction between their family and the family of any other child in your class;

● be prepared for them – have their place ready, name their tray and books;

● talk to the class before the new child arrives, just as you would about any new pupil;

● liaise closely with the support agencies and ask for help, advice and guidance.

For children of families in the forces, the same principles apply. The school may have a long-standing relationship with one of the services. If this is the case, it is likely that a number of service children will already be in the school and supportive, effective networks will be established. If so, use them. Decide what the child's needs are and organize the learning to best meet these. Always look at the positive and build on the strengths. Make their time in your class, however short, a happy and worthwhile period.

Children with learning difficulties

Records and general information about any child in your class with learning difficulties should be made available to you. Study the background notes and arrange to meet with the school's special needs teacher.

Make sure you:

- are aware of any children with learning difficulties;
- know exactly what these difficulties are;
- have a clear idea of the level they are working at;
- know what their planned programmes and targets are;
- are aware of all support available;
- know about any involvement with external agencies.

Whatever the child's difficulty:
- plan for appropriate learning;
- set achievable targets which are regularly reviewed and assessed;
- liaise closely with the special needs teacher, outside agencies and the child's parents;
- ensure that the child is, and feels, integrated as a valued member of the class.

Celebrate successes and achievements, however small they may appear compared with some other children's. Look for opportunities to promote the child within the class group and be sensitive at stressful times when there are class or school assessments.

Physically disabled children and children with health problems

It is probable that, by Year 5, any children who have a physical disability or suffer with health problems will be familiar with and to the school. This will be very helpful to you as you will be able to continue with the practices that have been established. The child, family and school should feel comfortable and confident with each other. You will need to have a sound knowledge of the child's case history, procedures to follow and how to respond in any emergency.

Again, your first task is to find out as much background information as you can about the child. If you have an opportunity, seek out the parents before they come looking for you. It is better that you take the initiative and that the parents feel you understand and care. After all, a change in teacher can be unsettling for any child. Parents of children who experience learning difficulties as a consequence of physical disabilities will be anxious and need reassurance.

By Year 5, children with physical disabilities or health problems will have developed coping strategies. Spend time talking openly and honestly with them. Establish what their strategies are, what they see as their needs and how they would like you to help. Once a relationship has been initiated, you should be able to start to enjoy each other's company and provide for them as you would for the able-bodied children in your class.

You will need to:
- maintain close links with the parents;
- seek advice when necessary;
- make sure any outside agencies which should be supporting are involved;
- remember to take precautions and make provision for the child when arranging visits or special events.

'Looked after' children

There may be children in your class who do not live with their natural parents but are cared for in a residential or foster home. School can have a strong and beneficial effect as your classroom will be one environment where the 'looked after' child will have largely the same experiences as other children of a similar age.

Your school should be informed by a social worker which adults share parental responsibility, the relevant parts of the care plan, and the child's particular needs that will require your attention in school. Make contact with the carers and, during the course of the child's time in your class, include the carers as you would any parent. Keep them informed about progress and invite them to class events. Liaise closely on a regular basis and follow up any concerns you may have, especially if they are related to attendance or a change in the child's behaviour. Work in partnership with staff from the children's home and carers. Keep yourself informed, seek support and advice

from the school's SENCO and be particularly vigilant about the child's well-being and any noticeable changes in mood or behaviour. If possible, you or the headteacher should attend the meetings about the child which are held regularly with the carers and social workers.

Reports

Report writing is not the most enjoyable part of your work but it is a duty and you should ensure that the reports are helpful and worthwhile for colleagues and children, as well as for parents.

Whatever the arrangements are at your school for compiling reports, be prepared. Collect the information you will need well in advance and follow these steps.

- Check when the 'hand in' date for the report is and work backwards, blocking in time so that you have a schedule, perhaps three reports a night for four nights a week over a three-week period.
- Give yourself a date by which all your assessments have to be completed.
- Check to see who else will need to write on your children's reports and agree a time scale with them.
- Gather all the information you will need to base your reports on.
- If possible, persuade a literate friend to check through your reports once you have written them. Or, at the very least, check your spelling and punctuation very carefully.

Reports should provide a summary of significant achievements, not complete coverage. Include some details of areas where the child has experienced difficulties, together with an indication of what they should focus on in the future. Comments about children's behaviour or attitude should not come as a surprise to parents. Avoid bland statements. Be positive. Be specific, to ensure that what you say is of value. Remember, other teachers who have your class after you have to live by what you say. Be as accurate as you can with the statements you make.

The parents
Communication with parents

If at all possible, meet the parents as a group before you take up your post or start the term with the new class. Use the opportunity to introduce yourself, to find out about their children and to start to develop trust between you.

At an early stage in the term, invite the parents into school so that you can talk to them about how you organize their children's learning. Parents will appreciate knowing:

- how you manage the class in terms of the groupings;
- curriculum division and class discipline;
- what the topics will be for the year;
- arrangements for homework;
- about any educational visits you may have planned;
- details of tests that may be taking place during the year;
- how they can help in school and at home;
- what to do if there is a problem and they need to contact you.

Keep a record of who attends and send a copy of notes about the meeting to parents unable to join you.

Be visible and available for parents at regular times, before and after school. You will often prevent a minor problem from developing if you can deal with it at an early opportunity.

However, by Year 5, a significant number of the children's parents do not bring them to school or collect them at the end of the day. This will be in response to the children's growing independence and also the likelihood that parents have returned to work. Casual conversations and regular contact will prove to be more difficult. Your chief contact will be through whole-

school events, specific evenings such as consultations, and through written communications.

At school events, make a point of seeking out parents of children in your class. Use these opportunities to be positive about their children's achievements, progress and general contributions to school life. If you need to, make an appointment for the parents to meet with you at a later time to discuss any matters that you need to share with them.

Evening meetings

When you do have an evening meeting with parents, ensure that they have had reasonable notice, that they are clear about the purpose of the meeting and the arrangements for the evening.

Before the meeting, decide where you will talk with parents (where other parents cannot overhear), where they will wait, whether there will be an opportunity for them to look through their child's work before the consultation, whether you want to share class achievements with them through such things as displays and class books.

At some point before your meeting with the parents, allow time for children to sort through and organize their tray or desk and any folders. It is surprising the number of non-essential items which find their way to the bottom!

Whatever the stage of the day or evening, imagine that each appointment is the first of the day. Be well prepared. Identify the main points you need to make for each parent. Check carefully beforehand that you have the information about each child that you will need. Parents will not be impressed if you spend part of the consultation rummaging through papers, searching for their child's tray or telling them what a hard day you have had. Appear fresh, alert and professional, even if you are not feeling at your best. Listen attentively to their responses and comments or concerns that they volunteer. Keep the discussion crisp and relevant and, at the end of the conversation, sum up and note anything that has been agreed.

Parents in the classroom

An increasing number of schools now rely on, and benefit from having, parents to help in the classrooms. It is very important that this is 'managed' by the school and by you.

First, establish what the school's policy is. Are parents generally welcomed? May they help in their child's class or do they have to provide support in another classroom? What vetting procedures are in place? Next, set down what your needs are, when the optimum times for support would be and how you intend to approach the parents.

Should parents volunteer, find out what particular skills or interests they have and when they would be available. Then marry your needs with the offers you have had. You might discuss the matter at this stage with the Year 4 teacher or any other colleague who is familiar with this particular group of parents.

For parents who will be helping:

● make them aware of school procedures for evacuation of the premises, access to the staffroom, school office, and so on;

- talk to them about confidentiality and what they should do if they are ever concerned about any child in the class because of something the child has confided in them or something they have seen;
- talk about what they should do if approached by another parent.

All the children should be aware that you have parent-helpers coming in and should have an idea of what they will be doing.

When parents arrive, make sure that they feel welcome and that they know what is expected of them. Show them how to support the children they are working with.

Some parents may be very nervous and find it initially a stressful experience. Be reassuring and do not forget to thank them at the end of their session with you. Remember how you treat them will influence their view of how you respond to the children. 'Talk' on the playground can have a negative as well as a positive effect. Use the situation to your advantage.

Dealing with problems

Not all parents will agree with or even want to understand school policies or practices. While major disputes will be directed at the headteacher or senior staff, you may be the first 'representative' parents focus their attention on. Should this be the case, outwardly remain calm and always be polite. Never raise your voice, even if the parent is shouting and screaming! Try and manoeuvre the parent away from children or other 'interested' parties, and make sure you call on an appropriate colleague for assistance. Listen to what the parent has to say. Take down notes. This can have a calming effect and will be helpful later. Assure the parent that you are interested and taking what they have to say seriously. Explain your position or the school's policy but avoid an argument. Advise the parent of correct procedures for any complaints and ask for them to be put in writing.

If you cannot calm an aggressive parent, seek help immediately. Again, try to lead the parent away from children and, if necessary, call the local police for assistance. Individuals can be totally unreasonable and their behaviour can be affected by drink or drugs. Often their grievance will not be directly school-related but you can be seen as a soft target. Whatever the situation you find yourself in, the safety of the children and your own safety is your first responsibility. Be cautious and always seek support.

The Year 5 year

A child in Year 5 is similar to a teenager; no longer an infant needing constant adult supervision but not yet old enough to be considered independent. As the year progresses and the Year 6 children's thoughts turn to their secondary schools, children in Year 5 will be jostling for their new positions. In some respects, Year 5 is a foundation year. A time when children are tested by degrees of responsibilities with further opportunities to experience independence and time to develop. Those who respond, and who demonstrate sufficient levels of maturity and positive attitudes, will lead the school in the year to come.

Curriculum and Classroom Planning

Materials and resources
Getting organized in advance

Get to know your classroom before you take over the class. Familiarize yourself with all available equipment and resources. Decide which you want in order to support teaching and learning and banish unwanted items into storage until they are needed.

As part of this exercise, spend time assessing the literature, reference material and 'scheme' books in the class library. Dispose of tatty, inappropriate examples or books that are obviously dated and unlikely to be read. If you are new to the school or the classroom, make a plea to the headteacher, PTA or school association for replacements.

Organize all your resources effectively. How you present the materials to the children will influence the way they present their work to you. Promote quality by demonstrating care and a genuine affinity with all the learning tools available to you.

Library

Your school may have an agreed policy for access to the library and an established system for how it operates. You should be familiar with both.

Do not assume just because the children are in Year 5 that they will know how to make the most of the library resources. Talk to them about library skills and give them opportunities to practise them. Library treasure hunts, where groups of children seek and search for information and materials from a prepared sheet, can be enthusiastically received. You could make it a competition between groups.

Arrange well in advance to withdraw books from the library and borrow collections of books from the school library service or local children's library to complement the work you are planning through the year.

Computers

Some of the children in your class may be using at home more sophisticated systems than the ones at school. Other children will have no out-of-school access to computers. Get to know the programs available to you so that you can match these with your teaching plans and the children's needs. Get rid of anything that you don't need and make sure that the remainder is properly organized and labelled.

When doing your planning, decide how and where computers will support learning and use

the word-processing package as a natural part of the children's education. Devise a recording system so you can check on the amount of time children spend on the computer. Inevitably, it tends to be the children who least need the practice who monopolize the equipment.

Audio visual

School televisions and video recorders always seem to have minds of their own and no two systems are ever the same. Get to know the peculiarities of your school's equipment so that you are not caught out. Practise beforehand and always make sure you have wound on to the right place on the tape.

Check any video and audio tapes in the classroom and trawl through the stock cupboard as well. You are most likely to find damaged and obsolete material, but you may find something really useful. It's exasperating to find that the school has the ideal video for one of your topics when it's too late to use it.

If you are going to use schools' broadcasts, build them into your plans, check to make sure that any back-up materials are available in school and order them if necessary.

People

People are your most important and valuable resource. Plan carefully how you can best make use of their time. If you are fortunate enough to have a class assistant, make sure that she is always actively involved. This should include time working with children and any administrative duties you may have identified for her. Don't waste her time sitting in assemblies or with extended breaks. There will always be boards to cover, books to make or repair and the inevitable filing.

Establish a book for anyone who is helping you, with the tasks identified. People like to know what is expected of them and this will give you a useful record for future use, or if you have difficulties related to their performance.

Visits

These should be planned for the year well in advance. Be careful that the visits do not make an unreasonable demand on limited finances. Have a varied mix of local, inexpensive visits as well as trips farther afield. It is a good idea to use an opportunity to talk to the parents early in the school year about visits. If you are arranging a longer trip or residential week, offer a 'pay as they learn' scheme so that parents can send in small amounts towards the cost on a weekly basis. (The school can then use any interest gained towards the cost of the trip.)

Always follow school procedures. Notify parents by letter with a consent slip. Check to see if you need insurance and that any transport arrangements satisfy local and school agreements.

Display

Planning for displays should form part of your preparation. Familiarize yourself with the school's written display policy – if there is one. Otherwise find out from a colleague what is expected and what the 'dos and don'ts' are.

Ensure that you have an appropriate range of materials, artefacts and a variety of fabrics available. Some of these can be obtained from the schools' museum service (order well in advance), others from car boot sales, market stalls and second-hand shops. Local sources should be exploited, including recycling centres. These can provide you with a range of unusual products at no cost!

If you are responsible for ordering your own backing materials, don't buy the cheapest paper. Paper that is a little more expensive will go up more easily, should not fade and will last longer. Invest in border strips and limit yourself to a range of colours that complement each other. A garish background will detract from the children's work.

Requirements of the curriculum

Your school will be used to adapting to change and adopting new practices. Seek advice and support from colleagues if you have any doubts or difficulties with planning. Share your draft timetable and termly plans with a colleague. This can be a reciprocal arrangement.

School-generated as well as national documentation will guide and instruct you. The recent literacy and numeracy initiatives clearly outline what you will be expected to cover. Use these frameworks and support materials to ensure that your planning is both appropriate and in accordance with policy.

Check on the school statement for the teaching of religious education. This is another sensitive area. You will need to be aware of any children, such as Jehovah's Witnesses, who will not be included (and who may have other restrictions about what they are able to do).

Time

Official recommendations

The DfEE's recommended minimum teaching time for Key Stage 2 children is 23½ hours a week. This does not include breaks, lunch time or the daily act of worship. When deciding on the percentage allocations for curriculum subjects, you will need to take account of the Numeracy and Literacy Hours, the National Curriculum, the school's curriculum and any established special priorities. For a typical Year 5 class, the breakdown might look like this:

	Engl	Maths	Sci	Tech	Hist	Geog	Art	Music	PE	RE	PSE
Hrs pw	6.5	5.5	2.5	1	1	1	1.5	1	2	1	0.5
%	28	24	11	4	4	4	6	4	8	4	2

This allows for a broad, balanced approach. A lot of English and IT are, of course, taught through other subjects. This allocation of time does not mean that you teach exactly so many hours of a particular subject per week but that, over a longer period of time, it will average out at roughly this amount of hours per week. You need to think in blocks of time so that you can do justice to a topic or activity.

Timetable

Before you decide on the details for your timetable, establish when the following will take place:
- assemblies/acts of worship;
- set PE times;
- times when another member of staff takes your class;
- Literacy and Numeracy Hours.

Ensure that your timetable shows a balance of activities. Organize your hall, PE and drama lessons on different days so that they break up any significant periods of intense work. Think about when the children's attention and concentration will be at their best and plan your timetable accordingly.

Long-/medium-/short-term Planning

There is no single approach to planning or any common understanding of what each stage should include. Your school will have developed an individual system that works for them and meets the needs of the children.

Long-term planning

Long-term planning may be included in a school's curriculum framework and in schemes of work for individual subjects. These will be quite specific and should form the core from which you take your plans.

You may be fortunate enough to be a member of a team for planning. This can provide you with opportunities to reflect together on past practices and activities, as well as to plan for the future. You can use each others' strengths, support each other and help with resource issues. Being a member of a team for planning will be particularly helpful for newly qualified teachers.

Medium-term planning

Medium-term planning might include an overview sheet for the half term that shows what you will be covering, subject by subject. This can be helpful for anyone looking at intended coverage and can be shared with parents. You will then need to break this planning down and add some more details. A half-termly grid is a helpful tool. If you use a grid, highlight what you have covered at the end of each week. This then gives you an immediate record, is visually reassuring, informative and very useful to any supply teacher who takes over your class.

Short-term planning

Short-term planning may be for a fortnight or just for a week. A sheet like the one shown below allows you to include as much information as you need to deliver the curriculum. You can show the assessments you intend to make and any evaluations that will help you in the future.

Fortnightly plan

Week beginning .... Group/Year group ....

Subj. ref	Learning intentions	Activities	Resources	Groupings	Evaluation

Your daily plans will be drawn from the fortnightly or weekly sheets. Normally it will be left to you to devise a format that will show you how you intend to organize the class or groups. In many respects these sheets will be a memory jogger.

You will need to decide if the children will have a homework diary, whether you will ask parents to check to see that the work is completed and how you will build time into your routine to mark the homework.

The teaching

Teach your children using a combination of strategies. The essential point is 'fitness for purpose'. Be clear what the learning intentions are. Plan how you can best encourage and enable learning and which approach will be the most effective, both for the children and in terms of your time.

Whole-class teaching

Teaching the class as a whole involves a high level of control. You need to provide instructions, pace the lesson so that attention does not wander and assess responses so that you can move the children on. Explanations need to be given in a logical, coherent manner.

If thoughtfully planned and approached, whole-class teaching will often prove to be both personally and professionally very satisfying and rewarding.

Group teaching

Teaching children in groups is an equally important strategy. It allows for resources to be shared and provides planned opportunities for children to interact together and with you. Focusing your teaching on selected groups while others work with an assistant on independent tasks is an effective approach.

However, group activities can be counter-productive if you have too many groups, too many different activities in operation at the same time, or if the criteria for grouping has not been carefully thought through.

Individual teaching

To teach every child in the class individually would be extremely difficult, if not impossible. Interaction with the child can be superficial and the real amount of teaching time the child

experiences is minimal. However, there will be times when it is appropriate to focus on and support the individual pupil. Children of all abilities, but particularly those with special educational needs, benefit from one-to-one teaching. It is up to you to decide if, while being best for the child, it is manageable. Can the other children in the class work independently and constructively without your immediate attention?

Teaching points

Whatever your method of organization, strategy or style of delivery, again, 'fitness for purpose' is your guiding consideration.

● Teach your class using a variety of methods, including to the whole class, in smaller groups of various compositions, and individually.

● Remember that no one exclusive method is ever appropriate.

● Ensure that you have a manageable number of groups and learning activities at any one time.

● Use your time effectively to instruct, question, explain, listen and assess.

Differentiation by task/outcome

Regardless of the age group you are responsible for, you should be aware of what to expect from each individual child. This will involve not only getting to know the child, but careful planning and evaluation. The evaluations you make at the end of any activity or assessment should then be used to form your future plans.

When you plan an activity for the whole class, their response or follow-up work may be 'open ended' with all the children working to their own level. An example of this would be a piece of creative writing on a set subject. Children will probably spend the same amount of time but write different amounts and produce a range of results. You will need to know the child to decide whether he/she has achieved an appropriate level .

With other activities, you may decide that, while your introduction will be for the whole class, the children should subsequently operate in ability groups. Your expectations for each group will be different. The more able will have extension activities, special needs children should be considered and you will have to decide which group or groups you will be focusing on.

Know exactly what it is that you intend the children should learn. Make sure that your class know what that learning intention is. (*We're going to see if you remember the work we did on apostrophes before half term.*) Ensure that the activity is thoughtfully planned and that you are meeting the needs of all the children in the class through a differentiated approach that is manageable and achieves your learning intentions.

Recording and presentation

Familiarize yourself with the school's policy on how work should be recorded and presented. Check this against examples of work from the previous year so that you can compare practice with policy.

When you first meet the children, agree a statement with them that sets the standards for the year. The main points will need to be taken from the school's policy or from a list that you have drawn up. The children should understand what is expected. There is little point in having a policy that they are unaware of. By Year 5, you should expect high standards of recording and presentation from most children. Many of them should be able to make their own decisions about the best ways to record and lay out information.

While the processes that the children have worked through are important, the presentation of the final product will say as much about their level of attainment as it will about you as their teacher. Use it to motivate and to build for the future.

Homework

Generally, you will need to adhere to the school's homework policy although, whatever it is, there will inevitably be occasions when you will ask the children to attempt or complete activities at home.

The Government now requires you to set homework, so establish sensible ground rules. Explain to the parents, as well as to the children, what they can expect, why it is important and what the procedures for distribution, collection and marking will be. Work set must be relevant, challenging and practical for children to attempt at home. (It is, for example, not practical to assume that all children have access to reference books at home.) If the school organizes a homework club, it will give you a wider range of opportunities for homework.

Homework for Year 5 children might include:

- finishing off a piece of work from class;
- learning multiplication tables or particular spellings;
- handwriting practice;
- a personal study area;
- a particular piece of research.

SATs and assessment

As a Year 5 teacher, it is unlikely that you will have to worry too much about the SATs testing, but you do have a very important responsibility. There will be the end of Key Stage 1 SATs information, together with any interim SATs levels from testing at the end of Year 4. These results will provide you with an assessment of where the children are and help you to identify individual targets before the SATs tests in Year 6.

Establish what the school's procedures are for any other testing as well as SATs. Teacher assessments will form a core of information for you. Keep on top of maintaining these as the term progresses. Develop formative assessment sheets for each child as well as other records. On the formative assessments, include details of significant achievements, particular difficulties and observations about personal and social development. You will be able to use this when report writing or if you are ever challenged. Formative assessment information will be your evidence!

At appropriate stages in any topic, include assessment opportunities in your planning for particular children. Organize this on a regular basis so that it is manageable. This information will be invaluable for end-of-year reports and consultation times with parents.

Towards the end of the summer term, on the basis of any interim SATs information and your own judgements, predict the final level of attainment you would expect each child to achieve at the end of the Key Stage. This can provide useful, additional information and a helpful reference for the Year 6 teacher.

English
including Literacy Hour

By the time they reach Year 5, children should realize that the way they speak and write will affect other people's understanding of them. Year 5 is a time for them to refine and develop their ability to speak and write with an audience in mind.

Most children should, at this stage, be capable of reading independently and of working out for themselves many of the problems which they encounter with unfamiliar words or phrases. However, there will still be a need for you to reinforce those strategies which provide graphophonic, semantic and syntactic clues for readers. You will need to emphasize the importance of being an independent reader and writer, while at the same time recognizing that children are still developing their literacy skills and need to be given ideas which will help them when they read and write outside the classroom.

It is important to remember that even those children who appear to be quite independent in their reading at Year 5 still need to develop skills which will enable them to cope with unfamiliar material. Reading development does not cease when a child begins to read without seeking help.

Make use of the Literacy Hour to demonstrate strategies and to focus children's attention on the structure of text, including sentence structure, punctuation, layout and organization. In addition, children should be shown ways of improving their writing and making it more interesting to the reader, both through greater accuracy and better presentation, and through more adventurous choice of vocabulary and sentence structure.

What should they be able to do?

Key area: Speaking

At Year 5, children should be capable of speaking in front of the whole class to answer questions or to present something which they have prepared. The direct teaching involved in the Literacy Hour should make extensive use of children's contributions and these should be used to take discussions forward and to allow children to express their own ideas and their queries about what they are learning.

Provide your class with plenty of opportunities to communicate with different audiences and to consider how the vocabulary, tone, pace and style which they use can be varied to improve their presentational skills. They may be involved in class assemblies or school productions which should allow them to work from prepared scripts.

Year 5 children should be given increasing opportunities to read aloud and to develop their ability to make use of expression and even dramatic devices to enhance their presentation. Indeed, drama work should be a feature of speaking and listening work at this stage. Drama should not be seen as being merely a fun activity which children undertake as a reward for good behaviour, nor should it be regarded as including only those activities which lead to school performances. Rather, you should use drama as a valuable way of bringing lessons to life for children, as well as offering them the chance to develop a sense of audience. The Speaking and Listening programmes of study in the National Curriculum English document offer many opportunities for work in drama and it can also be used in other subjects such as history and religious education. As in other subjects, there are skills which children need to develop in drama.

Key area: Listening

Give your class lots of opportunities to listen to stories, poems and other texts being read aloud and to respond to these in a variety of ways. They might make notes, discuss and compare with others their responses to the texts, and perhaps re-enact them before an audience or on tape. When they are listening to information presented by you or by other children, or to radio, television or drama, encourage children to identify key points and to evaluate what they hear and discuss its significance. You will need to remind them of the importance of listening to others and taking turns when participating in discussions.

Key area: Reading

The National Curriculum requires that children should be encouraged to develop as enthusiastic, independent and reflective readers. If this is to be achieved at Year 5, children will need to develop the skills which will enable them to read fluently. While there is no definitive method of teaching reading, there are strategies which children should be able to deploy by this stage. They should be familiar with a range of phonic strategies which will help them to break up words and determine how the words should sound. They should understand how they can look beyond a difficult word and seek help from surrounding text so that they can find additional clues when phonic strategies fail to help them, and derive meaning from text. At Year 5, a great deal of work should be done to enhance children's knowledge of these semantic or contextual strategies.

In addition, teach children to look at the text and examine aspects such as punctuation and word order to help them to understand what they read. Develop syntactical or grammatical strategies by spending time with children analysing passages of text and discussing with them the importance of word order and the significance of punctuation. Children will also need to build up their sight vocabularies so that they can recognize words quickly and easily without the need for elaborate decoding.

I like to read ...... because....

I like to read cookery books because
I want to find new recipes to try.
Robert

I like to read the William books
because they make me laugh
Jessica

I like to read scary stories like the Goosebumps
books because they make me shiver.
Raninder

I like to read 'The very hungry caterpillar'
to my little sister because she thinks its
great. Laura

I like to read comics
because they have lots
of pictures and funny
things happen.
Lee

I like to read
about competitions
because I
want to win
one Rosie

I like to read
the sports pages
because they tell
me about the
matches played
by my favourite
team - Chelsea!
Niko

I like to read
encyclopaedias because they
tell you interesting facts and you
can find out things that you
didn't know.
Martha

I like to read about competitions because I want
to win one. Rosie

The range of material which children have the opportunity to read should be wide, and they should be introduced to texts which are not necessarily written for children, such as newspapers and reference books. In some schools, they may also make use of the Internet to seek out information or have access to CD-ROMs which feature databases and encyclopaedias.

Key area: Writing

In writing, children should be developing further their ability to plan, draft, revise, proof-read and present their work in a manner appropriate for different audiences. They should increasingly be improving their note-taking abilities so that they are able to provide themselves with a starting point for their final drafts. The range and scope of their writing should increase and should incorporate stories, poems, journals, reports on real events, letters, persuasive writing and pamphlets and brochures.

Children at Year 5 should also be developing their knowledge of grammar so that they can understand, for example, the importance of word order and subject-verb agreement. Encourage them to look critically at examples of writing, including their own, and discuss ways in which they might be made more accurate and interesting. Whole-class teaching and group work during the Literacy Hour may be particularly useful here, since they will offer you the opportunity to look at and discuss texts with children and make teaching points about grammatical features.

At word level, Year 5 children should be increasing the bank of words which they are able to recognize and spell easily. Again, whole-class and group work can be invaluable in giving you the opportunity to show how similar spelling patterns can be found in different words and the significance of prefixes and suffixes in altering meaning. Children can also be shown that there are often many different ways of writing the same phoneme. For example, the e sound in *bed* may be made by *ea* in *bread*, and by *ai* in *said*, and the *ur* sound in *fur* can be made by *ir* in *dirt*, *er* in *fern* and *or* in *work*.

Activities which foster and develop children's interest in words and their meanings should be a feature of the Year 5 classroom and they should be encouraged to make their own collections and conduct their own research using dictionaries, thesauruses and encyclopedias.

Practical ideas

Literacy Hour

The teaching framework devised by the National Literacy Strategy is, of course, the foundation for the Literacy Hour. You must dedicate one hour a day to the teaching of reading and writing in a rhythmic transition from whole class teaching to small group work and back again.

During this hour, children should be engaged in work at:

▶ whole text level, involving comprehension and composition;

▶ sentence level, involving grammar and punctuation;

▶ word level, involving vocabulary and spelling.

Those of the following activities which are particularly suitable for use in the Literacy Hour are marked with a ⬤ in the margin.

Developing key areas
Speaking and listening

By the time they reach Year 5, most children should be capable of working co-operatively in a small group to find information, explore ideas or prepare a presentation. They should be encouraged to discuss what they have learned and to share information with other groups.

Technical vocabulary

Most Year 5 children should be familiar with many technical terms and be using them confidently when discussing their reading and writing. For some reason, teachers, who have been happy to assume that children can talk of *triangles* and *rectangles* from the reception class and *dodecahedrons* and *congruent polygons* by Year 5, have often been reluctant to use correct terminology in English and continue to talk of *describing words* rather than *adjectives* well into Key Stage 2.

Your class should be aware not only of the correct names for the parts of speech, but also increasingly of such terms as *alliteration, onomatopoeia, synonym, metaphor, simile, prefix, homophone, phoneme, prefix* and *suffix*.

The THRASS (*Teaching Handwriting Reading and Spelling Skills*, A Davies and D Ritchie) programme introduces the correct phonic terminology from the outset and children appear to become at ease with using it quite quickly.

Talking partners

⬤ Children can have regular talking partners with whom they consult, try out ideas, raise questions, share experiences and discuss what they have learned. This may be used as an alternative to news or diary sessions in which the whole class listen as people take turns to talk about what they have done recently. Inevitably, in such sessions, some children do not get an opportunity to discuss what they have done in much detail or at all, while others, who may have little of interest which they wish to share, may be forced to contribute when they do not wish to do so. Children can talk at much greater length when they only have one person in their audience, and the paired discussions can act as a prelude for whole-class talk with an alternative slant being provided by asking questions such as *Whose partner did something really exciting at the weekend?*

⬤ Paired discussion may lead on more gradually to the sharing of the ideas of each pair with another pair. This may progress so that groups of eight and then sixteen get together and report to each other before the whole class come together.

Brainstorming

Brainstorming can be a valuable starting point for a range of activities from writing to creating a game to planning a piece of drama. Children can work together in small groups to share ideas and record them quickly in note form and then use the notes as a starting point for other work. This may be done in pairs, groups or as a whole class with you as scribe.

Group discussions

By the time they reach Year 5, many children are capable of chairing discussions, thus enabling groups to come together to share ideas without your participation. Guidance should be given on ways of maintaining an orderly atmosphere and children could even engage in group discussions to determine some rules for speaking and listening, so that there is a reference point for the chairperson to draw attention to when discussions break down or become disorderly.

Jigsawing

A useful group activity, which encourages children to make use of information which can be obtained from books and information technology, is jigsawing. The class is organized into groups with each member of each group being given an aspect of the topic on

which to become expert. The experts from each group meet to share ideas and then report back to their groups. This encourages children to listen carefully to others' ideas and to evaluate what they have heard before reporting back to their groups. An alternative approach is to divide the class into groups and give each group an aspect of a topic to become 'expert' in. Groups may further subdivide the topics and should report back to the whole class.

Styles of speaking

In order to develop children's awareness of standard English, provide opportunities for them to listen to a range of styles of speaking, including regional dialects and standard English. Show the children how some dialects deviate from standard English and ask them to make collections of dialect words and phrases from literature and television and radio broadcasts. You could, for example, ask them to listen at home to soap operas which are set in different regions and countries, such as *Brookside* in Liverpool, *Coronation Street* in Manchester and *Eastenders* in London, *Neighbours* and *Home and Away* in Australia, and many programmes in America. They, or you, could bring in edited tape recordings to play to the class to illustrate instances of dialect which would not occur in standard English. (Remember to make the distinction between dialect – different words and syntax – and accent.) By discussing such examples, a greater understanding of standard English can be developed.

Drama

Speaking and listening skills can be developed and enhanced through the use of structured drama lessons, particularly when children are provided with opportunities to respond to what they have seen and heard and to evaluate their own and others' contributions. The following activities are designed to offer opportunities for group work leading to presentations and should also provide useful opportunities for discussions about the ways in which language use varies according to the nature of the activity.

Freeze frame

After reading a story or poem, ask children, in groups, to produce tableaux which depict a scene. The rest of the class can try to identify the scenes and each character can say a line or answer a question in character. This activity might be followed by a piece of writing in which the children describe different characters or scenes from the book in detail. They might go on to draw a tableau and use thought bubbles to show what each character might be thinking.

Historical events

After talking to the children about an historical event or a religious story (see the history and RE chapters), ask them to work in groups to plan a re-enactment of the story. This will help to reinforce the sequence of events in the story and should allow them to

explore the possible feelings of the principal characters. They might also engage in further research to find out more details about the characters to help them to portray them more accurately.

Conflict

Present children with scenarios in which there is potential for conflict to be explored through drama. For example, two members of a group might be told that they were to play the role of parents while another two were children. They could then be asked to develop a scene in which there was an argument over what time the children should go to bed or what they should be allowed to watch on television. Having developed the argument in an ad hoc way, they could go on to produce notes for a script and then perform for the rest of the class. This could lead to debates and discussions involving the whole class and may be further developed into pieces of persuasive writing, written in role.

Selling a robot

In this activity children work in pairs or small groups, one child taking the role of a salesperson while the others become robots. The salesperson's task is to demonstrate the robots' features to potential buyers while the robots, through their movements, show what they can do. You could show the children examples of television commercials which involve a persuasive salesperson demonstrating goods and ask the children to consider how tone of voice, pace of speech and use of vocabulary can be used to make an effective presentation. Some children may be able to provide their own renderings of sales patter used by market stallholders, for example.

Sports commentaries

Ask the children to take on the roles of commentators and players. The commentator describes the action which is performed by the players. Once again, examples of real sports commentaries may be recorded from television or radio and played to children to give them ideas. This could lead to a discussion about the ways in which commentators vary tone and pace according to the nature of the events. (Racing commentaries on the radio provide a very good example and can be heard on weekday afternoons.)

Reading

By the time they reach Year 5, many children have developed an ability to read texts but have yet to become 'real readers'. They may be able to read mechanically, but often they derive little meaning from what they read, and they may not read independently for pleasure or for information. It is important that you adopt a very positive approach, creating a literate environment in which children are surrounded by relevant and interesting print. Children should also be given lots of opportunities to encounter different genres of texts. Besides fiction, play scripts and poetry, children should have access to a range of other materials, which might include:

▶ catalogues;
▶ timetables;
▶ brochures and pamphlets;
▶ programmes for sports or drama events;
▶ reference books;
▶ newspapers and magazines;
▶ computer texts.

These items should be incorporated into practical activities such as planning a trip, making a shopping list for presents, finding out information about people and places, and producing databases of information on different topics.

While literature has an intrinsic value and is a source of entertainment, it also offers you opportunities to extend children's learning in a variety of ways. The children's own writing may well improve and develop as they experience the ways in which authors make use of language. They may also gain a greater insight into the world and into human relationships through reading stories, poems and plays. In this section, we will look at the reading skills which Year 5 children should be developing, as well as the kinds of literature and activities with which they might be involved.

Reading skills
Phonic knowledge
⊘ Children should have developed quite a considerable phonic knowledge by the time they reach Year 5, but many will need to revise this and develop further knowledge, both to enable them to read with greater fluency and to help them to develop spelling skills. All children need to be able to cope with the increasing number of irregularities in words which they meet as their reading increases in sophistication. Phonic development might be linked to the teaching of spelling, with words being examined in some detail, so that children may see which job each grapheme has.

⊘ Collections of words may be made and rhyming dictionaries can be used to show how similar sounds may be created in different ways. For example, the ew sound in *brew* may also be made by *ue* as in *clue*, *oup* as in *coup*, *ieu* as in *lieu*, *oe* as in *shoe*, *ough* as in *through*, *ut* as in *debut* (depending on pronunciation), *o* as in *do* and so on. The irregularities may prove a source of frustration for some children, but with careful guidance from you and a selection of interesting, creative activities which encourage children to find their own examples, they can also be a source of fascination.

Phonemes and graphemes
⊘ There is a range of activities related to developing a greater appreciation of phoneme/grapheme correspondence. The children might play bingo games in which they have cards with graphemes written on them and you say phonemes which they then try to match to the letters on their cards. They might also play a game based upon an idea used in the BBC's *A Question of Sport*, in which in one round competitors have to guess the identity of a sports personality whose picture is revealed slowly by small sections being uncovered at a time. A similar game could be played using multisyllabic words which are revealed one grapheme at a time, with children being invited to consider the possibilities for what

COO!
Find different spellings that make the <u>oo</u> sound

two   shoe
clue
through
canoe
brew   loo   do
Crewe
rendezvous

the word might be by studying the graphemes carefully and perhaps using a dictionary if the initial grapheme is revealed first. For example, *reporter* could be revealed as *re, port, er* with children looking both at the structure of the word as it is revealed and at the meaning of the prefix *re-*.

Onset and rime

The use of onset and rime will help children to analyse and break down words and make analogies between words with similar spelling patterns, such as *night, bright, light* and *fight*. (The onset is the initial consonant or consonant cluster of a word and the rime is the sound which follows it. For example, in *bright, br-* is the onset and *-ight* the rime.) Children usually find that they are able to decode more quickly if they 'chunk' words using onset and rime than if they break them down letter by letter.

Fiction
Analysing plots

Give the children in your Year 5 class plenty of opportunities to look closely at the plots of works of fiction and show them how to analyse these in simple ways. (For example, ask them to produce a flow chart to show the key events in a story.) They should also look at the ways in which authors develop their characters and you could ask them to draw a picture of one character and show what they feel about that person by surrounding the picture with appropriate adjectives. They then write sentences to justify their choices. It is this element of justifying ideas which children should increasingly attempt at Year 5.

In reading at Key Stage 2 they are expected to use inference and deduction in their response to texts, while in writing they are expected to write explanations and learn about the characteristics of argumentative writing.

Reading aloud

● For many children, there is a whole range of literature which they could enjoy but don't because of their limited reading abilities. It is important that you make time to read aloud to children, not only for the benefit of the poorer readers, but also because it enables you to bring text alive for everyone and read it in a way which the less experienced reader may not be able to manage. You can provide a model for children's own reading by using tone, pitch and stress to bring colour to the text, and you can make use of different accents and emphases to show how the author might have intended the written words to be read.

● Stories may be presented in a variety of different ways and by a variety of different people:
▶ you may read a story regularly as a serial;
▶ other adults may visit to read to children;
▶ children may take turns to read the story aloud to the class;
▶ children may share selected passages of favourite books;
▶ children may select passages on a particular theme from a range of books and make a tape recording of these for others to listen to and try to identify;
▶ stories may be told through radio, tape and TV presentations;
▶ a local author could be invited to visit to read and write with children;
▶ reading sessions may be held at the local library;
▶ children could read stories in groups, taking turns to read;
▶ children could watch a film or television version of a well-known story and then read or listen to the book version and compare the book with the film.

● Having presented a story to children, you can then go on to invite the children to take part in a range of related activities. These might include:
▶ using the story in conjunction with text books for topic work;
▶ retelling an extract as a radio play with sound effects;
▶ group discussions of the possibility of the book as a film – well-known actors might be cast (hypothetically!) in leading roles;
▶ producing a long collage to chart the story;
▶ retelling the story using puppets;
▶ prediction exercises;
▶ making models or drawing pictures of characters.

● Further responses might involve dramatizing the stories and exploring through drama the ways in which characters interact. This could lead to an investigation of published drama scripts and possibly the writing of scripts by the children. They might also keep a log book of the story. This could include a simple commentary on the storyline, predictions of what might happen next, or notes to help a fellow pupil who was absent when a particular section was read to the class.

Analysing novels

It has been suggested that analysing a novel with children can afford them various levels of understanding, for example:
▶ reading what is in the text, retelling what has been read;

▶ reading between the lines, considering possible or implied meanings;

▶ making associations with other knowledge, experience and reading;

▶ reflecting on what has been read, re-evaluating responses and perhaps modifying beliefs and understanding.

This approach demands that children gain a deeper level of understanding of what they read than they might acquire simply through independent reading and it requires your involvement and knowledge of the stories which the children read.

✅ One approach could involve a series of activities, related to a text, which are introduced gradually, perhaps as a story is being read to the children in serial form. Initially, children might be asked to speculate about what the story might be about, basing their predictions upon features of the book such as the cover, the publisher's blurb, the contents page, and the first page. They could also take into account any knowledge which they might have of other works by the same author.

✅ As the story progresses, invite children to make further predictions and ask for their views on the ways in which different characters behave. Character grids or charts might be produced with illustrations. You could ask the children to write about the person whom they like most, or the one whom they would most like to be if they were part of the story.

✅ Before the story is completed, you might, on a number of occasions, ask the children to write their own chapter endings or the ending for the story which they would like or which they predict. As they discover the author's version, they can then compare their own versions and consider which they find most satisfactory.

✅ Further activities could include making relationship charts which show how characters are related to each other by family ties or by actions. It might be useful at this point to discuss some of the soap operas which the children may watch and to ask them how they think the authors keep track of the characters' histories. They could also select a few of the principal soap characters and produce charts which show on which occasions they had dealings with each other. Relating an activity to television programmes may appear to deviate from literacy development, but it may well engender interest in some children who might otherwise have been reluctant participants. By moving from the familiar to the less familiar, children may gain a greater insight into methods of analysing stories.

✅ You might analyse and discuss the plot of the book in various ways. Children might produce a list of key events or a timeline to show the sequence of events. They could draw a storyboard and make notes on what is depicted in their pictures. (Discuss how this is done in films and television.) They could

make use of their storyboards as a starting point for dramatizing the story. You could encourage them to select key passages from the story and compare their ideas on what the major events were. They could also select particularly exciting passages and use these to advertise the book, in the same way that film makers take exciting parts of films and use them in promotional extractsat the cinema.

The events in a story can become the basis for the children to make a board game. For example, for *The Lion, The Witch and The Wardrobe*, 'The snow begins to melt, move on three spaces'. The board game might be based upon a snakes and ladders board, with children drawing a 'chance card' when they land at the top of a snake or the bottom of a ladder. Or children could design their own boards. Creating games encourages children to look closely at the story and identify key events in order to make appropriate cards.

A further activity might involve the children in selecting passages of speech and copying out and displaying them so that others could examine them and try to decide whom the speakers were. They could go on to write further dialogue in the style in which different characters might have spoken when discussing events which the author describes, but for which he or she did not write dialogue.

Once the book has been read, ask the children to consider what could happen to the characters in the future. For example, you could ask them to write about a further adventure for one person. There are several precedents for this in television, some of which children or their parents may have encountered (*Frasier* from *Cheers*, for example).

Authors' use of language

Look at the different ways in which an author avoids using 'he said' or 'she said' in speech. Ask the children to notice how the author sometimes doesn't say who is speaking at all if it is obvious from the context.

Ask the children to find examples where the author has used pronouns to replace characters' names to vary the vocabulary of the text.

Cloze work

This can take several forms with words taken out randomly, particular parts of speech removed, or key words removed. Provide passages which do not have only one possible answer and have children share their answers to promote discussion.

Word-a-day

Write an interesting word on the board each day and discuss it with the children. Encourage them to think of related words by choosing root words. For example, 'signature' might lead to discussion of 'sign', 'signal' and 'significant'. You could also suggest that they should try to use the word, correctly, as often as possible during the day.

Poetry

The Programme of Study and the National Literacy Strategy state that certain genres should be included in children's reading. Sometimes you might read extracts from works which are usually read only by adults. For example, Shakespeare, Keats and Wordsworth's works include passages which have relevance for children and which make use of exciting and interesting vocabulary and phrasing which children may find fascinating. The witches' brew in *Macbeth*, the beginning of Keats' 'Ode to Autumn', and Wordsworth's 'Daffodils' are all accessible for most KS2 children.

The poems listed below are intended to give examples of the kind of poetry which might be used both to entertain and enthuse listeners and to fulfil the National Curriculum and National Literacy Strategy requirements:

- Roald Dahl, 'The Centipede's Song';
- Eleanor Farjeon, 'Cats';
- T S Eliot, 'Macavity';
- Christina Rossetti, 'The Months';
- Ted Hughes, 'The Thought Fox', 'Autumn Song';
- Pam Ayres, 'Oh, I Wish I'd Looked After Me Teeth';
- Hilaire Belloc, 'Jim', 'Matilda';
- Wilfred Wilson Gibson, 'Flannan Isle';
- Alfred Noyes, 'The Highwayman';
- Lewis Carroll, 'The Jabberwocky';
- Michael Rosen, 'When You're a Grown Up';
- John Masefield, 'Sea Fever', 'Cargoes';
- Ogden Nash, 'Winter Morning';
- Thomas Hood, 'November';
- Marriott Edgar, 'The Lion and Albert';
- Mary O'Neill, 'Mimi's Fingers';
- John Keats, 'There Was a Naughty Boy'.

Other texts which are introduced might include prayers and hymns, folk songs, and extracts from the Bible and from other religious books.

In responding to poetry, children might attempt to do some of the following:
- dramatize or write the story of a narrative poem as a newspaper item;

- sequence segments;
- compare with other poems on a similar subject;
- read the poems aloud themselves;
- use cloze work to draw attention to rhyme and rhythm;
- draw or paint images from a poem;
- learn a poem or section of a poem.

Encourage discussion about poets' use of language and foster the use of terms which describe different types of poetry and different features of poems. For example, you might discuss the use of literal and figurative language, similes, metaphors and imagery. This could lead to the children having opportunities to write their own poems using some of these devices.

Introduce the children to sonnets, narrative poems, elegies, ballads and even raps. The THRASS raps may already be familiar to some children and their use may be a starting point for more adventurous word play.

'Lone Dog' by Irene McLeod is a good example of the skilful use of repetition, rhyme and rhythm, while 'Our Tree in Spring' by E Nesbit provides an example of the use of imagery. For a good example of similes, 'Deeds not Words' by an anonymous author should prove useful. All three poems may be found in *A Puffin Book of Verse*.

Introduce children to dialect and non-standard

English in poetry (look at Pam Ayres, Robert Burns and Benjamin Zephaniah) as this encourages them to consider the nature of standard English, too.

Limericks

Read some examples (be careful!) and ask children to make up their own either individually or in groups of five, passing the limericks round so that each child contributes a line. This activity can be linked to work on phoneme-grapheme correspondence and onset and rhyme. As part of a Literacy Hour, you could begin by introducing the limerick format and then go on to provide examples which require completion. Children could suggest possible rhymes and these could be written on the board and discussed with particular reference being made to the ways in which phonemes can be written in different ways. The children could make use of rhyming dictionaries to explore further possibilities and you could ask them to make collections of rhymes both at school and at home.

Adjective/noun poems

Ask children to write a piece of descriptive poetry confined to adjectives and nouns. Encourage them to make use of dictionaries, thesauruses and other sources to find interesting adjectives to describe nouns. The poems should be based upon a single theme such as a type of weather, a season or a holiday. For example:

Crunchy leaves, naked trees,
Swirling mist, soaking grass.

might be used to describe autumn. The poems might be left as they are or they could be starting points for more detailed descriptive work. The original poem could be displayed next to the more developed one to show the children and their parents how the work evolved.

Non-fiction

For some children, reading becomes difficult when they are faced with non-fiction texts because they have had a reading diet largely confined to stories. They will need to be shown that authors present materials differently according to their purpose. Show them how non-fiction texts work (see below) and give them extensive work on alphabetical order and the use of indexes and contents pages.

Examining the structure

Analyse the structure of a non-fiction book. Make a display of pages from an old book (or photocopies from a new one) to show features such as the title page; the publisher's details, publication date and ISBN; the contents page; the use of headings, sub-headings, illustrations and captions; the index; the publisher's blurb; and the biographical notes on the author. Place questions alongside the display which can be answered by studying it.

Look, too, at the structure of dictionaries. Use an enlarged dictionary page or an overhead projection to demonstrate how words are set out, how definitions are given, how the first and last word on each spread are usually printed at the top of the pages to make for easy reference, and how some dictionaries show how words should be pronounced, which parts of speech they are, and sometimes how they are adapted to different parts of speech. You could study different layouts from a range of examples and ask the children to decide which is the easiest to use and what age group each would be most suitable for.

Using catalogues

Reference skills may be developed through the use of mail order catalogues or by using street atlases and other maps. When children are able to relate their work to something familiar they often learn more quickly and, if you use catalogues which include toys and games, you should ensure interest and enthusiastic participation. You can incorporate this activity into mathematical work, giving them a budget with which they have to buy Christmas or birthday presents for family and friends without spending all their money. This will involve them in

finding items in the index, looking at prices, and seeking alternatives which enable them to stay within their budget limit.

Fact or fiction?

In this activity children use reference books to produce statements which may or may not be true; these can be displayed or placed, loose, in the fronts of the books. Others then have to use the same and other books to check the statements. This activity involves the children in initiating work for each other, therefore you will need to monitor it carefully. If children find the activity difficult, try providing some statements as a starting point and ask the whole class or group to check their veracity, preferably making use of a text book of which you have enough copies for everyone to see one.

Text reshuffle

Divide a passage into paragraphs or sentences, cut it up and then ask the children to work in pairs or small groups to organize it logically. This encourages consideration of the concepts of introduction and conclusion and invites children to make use of semantic skills to determine an appropriate order. A subsequent plenary session should allow for a sharing of ideas by different groups.

Advertisements

Provide a selection of advertisements from magazines and newspapers and ask children to look at the style and types of words used. They could conduct a survey of advertisements to find out which words were most commonly used. Ask them to produce their own for school performance events. You can also use advertisements to discuss the presentation of facts and opinions and the effectiveness of different layouts and presentations. This could lead to an exploration of the fonts and other presentational devices available on word processors.

Listening carefully

Provide a passage of writing and then read another version of the passage which contains errors or slight differences. Ask the children to mark the places in the text where they spot differences. This can be done by individuals or pairs or orally as a class with all of the children looking at an overhead projection of a passage while you read the other version. One strategy here might be to include lots of antonyms in the version which you read so that the meaning is altered. This could lead on to a discussion about opposites and the ways in which

prefixes may be used to give a root word a different meaning.

Writing

Developing range

Instructions

Children can write instructions for games, experiments, journeys and so on. This work could be developed out of research work such as that done in preparation for a school trip.

Diagrams and charts

Instead of always writing prose, children can report on visits and topics studied using flow charts, cartoon strips and so on. Collect examples of charts and diagrams from newspapers and magazines and display them to provide ideas.

Making a class dictionary

This can be associated with a topic or may be more general work, based upon words which the children use frequently. You should first do some work on the structure of dictionaries (see page 33). Children might begin by looking at their own writing and identifying those words which occur frequently. These could be written on individual slips of paper and be pinned to the wall under letter headings. Some children can then rearrange them into alphabetical order, making use of second and third letters to do this. Write the words on the board and the class or a group or pairs can work together to produce definitions before comparing them with those in published dictionaries. The work on the

structure of dictionaries will help to establish what features to incorporate and a suitable layout to use.

When a class dictionary has been produced in handwritten form, children can go on to enter their definitions in a computer file which can build up into a reference source to be added to regularly. Teach them to use the SORT function to ensure that lists are in correct alphabetical order.

Notices

A class noticeboard can encourage a variety of different styles of writing. For example, advertisements for exchanges of books, appeals for lost property or announcements about forthcoming events. Children could be asked to maintain the noticeboard themselves and to check each other's writing to ensure that there are no mistakes.

Jokes

Tell a joke and ask the children to retell it in writing, embellishing it as they see fit. This activity requires them to write chronologically and to plan the sequence of events before beginning their writing. Make a collection of jokes or a joke book and ask the children if they could rewrite some of the jokes to make them even funnier or ask them to enlarge a joke they like into a story. They could use the computer to produce a joke book and sell it in school in aid of a good cause.

Planning a trip

Provide atlases, timetables and so on and ask children to plan a journey. This might be related to a future school visit or to work in geography. Ask the children to write down instructions so that other pairs or small groups can check the routes.

Invented mysteries

In this activity, children 'find' a wallet, a letter or another item which has been specially prepared by you and placed in an unusual setting, and have to solve a mystery in writing. They might be asked to examine the contents of a wallet which has been left for them to discover and which contains various clues such as notes, train or bus tickets and addresses, which will involve them in detective work, looking at, perhaps, maps, timetables, newspapers and books to discover more about the owner of the wallet. They could go on to write descriptions of the owner and these could be displayed around the contents of the wallet. The activity requires inference and deduction as well as knowledge of different genres of writing.

Pictures

Unusual pictures can provide stimuli for written work. You could mount each one in the middle of a large piece of paper and ask pairs of children to make notes of their impressions and reactions around the edge as a form of drafting for later work. The children can pass on their notes and pictures so that another couple may add their ideas, and so on until the pictures are returned to the original pairs who make selections from all the ideas to produce pieces of descriptive writing which can be displayed near the pictures. This activity provides good practice in editing skills: selecting, organizing and writing coherently.

Adverb opposites

This activity is designed to encourage children to make use of different structures in their writing and it requires them to begin sentences with adverbs. The children work in pairs. Each child begins by writing a sentence which begins with, say, *Fortunately* and then the children exchange papers and write a sentence beginning with an opposite adverb, in this case, *Unfortunately*. It is important to stress to them that their sentence must follow on from what their partner has written and not from what they have just written. The activity may be started orally round the class before children go on to work with a partner.

Asking questions

After reading a story to the children, ask each one to write a question about the story for others to answer. Encourage questions which demand thought rather than one-word answers. This might be done in a reading log of which children make regular use following story reading.

Extra dialogue

Children write additional dialogue for a story. You might ask them, for example, *What did the three bears say when Goldilocks had gone*? and they then have to write appropriate dialogue. As a Literacy Hour activity this could involve a discussion about the use of speech marks as well as work on considering appropriate language for each of the characters.

Diaries

Apart from keeping their own diaries, children could make up diaries of historical figures, celebrities and so on. First, read them extracts from Pepys, Kilvert, Adrian Mole, *Diary of a Nobody*, Anne Frank or Irene Meggison (*Mud on my Doorstep* and *A Little Less Mud*, Hulton) or any other diaries you know of. They will have to find information about the celebrities by using books, magazines and newspapers and then write in an appropriate style. Where historical figures are used, this may lead to the children examining the way in which people used language in the period in question.

Missing adverbs and adjectives

Provide a passage from a piece of children's literature from which you have deleted the adverbs and adjectives and ask the class to add suitable descriptive words to 'bring it alive'. After they've written their versions, look together at the complete original and make comparisons. *Did you choose some of the same words as the author? Which words do you like best? Why?* This also provides a good opportunity to talk about adjectives and adverbs and remind children of their function and the difference between them.

This activity could precede narrative writing or poetry writing in which you invite children to make extensive use of adverbs and adjectives drawing on thesauruses. They could make collections of useful descriptive words and develop them into class thesauruses as reference points for use during writing lessons.

Punctuation

Year 5 children should be using full stops, capital letters and question marks accurately and should be becoming familiar with the use of speech marks, exclamation marks, colons and apostrophes. At this

stage, punctuation work might focus upon these as well as reinforcing work already learned.

Group reading and punctuation

Often, readers seem to pay little attention to some features of punctuation in their reading. This can lead to confusion and it may also mean that they do not have sufficient knowledge to be able to punctuate their own work accurately. Group reading may be used to encourage readers to look at text closely. For example, you can ask children to take turns to read a sentence each, or tell them that particular children will read only the dialogue spoken by a particular character and that someone else will read the text which is not spoken. This virtually forces readers to look for commas and speech marks so that they know when their turns begin and end.

Proof-reading

Encourage children to proof-read their work. This can help with punctuation, especially when they are provided with response partners. The necessity to communicate to someone else through writing can provide the stimulus many children require to develop punctuation skills. Tape-recording work may help some children to realize where it is necessary to indicate pauses, in much the same way as early printers devised schemes for doing the same. Such proof-reading may be easier for children to manage if they are given a check list for checking their work. This might take the form of a list of questions.

▶ *Have you put a capital letter at the beginning of each sentence?*
▶ *Does each sentence end with a full stop, question mark or exclamation mark?*
▶ *Have you used speech marks to show when someone was speaking? Did you start a new line for a new speaker?*
▶ *Have you used commas to separate items in lists?*
▶ *Have you used apostrophes to show words that have been shortened or that something belongs to somebody?*

Often, children who are simply asked to check their work go away and return a few minutes later having either done very little, or having added punctuation in a random way. By providing a checklist, we can enable them to focus on specific aspects of their writing rather than expecting them to spot mistakes in a more general way.

Exclamation marks

Exclamation marks may be introduced through an oral activity in which children pass a word around and try to say it in different ways, for example loudly, angrily, softly or humorously. They then discuss which are exclamations and are shown that these can be denoted in writing by using an exclamation mark to help readers to understand how they were spoken. The class might go on to write short drama scripts in which there are frequent exclamations.

Newspaper headlines are a rich source of exclamation marks and children could make collections of these for a classroom display.

Speech marks

Many children are confused about the placement of inverted commas when writing dialogue and may gain a greater understanding if they are introduced to them through speech bubbles in comics. They could be given copies of comic strip stories with the speech bubbles blanked out and then be asked to add dialogue. Subsequently, they could write the story using speech marks and adding text to show the identity of speakers. Tell them to think of the speech marks as an abbreviated bubble. Children

who are confident with speech marks can do more complex work on changing direct, to reported speech, and vice versa.

Grammar
Parts of speech
● Ask the children to look carefully at a passage of text and use highlighter pens of different colours to mark adjectives, nouns, verbs, adverbs and conjunctions. This could lead to a discussion of alternative words which could be substituted, or of the meanings of some less familiar words. It is particularly important that children realize that many words may be different parts of speech according to the way in which they are used, so get them to look at the functions of the words within their context. For example, it would be wrong to teach children that the word *fast* is an adjective as in *a fast car* without pointing out that it can also be a noun as in *I went on a fast*, a verb as in *I am going to fast for 24 hours*, and an adverb as in *My uncle drives too fast*.

● Encourage the children to notice instances of words which are being used as different parts of speech in what they hear or read.

Tenses
Children often mix tenses within the same piece of writing and may not appreciate when they need to use the past, present and future tenses. Some early reading books are written in the present tense and these may be used as a starting point for discussing the fact that most stories are written in the past tense. Children could be asked to rewrite texts in the past tense or to retell stories for younger readers using the past tense. For some children, much confusion surrounds the verb 'to be' and they may use incorrect forms such as 'we was' and 'I were'. Sometimes this is because of local dialect and discussion of dialects and standard English may be a starting point for exercises which require children to select verbs which agree with their subjects.

Double negatives
● Do the children know the classic example of double negatives – the song which begins *We don't need no education* which does, of course, mean in standard English: *We need education*. Tell the children that, in writing and formal speaking, you would have to say *We don't need education* or *We need no education* to get the singers' message across. Tell them to imagine a parent saying to a child *No sweets today* and the child wailing *I don't want no sweets*. The child is using the double negative correctly, to mean *I want some sweets*. There is widespread use of the double negative in speech – it adds emphasis – and some children may find it difficult to eradicate it from their writing or formal speaking – or see the need to do so. Provide various examples and ask the children, working in pairs, to look at the sentences closely and decide what they actually tell the reader: *I don't want you not to come* or *Jack won't not be going to Barnsley* or *Don't think I can't see you!* or (more difficult) *I haven't got no crisps today*.

Problems may arise when elision is used because some children may not see that the abbreviated form includes the negative. A discussion of elision and negatives can be a good starting point for looking at double negatives.

Spelling
● We often hear people talking about spelling rules, but, when asked to describe some, many people can only think of 'i before e except after c' – a rule with so many exceptions that it is little help. However, there are some useful rules which children could learn and you can introduce these by providing selections of words and asking the children to draw their own conclusions about the rules that apply. For example, you could provide a list of words in their original form and a modified form with -ing added. Some, such as *hope* and *hoping* and *race* and *racing*, drop the final e when adding the suffix, while others, such as *hop* and *hopping* and *drop* and *dropping*, double the final consonant before adding *-ing*. Ask the children to make collections of words which end in *-ing* and work out what the root words were and the rule that applied. Follow this by discussion and explanation as well as exercises to reinforce the rules.

● In Year 5, give children plenty of opportunities to explore vocabulary and to look at ways in which words can be modified through the use of prefixes and suffixes. Collections of words can be made and children should be encouraged to use the *look, say, cover, write, check* approach to learn to spell new words. Talk about the ways in which sounds can be represented and encourage children to attempt to pronounce new words by drawing upon their knowledge of sound-symbol correspondence.

The children might also make collections of words which have irregular sounds (*gnome, pneumatic,* and names such as *Sian* and *Siobhan*) and words which have been acquired from other languages (*anorak, ketchup, kiosk, caravan, ski, bungalow, paella*).

Assessment

Year 5 is, then, a year in which children should refine their written and oral communication skills. In order to assess their progress as readers, consider using miscue analysis and running records to determine where any problems may lie. You should also note any deficiencies which are preventing children from developing as independent readers and writers and pass on these records to Year 6 teachers together with comments on the strategies you have already tried.

What do they know?

By the end of Year 5 children should know the following things:
- how to use contextual clues to help them to read unfamiliar words;
- a wide range of graphemes, blends and digraphs;
- that there are significant differences between different types of books, for example, fiction and non-fiction;
- that there are often several possible graphemes to represent a single phoneme;
- how to use a dictionary to look up spellings and definitions;
- a range of strategies for learning spellings including look say cover write check;
- a variety of poems;
- a range of children's novels;
- how to proof-read their writing to check for mistakes.

What can they do?

They should be able to:
- read aloud to an audience with fluency and accuracy;
- present ideas orally and accept constructive advice;
- be increasingly aware of audience in speaking and in writing;
- understand that prefixes can be used to modify the meanings of words;
- write in joined and legible handwriting;
- punctuate their writing with increasing confidence and accuracy;
- break up words phonically to determine probable pronunciation;
- make notes and then develop these into finished pieces of work;
- draw upon an increasing sight vocabulary;
- use the word processor to help them to draft their writing.

What have they experienced?

They should have:
- read an increased range of different genres in both fiction and non-fiction;
- read independently and in groups;
- written in a variety of styles for real audiences;
- had frequent opportunities to talk about their work in groups and to the whole class;
- developed a positive attitude to literacy;
- made considerable use of reference sources;
- used non-fiction texts extensively and made use of indexes and contents pages to help them to find information.

Mathematics
including Numeracy Hour

The teaching and learning opportunities that you provide for your class in Year 5 build upon the mathematical foundations established in lower Key Stage 2. It is here that children continue to apply the pure mathematics (mathematical knowledge, skills and understanding) they have learned to more sophisticated real-life, problem-solving investigations.

Children also need to continue to develop a firm understanding of new mathematical concepts and make the necessary connections between the mathematical experiences they encounter. That is, between:

- **mathematical symbols**: x^2, $\sqrt{}$, % signs;

- **mathematical language**: *mean, square root, percentage*;

- **pictures** (recognize that $\frac{5}{10}$, $\frac{1}{2}$, 50% or 0.5 is shaded);

- **concrete situations**: *Seventy-five per cent of our class have school dinners. How many children have a packed lunch?*

The teaching and learning objectives contained in this chapter show progression throughout Year 5. It is about 'what' mathematics to teach. So often children's learning is lead by the activity rather than the learning intention that underpins the activity.

It is hoped that what follows will enable you to identify where children are in their stages of development, and where best to develop their learning in the future.

Generally, children should be familiar and successful with the materials, language and activities of one learning objective before starting on the next. Mathematics, however, is not a fixed, linear, hierarchical discipline: it is cumulative rather than sequential. Although the learning objectives presented in this chapter show a step-by-step sequence, they should be tailored to the strengths and abilities of individual children.

Language

Children need to experience mathematics in a rich oral environment, for it is through language that they make meaning out of their experiences.

While still developing the vast range of skills, knowledge and understanding learned from previous learning objectives, children are exposed to new mathematical concepts of ever-increasing difficulty. When they are asked to talk about what they are doing and thinking in mathematics, they not only show you how much they understand, but they also clarify and develop their own understanding. Encourage them to talk about their experiences and make the necessary connections between the language, pictures, symbols and concrete situations they encounter in their learning.

You need to be continually asking questions that will help children to:

● make connections in mathematics: *If you know what 25% of 12 is, what do you think 75% of 12 equals?*;

● develop a greater understanding of the learning objective: *What have you learned from the investigation you have just undertaken?*;

● make new discoveries in mathematics: *What have you done so far?*;

● apply their mathematical knowledge to other contexts: *If you know that $5^2 = 5 \times 5 = 25$, what do you think 6^2 is?*

Estimation and approximation

Development of the ability to estimate and approximate should be a regular part of the mathematics programme in all classes. It is important that you provide children with opportunities to estimate a 'rough answer' to a problem and approximate the 'range' an answer is likely to occur within. Only through practical activities aimed at developing their estimation and approximation techniques will they develop a 'feel for numbers' and know whether their answers are reasonable or not.

Estimation and approximation skills also play an important part in the ability of children to measure with understanding. Children should be continually exposed to real-life situations to develop their estimation and approximation skills.

Encourage your Year 5s to estimate as close to the actual answer as possible. By this stage they should be acquiring greater accuracy in estimating numbers and measurements, in a variety of contexts, with a range of materials and units.

Do they still need apparatus?

Children need to develop their initial understanding of mathematical concepts through the manipulation of concrete materials in everyday contexts that are relevant and practical to their own experiences. Such experiences enable them to 'see and touch' the mathematics they are engaging in.

By Year 5, most children are ready to move away from manipulating concrete apparatus and begin to internalize their understanding and develop more sophisticated 'mental mathematics' strategies. However, when a new concept is introduced, some children may initially need to work with concrete apparatus.

Children's recording

When introducing a new mathematics topic in Year 5 the emphasis should be on consolidating children's mental and written methods and talking about mathematics. However, by now they should be able to record their results confidently using both their own methods of recording and the more conventional mathematical recording techniques.

The Numeracy Hour

During the Numeracy Hour, all the children should be working on mathematics at the same time for the whole period. The mathematics you do will not be part of a general theme or integrated work but is focused on teaching specific mathematical concepts and methods.

You will spend most of the time directly teaching and questioning the class. Children should spend approximately half of their time in a direct teaching relationship with you and the rest of the time working independently either in groups, pairs or individually. Each lesson should follow the following structure.

Introduction: Oral work and mental calculation (about 10 minutes)

Aimed at:
- developing mental fluency in previously taught concepts/methods and developing children's oral skills (whole class).

Main teaching and pupil activities (about 30–40 minutes)

Aimed at:
- introducing children to new mathematical concepts/methods (whole class, group); or
- consolidating previously taught concepts/methods (whole class, group); and
- providing children with opportunities to practise, consolidate, use and apply taught mathematical concepts/methods (groups, pairs, individuals).

Plenary (about 10 minutes)

Aimed at:
- drawing together the main teaching points of the lesson (whole class).

What should they be able to do?

By the end of Year 5, children should have had appropriate and sufficient experiences to help them in the following key areas. The statement 'Children should' refers to the majority of children.

Key area: Using and applying mathematics

You need to provide children with opportunities to:
- use and apply mathematical knowledge, skills and understanding, that have been previously taught, practised and consolidated, in problem-solving situations;
- acquire knowledge, skills and understandings through 'real-life', meaningful, problem-solving investigations.

Making and monitoring decisions to solve problems

Children should be able to:
- plan strategies for working methodically through a problem;
- select the materials and mathematics to use for a task when the information given leaves opportunity for choice;
- develop their own strategies for solving problems when working within mathematics;
- develop their own strategies for solving problems when applying mathematics to practical contexts.

Developing mathematical language and communication

Children should be able to:
- present information and results in a clear and organized way in oral, written and visual form;
- decide on appropriate methods of recording;
- explain reasons for presentation of information and results;
- begin to interpret mathematical information presented in a variety of ways.

Developing mathematical reasoning

Children should be able to:
- investigate, make and test rules, statements and predictions;
- work systematically;
- develop more sophisticated strategies.

Key area: Number

Children should be given opportunities to develop both their own and standard methods of working, mentally, orally and in the written form, in a variety of contexts and using a range of practical resources.

To make sure that children receive a broad and balanced range of experiences, you need to provide your class with activities that employ the following tools:
- concrete materials;
- mental mathematics;
- paper and pencil;
- information technology.

Developing an understanding of place value and extending the number system

Children should be able to:
- recognize, read, write, count and order in figures and words any whole number, including five-, six- and seven-digit numbers;
- identify what each digit in a number represents and partition a number into millions, hundreds of thousands, tens of thousands, thousands, hundreds, tens and units (M, HTh, TTh, Th, H, T, U);
- compare two numbers saying which is more or less and giving a number which lies between them;
- make sensible estimates and approximates of large numbers;
- round a three- or four-digit number to the nearest 10, 100 or 1 000.

Money

Children should be able to:
- use all four operations to solve word problems involving money;
- use percentages to solve problems involving money;
- make simple conversions to foreign currency.

Fractions

Children should be able to:
- use fractional notation;
- use and order mixed numbers, for example, $5\frac{1}{2}$;
- use the terms numerator and denominator;
- recognize equivalence between simple fractions;
- relate hundredths to tenths, for example, $\frac{60}{100} = \frac{6}{10}$;
- change a 'top heavy' fraction to a mixed number, for example, $\frac{14}{10} = 1\frac{4}{10}$;
- recognize whether fractions such as $\frac{3}{8}$ or $\frac{6}{10}$ are more or less than $\frac{1}{2}$;
- find simple fractions, including tenths and hundredths of numbers and quantities, for example, $\frac{3}{4}$ of 16, $\frac{1}{10}$ of 70, $\frac{1}{100}$ of £7.

Decimals

Children should be able to:
- use decimal notation for tenths and hundredths;
- know what each digit represents in a number with up to two decimal places;
- order a set of decimal numbers with the same number of decimal places;
- round a number with one decimal place to the nearest whole number.

Fractions and decimals

Children should be able to:
- recognize the equivalence between the decimal and fraction forms of one-half, one-quarter, three-quarters, and tenths and hundredths.

Percentages

Children should be able to:
- begin to understand percentage as a fraction of 100;
- express one-half, one-quarter, three-quarters, tenths and hundredths as percentages, for example, know that $\frac{3}{4} = 75\%$;
- find simple percentages of whole number quantities, for example, 25% of £4.

Negative numbers

Children should be able to:
- order negative numbers in context;
- calculate a temperature rise or fall across 0°C.

Understanding relationships between numbers and developing methods of computation

Patterns

Children should be able to:
- recognize and extend number sequences formed by counting from any number in steps of constant size;
- recognize and extend the number sequence beyond zero when counting backwards;
- make general statements about odd and even numbers including the outcomes of sums, differences and products;
- recognize multiples of 2, 3, 4, 5, 6, 7, 8, 9, 10, 100 and 1 000, including beyond the tenth multiple;
- know and apply simple tests of divisibility;
- recognize square numbers to 10 x 10 and beyond;
- recognize two-digit prime numbers;
- find all the pairs of factors of any number up to 100;
- make generalizations about patterns;
- make predictions about patterns;
- record observations.

Addition

Children should be able to:
- extend understanding and use of the vocabulary associated with addition;
- understand the principles of the arithmetic laws applying to addition;
- understand doubles of all numbers 1 to 50;
- understand all number pairs that total 100;
- understand and use all the addition facts to 20;
- use knowledge of number facts and place value to add a pair of numbers mentally;
- extend and refine paper and pencil methods to record, explain and support partial mental methods involving addition of:
  - two or more three- or four-digit numbers;
  - a pair of decimal fractions, both with one decimal place or both with two decimal places, for example, £4.67 + £6.86.

Subtraction

Children should be able to:

- extend understanding and use of the vocabulary associated with subtraction;
- understand the principles of the arithmetic laws applying to subtraction;
- understand and use all subtraction facts to 20;
- use knowledge of number facts and place value to subtract a pair of numbers mentally;
- extend and refine paper and pencil methods to record, explain and support partial mental methods involving subtraction of a pair of:
  - three- or four-digit numbers;
  - decimal fractions, both with one decimal places or both with two decimal places, for example, £4.67 – £3.86.

Addition and subtraction

Children should be able to:

- extend understanding of the relationship between addition and subtraction;
- further develop mental strategies for addition and subtraction;
- further develop paper and pencil methods for calculations;
- solve problems involving addition and subtraction.

Multiplication

Children should be able to:

- extend understanding and use of the vocabulary associated with multiplication;
- understand the principles of the arithmetic laws applying to multiplication;
- recall multiplication tables up to 10 x 10;
- recall doubles of whole numbers to 50;
- use paper and pencil methods, estimating by approximating first, to record, explain and support partial mental methods involving multiplication of:
  - TU x U, extending to HTU x U (short multiplication);
  - TU x TU (long multiplication).

Division

Children should be able to:

- extend understanding and use of the vocabulary associated with division;
- understand the principles of the arithmetic laws applying to division;
- understand the remainder expressed as a whole number;
- understand the remainder expressed as a decimal;
- develop an understanding of the remainder expressed as a fraction;
- make sensible decisions about rounding up and down after division, including what to do with the remainder;
- understand halves of whole numbers to 100;
- recall division facts related to the 2x, 3x, 4x, 5x, 6x, 7x, 8x, 9x and 10x multiplication tables;
- use paper and pencil methods, estimating by approximating first, to record, explain and support partial mental methods involving division of TU by U, extending to HTU by U (short division).

Multiplication and division

Children should be able to:

- extend understanding of the relationship between multiplication and division;
- further develop mental strategies for multiplication and division;
- further develop paper and pencil methods for calculations;
- solve problems involving known multiplication and division facts;
- choose the appropriate operation when solving multiplication and division problems.

Solving numerical problems

Children should be able to:
* solve numerical problems involving known addition, subtraction, multiplication and division facts in the context of real-life, investigative problems about money, length, mass, volume and capacity, perimeter, area and time.

Key area: Shape, space and measures
Understanding and using properties of shape

3-D solids

Children should be able to:
* extend understanding and use of the vocabulary associated with 3-D solids;
* continue to recognize, name and describe the properties of 3-D solids;
* deduce Euler's relationship between faces, edges and vertices: $F + V = E + 2$;
* sketch nets of a closed cube and other polyhedra;
* construct 3-D solids using various apparatus.

2-D shapes

Children should be able to:
* extend understanding and use of the vocabulary associated with 2-D shapes;
* continue to recognize and name 2-D shapes;
* classify polygons by number of sides;
* distinguish between regular and irregular polygons;
* classify triangles as equilateral, isosceles, scalene or right-angled and know their properties;
* construct rectangles and right-angled triangles using a set square and a ruler;
* draw 2-D shapes in different orientations on grids;
* identify shapes that are congruent.

Symmetry

Children should be able to:
* extend understanding and use of the vocabulary associated with symmetry;
* begin to recognize planes of symmetry in the environment and in 3-D solids such as a cuboid and a square-based pyramid;
* draw the reflections of a simple shape using mirrors.

Understanding and using properties of position and movement

Position

Children should be able to:
* extend understanding and use of the vocabulary associated with position;
* read and plot points using co-ordinates in the first quadrant;
* recognize the 16 points on a compass.

Movement

Children should be able to:
* extend understanding and use of the vocabulary associated with movement;
* recognize simple cases of rotational symmetry;
* collect, make and discuss rotational patterns.

Mathematics

Angle

Children should be able to:

- extend understanding and use of the vocabulary associated with angle;
- understand acute and obtuse angles;
- estimate, measure and draw angles up to 90°, using a protractor;
- calculate angles in a straight line;
- recognize and draw parallel and perpendicular lines, using a set square and ruler.

Understanding and using measures

Length

Children should be able to:

- extend understanding and use of the vocabulary associated with length;
- recognize the centimetre (cm), metre (m), kilometre (km), millimetre (mm) and mile lengths;
- estimate and measure using millimetres, centimetres, metres and kilometres;
- know the relationship between familiar metric units;
- convert larger to smaller units, for example, kilometre to metre, metre to centimetre or millimetre;
- choose and use the appropriate unit and measuring apparatus;
- record estimates and measurements;
- use the four operations to solve problems involving length.

Mass (weight)

In the National Curriculum for mathematics the term 'weight' no longer appears, but has been replaced by the term 'mass'. 'Weight', the amount of pull something exerts, is properly measured in newtons; 'mass', the amount of substance, is measured in grams.

Children should be able to:

- extend understanding and use of the vocabulary associated with mass;
- recognize the gram (g) and kilogram (kg) measures;
- estimate and measure, using grams and kilograms;
- know the relationship between familiar metric units;
- convert larger to smaller units, for example, kilograms to grams;
- choose and use the appropriate unit and measuring apparatus;
- record estimates and measurements;
- use the four operations to solve problems involving mass.

Volume and capacity

Children should be able to:

- extend understanding and use of the vocabulary associated with volume and capacity;
- recognize the litre (l) and millilitre (ml) measures and the pint measure;
- estimate and measure using litres and millilitres;
- know the relationship between familiar metric units;
- know about the imperial gallon;
- find the volume of cuboids;
- use the standard measure centimetre cube (cm³) to measure volume;
- convert larger to smaller units, for example, litre to millilitre;
- choose and use the appropriate unit and measuring apparatus;
- record estimates and measurements;
- use the four operations to solve problems involving volume and capacity.

Perimeter

Children should be able to:

● measure and calculate the perimeter of rectangles and other simple shapes using counting methods and the standard units of metre (m), centimetre (cm), millimetre (mm).

Area

Children should be able to:

● measure and calculate the area of rectangles and other simple shapes using counting methods and the standard units of cm², mm².

Time

Children should be able to:

● extend their understanding and use of the vocabulary associated with time;

● tell the time, using digital and analogue clocks, to the nearest minute;

● estimate and check time, using seconds, minutes and hours;

● use am and pm;

● tell the time using a 24-hour clock;

● use the notation 16:46;

● use timetables;

● use the four operations to solve problems involving time.

Key area: Handling data

In Year 5 children need to formulate questions and use simple statistical methods. They should be given opportunities to access and collect data through purposeful enquiries. The use of computers should be encouraged as a source of interesting data and as a tool for representing data.

Collecting, representing and interpreting data

Handling data

Children should be able to:

● collect, record, discuss and predict numerical data frequency tables with grouped data;

● collect, record, discuss and predict numerical data using bar line graphs involving vertical axes labelled in 2s, 5s 10s or 20s, first where intermediate points have no meaning (for example, scores on a dice rolled 400 times) then where they may have meaning (for example, room temperature over time);

● collect, record, discuss and predict numerical data using pictograms (with the symbol representing 2, 5, 10 or 20 units);

● find the mode, median and range of a set of data.

Probability

Children should be able to:

● classify events according to their degree of likelihood, using appropriate vocabulary;

● begin to recognize and predict the outcome of equally likely events such as choosing a black playing card or rolling a six on a die.

Practical ideas

Numeracy Hour

Virtually all of the practical ideas which follow are suitable for using in Numeracy Hour. If, for example, your objective was to provide children with the opportunity to solve word problems about money, you might plan your Numeracy Hour in the following way.

Introduction: Oral work and mental calculation (10 minutes)

Play Bingo with addition, subtraction, multiplication and division questions, including some about money (see page 61).

Main teaching and pupil activities (30–40 minutes)

▶ Give the class a word problem involving money (see page 52);
▶ ask the children to solve the problem, individually or in pairs;
▶ invite individual children to give their answer to the question and explain how they arrived at it;
▶ discuss the answer(s) and method(s);
▶ provide another example, if necessary;
▶ give the children a worksheet containing a number of word problems about money.

Plenary (10 minutes)

▶ Ask individual children to offer answers and methods to various questions from the worksheet;
▶ discuss the answers and methods with the class.

Assessment

Most of the activities can be used for some form of assessment. However, those that have the ○ symbol in the margin alongside them are particularly useful for assessment purposes.

Making a start

The first activities under each main heading are particularly suitable for introducing the concept. Generally speaking there is progression within the group of activities under each main heading, and therefore you may want to follow the sequence shown.

Developing key areas
Number

Place value
Knowing numbers

○ Count round the room from any whole number, including five-, six- and seven-digit numbers, forwards and backwards.

● Display place value posters for any whole number, including five-, six- and seven-digit numbers, to familiarize children with place value. On the place value poster display the number, number name and place value representation.

TTh	Th	H	T	U

45 758

forty-five thousand, seven hundred and fifty-eight

HTh	TTh	Th	H	T	U

865 789

eight hundred and sixty-five thousand, seven hundred and eighty-nine

M	HTh	TTh	Th	H	T	U

3 521 426

three million, five hundred and twenty-one thousand, four hundred and twenty-six

Number charts and squares

☼ Use a 1–100 chart, 10–1 000 chart, 100–10 000 chart, 1 000–100 000 chart, 10 000–1 000 000 chart for the following activities.

● Count forwards/backwards in 1s, 10s, 100s, 1 000s, 10 000s.

● Identify the patterns that occur in the columns and rows: for example, the pattern of 500s in the hundreds column and the pattern of 2 000s in the thousands row:

100	200	300	400	**500**	600	700	800	900	1000
1 100	1 200	1 300	1 400	**1 500**	1 600	1 700	1 800	1 900	2 000
2 100	2 200	2 300	2 400	**2 500**	2 600	2 700	2 800	2 900	3 000
3 100	3 200	3 300	3 400	**3 500**	3 600	3 700	3 800	3 900	4 000

100	1100	**2 100**	3 100	4 100	5 100	6 100	7 100	8 100	9 100
200	1200	**2 200**	3 200	4 200	5 200	6 200	7 200	8 200	9 200
300	1300	**2 300**	3 300	4 300	5 300	6 300	7 300	8 300	9 300
400	1400	**2 400**	3 400	4 400	5 400	6 400	7 400	8 400	9 400

● Ask the children to complete an incomplete square of the type listed below. Alternatively, they could complete an incomplete square which follows a different pattern.

200		400	500	600	700		900	1000	
1 100	1 200	1 300		1 500	1 600	1 700	1 800	1 900	2 000
	2 200	2 300	2 400	2 500		2 700	2 800		3 000
3 100	3 200		3 400	3 500	3 600		3 800	3 900	4 000

● Cover up a number or numbers and ask the children to identify the covered number(s).

100	200	300	400	500	600	700	800	900	1 000
1 100	1 200	1 300	1 400	1 500	1 600	1 700	1 800	1 900	2 000
2 100	2 200	2 300	2 400	2 500	2 600	2 700	2 800	2 900	3 000
3 100	3 200	3 300	3 400	3 500	3 600	3 700	3 800	3 900	4 000

● Give the children a completed square with jigsaw markings that they have to cut and put back together as in the example above. Alternatively, the children can make their own number square jigsaws.

Number cards

● Using a set of number cards in the range 0–1 000 000, display two number cards. *Can you tell me any number that lies between 402 656 and 456 627? Which number is more/less?* Repeat.

● Make any number in the range 0–1 000 000 using 0–10 number cards. Discuss the value of each digit. *What is the value of the 5 in 3 567? How many tens of thousands are there in 3 567 501?*

● Using a selection of number cards in the range 0–1 000 000, ask the children to place them in order. For example:

》 47 235; 354 604; 2 436 080;

》 24 646; 25 364; 2 756; 654; 4 657.

Less and more than

✪ Ask the children what is 1, 10, 100, 1 000, 10 000, 100 000 or 1 000 000 **more than** any number in the range 1–1 000 000. *What is 100 more than 566 707?*

● Ask the children what is 1, 10, 100, 1 000, 10 000, or 100 000 **less than** any number in the range 1–1 000 000 (not involving negative numbers). *What is 1 000 less than 5 343?*

Calculators

Using a calculator, children should be able to:

》 use the clear key, all four operation keys, the equals key and the decimal point to calculate with realistic data;

》 select the correct key sequence to carry out calculations involving more than one operation, for example $(84 \times 9) - 64 = \square$;

》 key in fractions, recognize the equivalent decimal form and use this to compare two fractions;

》 recognize simple decimal notation, for example, $\frac{1}{2} = 0.5$, $\frac{1}{4} = 0.25$, $\frac{1}{3} = 0.33$;

》 key in and interpret the outcome of calculations with money, for example, 0.6 = 60p;

》 identify 67.333333333 as '67 point 3 recurring';

》 round numbers to the nearest whole when displayed on a calculator, for example, 5.78 as 6;

》 know that 34.75 lies between 34 and 35;

》 recognize simple decimal notation involving money for example, £5.36 + £4.94 = 10.3 is the same as £10.30;

》 use the constant key for repeated addition, subtraction, multiplication and division;

》 understand a negative number output;

》 use the square root key;

》 have a feel for the approximate size of an answer after a calculation;

》 check a calculation by performing the inverse calculation.

Estimation and approximation

● Encourage children to develop their estimation and approximation skills involving large numbers by asking questions such as:

How many children are there in the school?
How many letters are on this newspaper page?
How many counters are in this container?
How many days to Christmas/Easter/the summer holidays?
How many hours in a year?
How far is it from the farthest football goal to the front gate?
What is 3 782 + 8 549?
What is half of 79 896?
What is 393 multiplied by 7?

Encourage children to explain how they arrived at their estimate. They can then record their estimates and find the difference between the estimate and the actual answer.

● Show children a three- or four- digit number card and ask them to round it to the nearest 10, 100 or 1 000. For example, 5 785 rounded to the nearest 10 is 5 790, to the nearest 100 is 5800 and to the nearest 1 000 is 6 000.

Money

✪ Ask the children to name and identify all the British coins and notes to make sure that there are no gaps in anyone's knowledge.

● Encourage children to apply their knowledge of addition, subtraction, multiplication and division number facts to solve calculations involving money, such as finding totals and giving change. *In the newsagents Jason bought two papers at 32p each and one magazine at £2.30. How much did he spend altogether? How much change would he get from £5?*

● Ask children to use notes and coins in simple contexts, adding, subtracting, multiplying and dividing, as well as calculating with fractions, decimals and percentages in both single- and multistep operations.

If all items in a shop have 25% off, how much would you get off £34? How much off £16?
If five bags of oranges cost £5.50, how much does three bags cost?
What is 20% of £5.60?
Simone is able to save 60p a week. She wants to buy a CD that costs £4.40. If she already has £1.50,

how many weeks will it take her to save enough money to buy the CD?

● Give children practice in converting pounds to pence and vice versa:
£1.67 = 167p; 467p = £4.67; £31.87 = 3 187p; 8 407p = £84.07.

● Use a geography project on another country to offer problems involving foreign currency. Ask them to suppose that exchange rates for £1 are: 1.6 US dollars; 9.5 French francs; 280 Spanish pesetas. *How many dollars, French francs and Spanish pesetas do you get for £5?*

● Bring in a list of exchange rates from a newspaper and ask children to 'buy' £10 worth of any currency. Record how much everyone would get in the currency of their choice. (If you have the time, you could give them paper 'money' with the denomination and currency name on it.) Ask children to bring in real, low value, coins in any currency for a display. They can check exchange rates every week (in the same paper), and at the end of the term can 'sell' their currency back to you at current rates. *Who still has £10? Who has more? Who has less?* (Most children will have less because of the difference between buying and selling rates – a useful lesson to learn.)

Some children might like to check rates in local banks to see if they got a good rate from you!

Fractions
Representing fractions
Dictate fractions and ask children to write them in both words and numerals. (Five-tenths and $\frac{5}{10}$. Two wholes and three-quarters and $2\frac{3}{4}$.) Identify children who are having problems with this and give them practice with colouring in grids and so on.

Equivalent fractions
● Teach the children how to reduce a fraction to an equivalent fraction by dividing both the numerator and denominator by the same number (cancelling). For example, $\frac{4}{10}$ is equivalent to $\frac{2}{5}$. Again, have squared paper ready so that doubtful children can experiment and see that the fractions really are equivalent.

● Teach them that, for example, $\frac{4}{10}$ can be changed to an equivalent fraction, such as $\frac{40}{100}$ by multiplying the numerator and denominator by the same number. (They can colour in 100 squares to check the equivalence.) Ask them for the equivalents in

hundredths for $\frac{1}{10}$, $\frac{3}{10}$, $\frac{1}{4}$, $\frac{5}{10}$ or $\frac{1}{2}$ and $\frac{3}{4}$. Some children will find this simple. Others may struggle. Pair the strugglers with the confident children. *Can you find a good way to help your partner to understand these equivalents?*

● Show children the patterns in equivalent fractions for $\frac{1}{2}$, $\frac{1}{3}$, $\frac{1}{4}$, $\frac{1}{5}$ and $\frac{1}{10}$. For example, $\frac{1}{5}$ = $\frac{2}{10}$ = $\frac{3}{15}$ = $\frac{4}{20}$. *Can you see the pattern? What do you think the next equivalents will be? Now try it for another fraction.*

Improper fractions
● Teach the children the difference between a 'proper' and an 'improper' fraction. An improper fraction is top heavy. Explain that proper fractions always have a smaller number above the line than below
Write an improper fraction, say $\frac{12}{5}$, on the board and demonstrate it by colouring in grids of five. The children can see that there are twelve-fifths, but also that there are enough fifths to make whole numbers. *How many whole numbers? How many fifths left over?* Write $2\frac{2}{5}$. Some children will be able to see immediately that this is equivalent to dividing the numerator by the denominator. Others may have to colour in more grids before they are convinced of this.

● Show the children, too, how to convert a mixed number to an improper fraction. *If we have $3\frac{2}{3}$, how many thirds are there in the three wholes?* (9). *And then we add on the two other thirds. How many thirds altogether?* ($\frac{11}{3}$).

Working with fractions
● Children need to be able to add to, or subtract from, any familiar fraction:
$4\frac{3}{4} + \square = 6$;
$8 - \frac{4}{5} = \square$, and so on.
Once again, work with colouring grids or segmented circles will help those with difficulties.

● Help children to see the relationship between fractions and division:
$\frac{1}{2}$ x 8 is the same as 8 ÷ 2;
one muesli bar divided four ways is the same as $\frac{1}{4}$ or 1 ÷ 4;
$\frac{12}{3}$ is the same as 12 ÷ 3.

◯ Ask the children to count on from 0 and back from 10 in halves, quarters, thirds, fifths and tenths.

● Ask the children to make a number line showing wholes, thirds, sixths, twelfths.

● Give them a number line marked from 0 to 1 with 20 divisions, and ask them to mark different fractions on it.

● Ask them to order a set of familiar fractions and mixed numbers, for example, $2\frac{3}{4}$, $1\frac{1}{2}$, $\frac{1}{2}$, $1\frac{3}{4}$, $\frac{1}{4}$, $\frac{4}{5}$, $\frac{1}{3}$.

● Give them familiar fractions and mixed numbers to round to the nearest whole number ($\frac{1}{2}$ rounds up).

● Make sure that the children can find fractions of numbers or measurements.
What is $\frac{1}{10}$ of 100, 40, 600 ...?
What is $\frac{1}{5}$ of 20, 10, 60 ...?
What is $\frac{1}{4}$ of 16, 20, 40 ...?
What is $\frac{1}{10}$ of 70, 20, 500 ...?
What is $\frac{1}{100}$ of 200, 700, 1 000 ...?
What is $\frac{1}{10}$, $\frac{1}{5}$, $\frac{1}{4}$, $\frac{1}{3}$, $\frac{1}{2}$ of £1, 1 metre ...?
What fraction of £1 is 20p?
What fraction of 1 metre is 50 cm?
What fraction of the larger shape is the smaller shape?

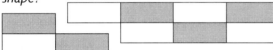

Decimals

✪ Ask the children to count from zero in steps of one-tenth.

Place value

● Look at a decimal number with the class, say 4.8. *What is the value of the 4? What is the value of the 8? How could we write it as a fraction?* ($4\frac{8}{10}$) *What if it was 4.83? What is the value of the 3?* ($\frac{3}{100}$). *If we have 4 and $\frac{8}{10}$ and $\frac{3}{100}$, how could we write that? Could we convert the $\frac{8}{10}$ to hundredths? Then how many hundredths would we have altogether?*

● Repeat this with different numbers, up to two decimal places, making sure the children understand the value of the different numbers and can write them as fractions.

● Go on to look at the value of the 5, 2, 6 and the 4 in £52.64; the 1, 2 and the 5 in 12.5m and so on.

● Then try converting fractions to decimals. Many children find this easier. *Write $\frac{3}{10}$ and $\frac{4}{100}$ as a decimal. What about $\frac{2717}{100}$ and $\frac{8}{100}$?* If children find this difficult, try presenting it as money. *How would you write seventeen pounds and eight pence?*

Working with decimals

● Using a calculator, ask children to change:
2.56 to 2.69;   12.56 to 12.76;
6.4 to 65;   23 to 2.3.

✪ Ask the children to start at 4.1 and count back in steps of 0.1.

● Can they continue the pattern: 1.1, 1.3, 1.5, 1.7, 1.9 ... ?

● At odd times, ask questions like: *Who can tell me a decimal fraction between 6 and 7?* Alternatively, place decimals on a number line between 0 and 1. For example:

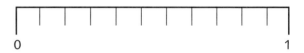

● Ask the children to put in order decimal amounts, smallest first. For example:
£3.99, 30p, £3, 33p; 4.5m, 2.3m, 4.7m, 2.9m; 2.3, 5.6, 2.4, 6.7.

● Ask the children to convert:
▶ pounds to pence and vice versa;
▶ grams to kilograms and vice versa;
▶ millilitres to litres and vice versa;
▶ centimetres to metres and vice versa.

● Ask the children to round a decimal to the nearest whole number (4.2 = 4; £4.76 = £5; 6.8m = 7m).

Word problems

Make up word problems which require children to solve calculations involving mixed units, such as 73p + £2.89 or 7.5m + 20cm or 6kg + 250g. The children can also make them up for their friends. (Setters must know the answers!)

Fractions and decimals

● Give the children calculators and ask them to experiment with finding the decimal equivalent of different fractions. *How do you convert a fraction to a decimal?* (Divide the numerator by the denominator. Some children – and adults – have difficulty in remembering which is which, so you can also say 'Divide the top by the bottom'.) *Which fractions show as two decimal places or less?* (Any fractions that can be expressed in hundredths.)

● Now ask children, without calculators, to convert halves, fifths, tenths and hundredths to decimals and vice versa. For example, $\frac{26}{100}$ = 0.26, 0.45 = $\frac{45}{100}$.

Matching game
● Children shuffle a selection of fraction cards and corresponding decimal cards together and play Pelmanism or Snap with them.

Percentages
● Introduce the children to the term 'percentage'. Then show them the % sign. *Have you ever seen this sign before? Where? What do you think it means?* Tell the children that 'per cent' means 'for every hundred' or 'out of 100'.

● Spread 100 red, blue, green and yellow multilink cubes on a desk. Tell the children that there are 100 altogether. Ask them to count the number of cubes of each colour to themselves and record what 'percentage' there is of each colour. Then check the answers. There may have been the odd miscount but everyone should have got roughly the same percentage.

● Children can start by learning simple percentages in terms of fractions. Ask them *What is $\frac{1}{2}$ of 100? What is $\frac{1}{4}$ of 100? What is $\frac{1}{10}$ of 100?* Write the answers on the board and then below write: 1 = 100%; $\frac{1}{2}$ = 50%; $\frac{1}{4}$ = 25%; $\frac{1}{10}$ = 10%.
  Then ask children appropriate questions while they can see this list. *If there are 30 children in the class and 50% are boys, how many boys are there? I went on holiday for 12 days and it rained for 25% of the time. How many wet days did I have? Martin gets 80p pocket money and he saves 10% of it. How much does he save?*

● Use shaded grids and ask children to say what percentage is shaded/not shaded. For example:

● Make sure that children know the relationship between percentages and fractions and decimals. Draw up a chart together, then the children can copy it in their books.

  1% = $\frac{1}{100}$ = 0.01;
  10% = $\frac{1}{10}$ = 0.1;
  20% = $\frac{2}{10}$ = 0.2;
  25% = $\frac{1}{4}$ = 0.25;
  50% = $\frac{1}{2}$ = 0.5;
  75% = $\frac{3}{4}$ = 0.75;
  100% = 1 = 1.

Encourage the chidren to use their knowledge of fractions to solve problems such as 30% of 60:
  $\frac{30}{100}$ x 60   = $\frac{3}{10}$ x 6   = 18.

● Ask children to solve calculations involving percentages in the context of word problems, including money and measurements: *45% of the class are boys. What percentage are girls? What is 10% of 4 metres? A jumper was marked '50% off'. If its original price was £15.00, how much does it cost now?*

Negative numbers
● Re-introduce the concept of negative numbers using a number line. Re-introduce the terms 'positive numbers' and 'negative numbers'.

● Discuss with the children the concept of negative numbers in familiar contexts such as temperature and on a calculator display.

Number line
● Discuss the fact that numbers go on forever in both directions, hence the arrows on the number line.

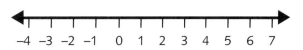

● Ask children to complete a number line with missing positive and negative numbers.

Reach −2
Each child has a number line similar to the one above but extending to, say, −7, and a counter. Children place their counter on any number on the number line. Throw a die, calling either 'add' or 'subtract' before you call the number thrown, say, 'add 4'. The children then have to move their counter along the corresponding number of spaces. Keep throwing the die and calling out 'add' or 'subtract' until a child lands on −2.

Working with negative numbers
◎ Ask the children to write down all the whole numbers between −10 and 5.

◎ Give the children a set of jumbled cards, −20 to 10, to put in order.

● Ask them which temperature is lower: −13°C or −15°C?

● Ask the children to take temperature readings using a thermometer and record the data in a graph.

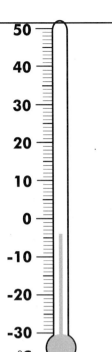

For example, body temperatures, inside a fridge, inside a freezer, from a cold drink, from a cup of coffee, and so on.

● Ask them to calculate a temperature rise or fall across 0°C. *The current temperature rises by 10°C. What is the new temperature?*

● Compare winter temperatures in this country with those in Canada (below). Calculate the differences in temperature and discuss.

Quebec			Temperature °C
Highest recorded	Average daily		Lowest recorded
	max.	min.	
J 11	-8	-17	-37
F 9	-7	-16	-36
M 18	-1	-9	-30
A 27	7	-2	-18
M 33	16	5	-7
J 34	22	11	-1
J 36	24	14	4
A 36	23	12	3
S 31	18	8	-3
O 25	11	3	-10
N 22	2	-4	-29
D 12	-6	-13	-36

Methods of computation
Patterns
✿ Children identify the place value patterns in one-, two-, up to seven-digit numbers.

✿ The class counts forwards and backwards in 1s, 10s and 100s from any two- or three-digit number and in repeated steps from any number in the range 0–1 000 000.

✿ Ask the children to describe and extend sequences such as: 57, 64, 71, 78 …; 35, 31, 27, 23 … *What is the rule?* Children can make up their own sequences and ask others to describe and extend them.

✿ Children find the missing numbers in sequences such as: □, □, 38, 41, 44, □, 50. *What is the rule?* Children can make up their own and ask others to describe and extend them.

● Discuss with the children some general principles of odd and even numbers:
▶ the sum of three even numbers is even;
▶ the sum of three odd numbers is odd;
▶ the difference between one odd and one even number is odd;
▶ the product of two even numbers is even;
▶ the product of two odd numbers is odd;
▶ the product of one even number and one odd number is even;
▶ an odd number can be written as twice a number plus one, for example, 21 = 2 x 10 + 1.

✿ Give children practice in continuing sequences involving odd and even numbers, such as 147, 149, 151, 153 … ; 362, 364, 366, 368 …

✿ Ask: *What odd number comes before 574? What even number comes after 371?*

✿ Children should be able to recognize multiples in all the multiplication tables to 10 x 10. For example, *Ring all the numbers divisible by 3.*

2	3	5	12	16	18	20	24

Which numbers in the box are also divisible by 6?

● Ask the children to identify the patterns in all the multiplication tables to 10 x 10 and the related division facts. For example:

1 x 7 = 7   7 ÷ 7 = 1;
2 x 7 = 14   14 ÷ 7 = 2;
3 x 7 = 21   21 ÷ 7 = 3, and so on.

● Discuss with the children the relationship between the various multiplication tables:

2x, 4x, 8x   (fours are double twos, eights are double fours);
3x, 6x, 9x   (sixes are double threes, nines are treble threes);
5x, 10x   (tens are double fives).

● Can the children recognize the multiples of 10, 100, 1 000 and 10 000, 100 000 and 1 000 000? For example:

60   is a multiple of 10;
400   is a multiple of 10 and of 100;
9 000   is a multiple of 10, of 100 and a multiple of 1 000.

Square roots
● Introduce children to the square root symbol: √. Explain that a square root of a number is another

number which, when multiplied by itself, will equal the first number. For example, the square root of 36 is 6, since 6 x 6 = 36, and it can be written as $\sqrt{36} = 6$. Look at the square numbers they know from their tables: 4, 9, 16, 25, 36, 49, 64, 81, 100. *Can you tell me the square root of ...?*

● Give children the opportunity to find the square roots of larger numbers using a calculator and the square root function.

Factors

● Children should be able to find all the pairs of factors of any number to 100. For example, the factors of 20 are 2 and 10, 4 and 5 and 20. *Which tables does '20' come in?*

Prime numbers

Explain to the children that a prime number is a number that does not break down into smaller, equal parts. They are numbers that do not appear in the answers to multiplication tables except when they are multiplied by 1. Prime numbers will only divide exactly by themselves and 1.

● Ask the children to name a prime number (for example, 2, 3, 5, 7, 11, 13, 17, 19, 23, 29, 31...).

● Ask the children, working in pairs or groups, to list all the prime numbers to 100.

● Children should be able to identify and recognize two- and three-digit prime numbers.

Addition
Mental calculation strategies

When adding mentally, children find crossing the 10s, 100s or 1 000s boundary difficult. Remind them of the range of mental strategies that will help them to solve these types of calculations more easily.

▶ Start with the largest number first.
▶ Count forward in repeated steps.
▶ Count up through the next multiple of 10, 100 or 1 000.
▶ Use two stages to add 9 (+10 −1), 19 (+20 −1), 29 (+30 −1) and so on.
▶ Use two stages to add 11 (+10 +1), 21 (+20 +1), 31 (+30 +1) and so on.
▶ Partition into hundred, tens and units, adding the most significant digits first:

    524 + 58
   (520 + 50) = 570
     4 + 8 = 12
   570 +12 = 582.

▶ Add nearest multiple of 10 or 100 and adjust:

   365 +86
  (365 + 100) – 14
   465 – 14
   451

▶ Use patterns of similar calculations.
▶ Use the relationship between addition and subtraction.
▶ Use knowledge of number facts and place value to add pairs of: three-digit multiples of 100; two-digit numbers to one decimal place.

● Teach the children to solve the following types of addition calculations using the mental calculation strategies mentioned above.
▶ Addition of a pair of three-digit multiples of 10, crossing the 100s boundary, but not 1 000.
▶ Addition of three or more three-digit multiples of 100, crossing 1 000.
▶ Addition of a multiple of 100 to a three- or four-digit number, crossing 1 000.
▶ Addition of a three-digit multiple of 10 to a three-digit number, without crossing the 100s boundary.
▶ Finding what must be added to a three-digit number to make the next higher multiple of 100.
▶ Finding what must be added to a decimal fraction with units and tenths to make the next higher whole number: $7.3 + \square = 8$.
▶ Addition of a pair of decimal fractions each with units and tenths, or each with tenths and hundredths: $0.45 + 0.62 = \square$.

Paper and pencil procedures

● Teach children to solve addition calculations using paper and pencil procedures to record, support and explain mental methods, building on established mental strategies. Encourage them to discuss and compare their methods.

● Teach children, when they are setting out work in columns, to line up units under units, tens under tens, and so on. Encourage the following paper and pencil procedures for the addition of:

HTU + HTU   crossing the 10s or 100s
                       boundary;
ThHTU + ThHTU   crossing the 10s, 100s or 1 000s
                       boundary.

Method 1: Most significant digit first:

648 +	5 462 +	
175	859	
700	5 000	Add
110	1 200	mentally
13	110	from top
823	11	
	6 321	

Method 2: Crossing through a multiple of 100:

```
  684 +
  547
  700      (684 + 16)   add 16 to get to a multiple of 100
  531 +    (547 – 16)   leaves 531 to add on
1 231
```

Method 3: Adding the least significant digits first and preparing for 'carrying':

```
  684 +
  547
1 231
  1 1
```

```
7 465 +
  558
8 023
  1 1 1
```

Subtraction
Mental calculation strategies

Remind the children of the range of mental strategies that will help them to solve subtraction calculations easily.

▶ Count backwards in repeated steps.

▶ If you know that 6 + 5 = 11, then you also know what 11 – 5 and 11 – 6 are, as all three calculations involve the same three numbers (5, 6, 11).

▶ Find a small difference by counting up from the smaller to the larger number.

▶ Use two stages to subtract 9 (–10 +1), 19 (–20 +1), 29 (–30 +1) and so on.

▶ Use two stages to subtract 11 (–10 –1), 21 (–20 –1), 31 (–30 –1) and so on.

▶ Decrease the largest number to the next multiple of 10 or 100 and subtract the remainder:

```
     7 894 – 5 324
   (7 894 – 5 300) – 24
       2 594 – 24
         2 570.
```

▶ Use patterns of similar calculations.

▶ Use the relationship between addition and subtraction.

▶ Use knowledge of number facts and place value to subtract a pair of numbers mentally.

● Teach children to solve the following types of subtraction calculations using the mental calculation strategies mentioned above.

▶ Subtraction of a pair of three-digit multiples of 10, crossing the 100s boundary, but not 1 000.

▶ Subtraction of three or more three-digit multiples of 100, crossing 1 000.

▶ Subtraction of a single-digit multiple of 100 from a three- or four-digit number, crossing 1 000.

▶ Subtraction of a three-digit multiple of 10 from a three-digit number, without crossing the 100s boundary.

▶ Finding the difference between a pair of numbers lying either side of a multiple of 1 000.

▶ Subtraction of a pair of decimal fractions each with units and tenths, or each with tenths and hundredths: 7.3 – 2.6 = ☐; 0.56 – ☐ = 0.38.

Paper and pencil procedures

Teach children to solve subtraction calculations using paper and pencil procedures to record, support and explain mental methods, building on established mental strategies. Encourage them to discuss and compare their methods.

The following paper and pencil procedures should be encouraged for subtraction of HTU – HTU and ThHTU – ThHTU crossing the 10s, 100s or 1 000s boundary.

865 – 397 =

Method 1: Counting up:

```
865 –                       Leading to
397                         865 –
  3   To make 400           397
400   To make 800             3  To make 400
 65   To make 865           465  To make 865
468                         468
```

Method 2: Crossing down through a multiple of 100:

```
  865 –
  397
  500   (865 – 365)
–  32   (397 – 365)
  468
```

Method 3: Approximating by taking away 100:

```
  865 –
  397
  465   (865 – 400)
+   3   (400 – 397)
  468
```

Method 4: Decomposition:

```
  865 =    800 + 60 + 5
– 397  =–  300 + 90 + 7
                                      Leading to
                                      7 15 15
     =    800 + 50 + 15  { adjusting   865 –
          – 300 + 90 + 7   from T to U } 397
                                        468
     =    700 + 150 + 15 { adjusting
          – 300 + 90 + 7   from H to T }
          400 + 60 + 8   = 468
```

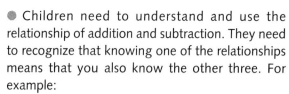

● Children need to understand and use the relationship of addition and subtraction. They need to recognize that knowing one of the relationships means that you also know the other three. For example:

$$36 + 27 = 63$$
$$27 + 36 = 63$$
$$63 - 36 = 27$$
$$63 - 27 = 36$$

Show them how they can use those relationships to check their calculations.

Multiplication
Mental calculation strategies

Remind children of a range of mental strategies that will help them to solve multiplication calculations easily.

▶ To multiply a number by 10/100, shift its digits one/two places to the left.

▶ Use doubling, starting from known facts (such as 8 x 4 is double 4 x 4);

▶ Double any two-digit number by doubling the tens first.

▶ Use factors (8 x 12 = 8 x 4 x 3).

▶ Use closely related facts (multiply by 9 or 11 by multiplying by 10 and adjusting; add facts from the 2x and 4x tables to work out the 6x tables).

▶ Partition (25 x 4 = [20 x 4] + [5 x 4]).

▶ Use the relationship between multiplication and division.

▶ Use knowledge of number facts and place.

● Teach children to solve the following multiplication calculations using the mental calculation strategies mentioned above.

▶ Multiply a two-digit multiple of 10 by a three-digit multiple of 10.

▶ Double any multiple of 5 up to 500.

▶ Consolidate multiplication facts up to 10 x 10.

▶ Multiply a two-digit multiple of 10 or a three-digit multiple of 100 by a single digit.

▶ Multiply a two-digit number by any single-digit number, crossing the 10s boundary.

Paper and pencil procedures

Teach the children to solve multiplication calculations using paper and pencil procedures to record, support and explain mental methods, building on established mental strategies. Encourage them to discuss and compare their methods.

The following paper and pencil procedures should be encouraged for multiplication of TU x U and HTU x U by the children.

Method 1: Partitioning: using the standard algorithm:

```
78 x 6 =              435 x 7 =
   78                    435
 x  6                  x   7
 ----                  -----
  420  (70 x 6)        2 800  (400 x 7)
   48   (8 x 6)          210  ( 30 x 7)
 ----                     35  (  5 x 7)
  468                  -----
                       3 045
```

Method 2: Partitioning: area method:

78 x 6 =

x	70	8	
6	420	48	= 468

435 x 7 =

x	400	30	5	
7	2 800	210	35	= 3 045

Method 3: Halving smaller numbers, doubling others:

```
48 x 6 =   48 x 6
           96 x 3 = 270 + 18
                  = 288
```

● Children should begin to extend one or more of the above methods for multiplication of TU x TU. For example:

46 x 38 =

x	40	6	
30	1200	180	1380
8	320	48	+ 368
			1748

Laws

Children need to understand and use, when appropriate, the principles (but not the names) of the commutative, associative and distributive laws as they apply to multiplication:

Commutative law: 13 x 4 = 4 x 13;

Associative law: 16 x 6 = 16 x (3 x 2) or (16 x 3) x 2;

Distributive law: 14 x 6 = (10 + 4) x 6 = (10 x 6) + (4 x 6) = 60 + 24 = 84.

Division
Tests of divisibility

How many divisibility tests can the children remember? Whole numbers are divisible by:

▶ 100 if the last two digits are 00;

▶ 25 if the last two digits are 00, 25, 50 or 75;

▶ 10 if the last digit is 0;

▶ 9 if the sum of the digits is divisible by 9;

▶ 8 if half of it is divisible by 4 or if the last three digits are divisible by 8;

▶ 6 if it is even and also divisible by 3;

- 5 if the last digit is a 0 or 5;
- 4 if the last two digits are divisible by 4;
- 3 if the sum of the digits is divisible by 3;
- 2 if the last digit is a 0, 2, 4, 6 or 8.

Mental calculation strategies

● Teach children a range of mental strategies that will help them to solve division calculations easily.
- Use halving, starting from known facts (for example, find quarters by halving halves).
- Use the relationship between multiplication and division.
- Use knowledge of number facts and place.

● Teach children to solve division calculations using mental calculation strategies above.
- Divide a four digit multiple of 1 000 by 1 000, 100 or 10.
- Halve a three-digit multiple of 10.
- Consolidate division facts related to the multiplication tables up to 10 x 10.

Paper and pencil procedures

Teach children to solve division calculations using paper and pencil procedures to record, support and explain mental methods, building on established mental strategies. They should be encouraged to discuss and compare their methods. The following paper and pencil procedures should be encouraged for HTU ÷ U.

Method 1: Using repeated subtraction:

$$
\begin{array}{rl}
156 \div 7 = & 156 \\
& -140 \quad (7 \times 20) \\ \hline
& 16 \\
& -\ 14 \quad (7 \times 2) \\ \hline
& 2
\end{array}
$$

Answer = 22 remainder 2

Method 2: Using the standard algorithm, developed from repeated subtraction:

$$
\begin{array}{rl}
156 \div 7 = & \quad\ 22 \\
& 7\,)\overline{156} \\
& -140 \quad (7 \times 20) \\ \hline
& 16 \\
& -\ 14 \quad (7 \times 2) \\ \hline
& 2
\end{array}
$$

Answer = 22 remainder 2

● Children need to understand that, unlike multiplication, division cannot be carried out in any order: 3 x 4 = 4 x 3 but 12 ÷ 3 ≠ 3 ÷ 12.

Remainder

Y5 children should understand the idea of a remainder, when to round up or down after division and what to do with it. They should be able to:
- give a remainder as a whole number: 45 ÷ 4 = 11 remainder 1; 467 ÷ 100 = 4 remainder 67;
- give a remainder as a decimal fraction when dividing by 10 or 2: 45 ÷ 10 = 4.5; 21 ÷ 2 = 10.5;
- give a remainder as a decimal fraction when dividing pounds and pence;
- begin to give a remainder as a fraction: 45 ÷ 4 = $11\frac{1}{4}$;
- find the remainder when dividing with a calculator;
- round decimals to the nearest whole number: 4.2 is between 4 and 5, but nearer to 4;
- decide what to do about a remainder after division and round up or down accordingly.

Consolidating understanding of the four rules

✪ Use flash cards with addition, subtraction, multiplication, division, fraction, decimal or percentage number facts to produce instant recall.

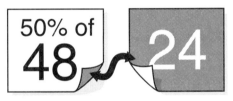

✪ *Can you make 246 ten different ways using as many of the four rules as possible?*
Variation: any number in the range 0–1 000 000.

✪ Ask the children to write examples of addition, subtraction, multiplication, division, fraction, decimal or percentage facts in real contexts.

> The Lottery Commission had £20m. They gave 25% of it for a sports complex in our town, 15% to build cycle tracks, 35% to plant a new forest and they have £5m left

Insist that children write examples which are at the limits of their ability.

● Display addition, subtraction, multiplication, division, fraction, decimal or percentage number facts on wall charts.

☼ Have a number of the day. Throughout the day, challenge children to give different number statements for a particular number using any operation or computational method they can that hasn't been used before.

Bingo

Play Bingo. Using a blank 6x6 grid children choose and write down any 36 numbers from a range you give them of about 50 numbers from 0 to 1 000 000. An example is shown in the next column. Have some number statements prepared which cover all the 50 numbers. Present them to the children in one of the following ways:

▶ a number card, for example: 4000 + 600 + 90 + 1 = □ ;

▶ a spoken addition statement, for example: *Five hundred thousand plus one hundred and eighty-seven thousand and five*;

▶ in a problem-solving context, for example: *The*

45	3 445	65798	65	12	2
456	32	456 087	647	4 961	692
755	3	673 068	32 687	668	7 006
76	4 691	54 607	1 297	687 005	98 001
5	14 555	40 695	4 079	901	590
8 964	43 758	186 795	11	89 334	17

school raised £510 and then were given another £82. How much money did they have altogether? The children have to work out the answer and, if they have that answer on their grid, they cross it out. When a child has crossed out any six numbers that are in a line vertically, horizontally or diagonally, it's 'Bingo!' You can continue until someone has crossed out all of his/her numbers on the grid.
Variation: Ask questions that relate to any one or combination of the following: place value, addition, subtraction, multiplication, division, fractions, decimals, percentages, money, measures, and so on.

20 questions

☼ Give the children 20 quick-fire questions orally, using a range of appropriate mathematical vocabulary. Ask them to write down the answer only. Repeat the next day. *Did you get them all finished? How many did you get correct today/yesterday?*

Beat the clock

☼ Give the children a strip of paper containing 20 simple calculations. Ask the children to complete it in a specified time (say, four minutes). Repeat the next day. *Did you get them all finished? How many did you get correct today/ yesterday?* Give different questions to different groups.

Mathematics

Countdown

○ Work out a calculation involving known number facts and operations. Say, (81 ÷ 9) x 70 – 234 = 396. Don't tell the children – keep it to yourself. Write the numbers 9, 70, 81 and 234 on the board. Tell the children that, using each of these numbers once only, in any order, and using some or all of the four operations, they have to reach the total of 396. You can give the same numbers but different totals to different groups. For example, (81–70) x 9 + 234 = 333. Children can make up their own and give them to each other. *Can you find different ways to reach the total?*

○ Children find four corner numbers which will total the centre number.

Can you find six different ways to make 20 579 using four numbers? Use subtraction, division and multiplication as well as addition. You can change the centre number, change the square to a triangle, a pentagon and so on.

Solving numerical problems

Children should have experiences of applying their knowledge of number in a variety of contexts including: money; length; mass; volume and capacity; perimeter; area; time.

Shape, space and measures

Properties of shape

3-D solids

● Revise 3-D solids by asking volunteers in turn to choose a 3-D solid and name and label it. The class, led by you when necessary, asks the chooser questions about the properties of the chosen shape in relation to its faces, edges and vertices. In this way, you can check their understanding of a cube, cuboid, cylinder, sphere, pyramid, cone, prism, hemisphere, tetrahedron and a square-based pyramid.

● Ask an appropriate group or groups of children to investigate the relationship between the number of faces, edges and vertices of 3-D solids. *Can you find a formula?* (It is: Faces + Vertices = Edges + 2 (F + V = E + 2) and is known as Euler's Formula.) The group explain the formula and the class check it against various shapes. *Is it always true?*

○ Play *What am I?* Children describe the attributes of a shape/object and the class have to try and identify the shape/object.

● Collect boxes of various shapes (including cuboids, pyramids and prisms). *Who can sketch the nets of these?* Children who are unable to attempt sketches can pull the boxes apart and then trace around the nets on to a sheet of card, cut around the net and assemble the shape. The sketchers can check their sketches against the traced nets.

● Children construct 3-D solids using various construction material, including paper.

2-D shapes
● Revise 2-D shapes in the same way as 3-D solids by asking children to draw a 2-D shape on the board, name it, label it and explain its properties in relation to sides and corners. In this way, reminding them as necessary, check their understanding of regular and irregular squares, rectangles, circles, triangles, quadrilaterals, pentagons, hexagons, heptagons, octagons, and other regular polygons.

✪ Ask the children to sort and classify a collection of 2-D shapes (regular and irregular) according to faces, edges and corners.

● Give the children a wide range of different types of triangles. Ask them to find different ways of sorting the triangles. When they have done this, teach them the names of the different types of triangle.
Equilateral – all sides and angles equal.
Isosceles – two sides are equal, angles opposite these sides are equal.
Scalene – all sides and angles are of different length.
Right-angled – has an angle of 90°, and the longest side is opposite the angle (hypotenuse).
Ask them to draw the different kinds of triangles using a different colour of paper for each. They can cut these out and display them under headings with the descriptions written underneath.

Construction and drawing
✪ Give children appropriate apparatus (pencils, rulers, dotted paper and geoboards) and ask them to draw pentagons, hexagons, heptagons (7-sided polygons), octagons (8-sided), nonagons (9-sided), decagons (10-sided), hendecagons (11-sided), dodecagons (12-sided). In Year 5 they should be drawing with increasing accuracy. Remind them to use sharp pencils and to hold rulers firmly with spread fingers and thumb.

● Ask them to construct rectangles and right-angled triangles using a set square and a ruler.

● Ask them to draw 2-D shapes in different orientations on various types of grid paper, drawing along the lines only.

● Give them isometric paper and ask them to draw objects and shapes, drawing along the lines only.

● Children need to be able to identify shapes that are congruent (exactly the same in size and shape). If they have difficulty with this, give them numbered shapes cut from paper or card so, after they have listed which are congruent, they can check by putting the shapes on top of each other to see if they are an exact fit.

Symmetry
✪ Revise symmetry by discussing it with the children. Decide what are the important points about symmetry. (Certain shapes have symmetry. They have a fold line, called 'the line of symmetry' or an axis of symmetry, which divides the shape into two identical halves.) Then ask children to make their own symmetrical shapes/patterns involving two or more lines of symmetry.

Planes of symmetry
● Explain to the children that a plane of symmetry is the symmetry of a 3-D solid on which a plane (flat) mirror could be placed so that the reflection looked exactly the same as the part of the shape behind the mirror. A shape can have several planes of symmetry.

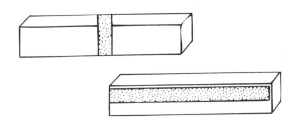

● Look together at a cuboid and a square-based pyramid and find the planes of symmetry on them. Find planes of symmetry in the environment.

● Using two mirrors at right angles, children sketch the reflections of a simple shape.

Properties of position and movement
Position
● By Year 5 children should have a wide 'position' vocabulary which enables them to describe the position of objects in relation to themselves and other subjects and in models, pictures and diagrams. Encourage them to use terms such as *clockwise, anti-clockwise, grid, row, column, vertical, horizontal, diagonal, compass point*.

● Give them practice in using a Roamer/Turtle/LOGO package to show position.

Co-ordinates

● Revise reading and plotting of points using co-ordinates (in the first quadrant). The first quadrant is defined as that where both points of a position have positive values. Draw a grid on the board.

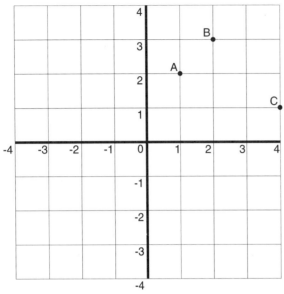

Remind the class that to find a point using co-ordinates we look *along* the columns and then *up* the rows and that a way to help us remember is 'Along the hall then up the stairs!'.

Now ask volunteers to describe the positions of the letters. (The co-ordinates for Point A are 1 line along and 2 lines up) and then to write the co-ordinates on the board. (A is at 1, 2.)

○ Add more letters to other locations in the grid and ask individuals to name the location of the letters using co-ordinates.

○ Give the children worksheets with various pictures or letters on a grid (in the first quadrant) similar to the one shown above. Ask the children to name the location of each of the pictures/letters using co-ordinates.

○ Ask the children to plot the points of a shape, for example, (1, 5), (2, 5), (4, 3), (2, 1), (1, 1). *What is the name of the shape?*

Direction

● Draw a large circle on the board or a large sheet of paper. Mark N, E, S, W on it. *Who can tell me what the letters stand for? Where do we see them? Who can remember the phrase that helps us to remember the order of the compass points?* (**N**ever **E**at **S**limy **W**orms.) *Does anyone have another way of remembering?*

Mark directional arrows for NE, NW, SW and SE on the compass. *Who can fill in the compass points at the end of these arrows?* Then draw arrows for NNE, ENE, ESE, SSE, SSW, WSW, WNW and NNW. *Does anyone know what compass points belong on these arrows?* If no one knows, ask the children to try to work it out. *This arrow is pointing to the north side of north east. What might that be called?*

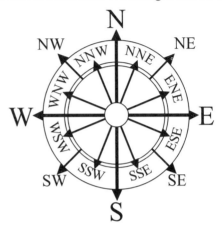

● Give pairs of children directional compasses. Remind them how to orientate their compasses and get them all facing North. Then ask individuals: *Point to south west, point to north north east,* and so on. If they are all clear about the compass points, take them out into the grounds and ask them to choose a position and mark it as theirs. They are then to get their compasses orientated and make a list of the direction of about six objects or landmarks that they can see from their chosen point. Each pair then gives a list of compass points to another pair who have to stand in the right place and identify the landmarks on the list.

IT

Draw a directional compass on a large sheet of paper, and use a Roamer. Children have to move it in various given directions, for example: *Starting at north move the Roamer east, then south, then west and finally north.*

Encourage children to describe the direction in which the Roamer is turning and travelling, using vocabulary such as 'clockwise' and 'anti-clockwise'. Children can give instructions to each other. Encourage them to use all 16 points of the compass.

Movement

● Re-introduce rotational symmetry (the symmetry of shape which has been turned and fitted on to itself somewhere other than in its original position) by asking the children to trace round 3-D solids and shapes. Children draw around the solid or shape, rotate it a little, draw around it again and repeat. Try this again using different solids and shapes.

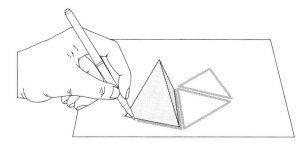

● Collect and discuss rotating patterns in fabric and wallpaper designs.

☼ Ask the children to combine translations and rotations to create their own patterns.

IT

Use a Roamer/Turtle/LOGO package to draw various movement patterns.

Angle

● Check that children understand the term 'right angle' and can point out right angles in the classroom. Remind them that a right angle measures exactly 90°.

● Introduce the children to the terms 'acute angle' (less than a right angle, < 90°), and 'obtuse angle' (more than a right angle, > 90°).

Have ready a range of angles drawn on the board and ask them to decide whether they are acute, right or obtuse angles. (Point out the arc that is used to show which angle is being examined.) Children can use a set square to check angles that puzzle them. Then clean the board and ask children, in turn, to draw an obtuse, acute or right angle on it.

● Give the children 180° protractors. The demonstrate (on an OHP, if possible) how a protractor is used to measure or draw angles. (Decide whether they are going to measure to the nearest 5° or to the nearest 1°.)

● Give them a worksheet with right and acute angles to measure. (Make sure the lines are long enough to extend beyond the edge of a protractor.) Children who manage to do this reasonably accurately can go on to use a sharp pencil, ruler and protractor to draw and measure some angles of their own. They can exchange papers with friends and check each other's measurements. Meanwhile, you can work with any children who couldn't manage the worksheet.

● Ask the children to draw some large triangles, measure all three angles and add up the measurements. *What total did you get?* Continue

until everyone is convinced that the sum of the angles of a triangle is always 180°.

● Introduce the children to the symbol ∠.

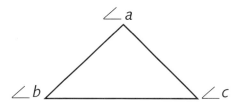

● Ask them to draw a triangle, labelled inside the angles, on a piece of scrap paper. *What do you think will happen if you cut out the triangle, tear off the three angles and fit them together?* When they have predicted the answer, let them try. Discuss how this is another way of showing that the sum of the angles of a triangle is 180° – or a straight line.

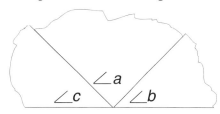

Parallel and perpendicular

Explain the terms 'parallel' and 'perpendicular' to the children. Then show them how they can draw parallel lines and perpendicular lines using a set square and a ruler.

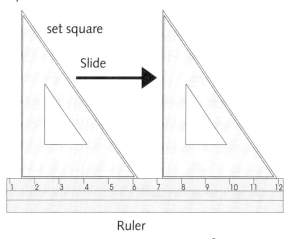

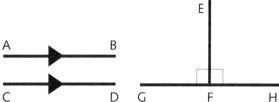

Lines AB and CD are parallel.
Angles EFG and EFH are right angles.
Line EF is perpendicular to Line GH.

Understanding and using measures

Length

☉ Working in pairs, children measure the length, height and distance of/between various objects/ people in and around the classroom using centimetre and metre rulers as appropriate. Encourage them to:

❯ find objects of specified lengths;

❯ estimate the length of objects before measuring them with the ruler;

❯ record both their estimates and actual measurements.

Discuss with the children the differences between their estimates and actual measurements and the concept of rounding measurements to the nearest centimetre.

● Using road maps that show distances in kilometres, the children can find distances between various destinations. Show them how to use the keys on maps to understand the systems of marking distances. Give them problems involving finding the shortest route between two places. Discuss with them whether the shortest distance always means the quickest journey.

● Check that the children can convert larger units to smaller units (kilometres to metres/metres to centimetres/metres to millimetres/centimetres to millimetres).

● Give the children opportunities to use the four operations to solve problems involving length, using the standard measures: centimetres, metres, kilometres and millimetres.

Miles

● Although schools work in kilometres, the children do, of course, live in a country where miles and not kilometres are used. They can look again at the road maps and find the figures showing miles and then calculate the distances between the same two places, but in miles this time. *Can you work out how many kilometres there are in a mile? Have a look at a car speedometer – does it show kph as well as mph? Would you be going faster if you went at 30mph or 40kph? Do our signposts show miles or kilometres?*

● Tell the children that miles are part of the old imperial measurement system. *Do you know any other measurements in the old system? What about yards, feet and inches? Are they still used? Ask some grown-ups how tall they are. Do they tell you in metres or in feet and inches?*

Mass (weight)

☉ Working in pairs, children weigh various objects in and around the classroom using both grams and kilograms. Encourage them to:

❯ find objects of specified mass;

❯ use a variety of weighing apparatus: balances, scales, dial scales;

❯ estimate the mass of objects before weighing them;

❯ record both their estimates and actual measurements;

❯ use measuring apparatus with increasing accuracy.

● By Year 5, children's estimates should be becoming increasingly accurate. If their estimates are still very inaccurate, discuss with them their strategies for estimating. Try to establish a mass that they know the feel of well (this might be a kilogram weight, a pound of sugar, a plastic or leather football) and suggest that they have that in mind when they are estimating weights.

● Check that they can convert grams to kilograms and vice versa.

● Give children opportunities to use the four operations to solve problems involving mass, using the standard measures gram and kilogram.

Capacity

☉ Working in pairs, children estimate and record how many litres and/or millilitres will be needed to fill various containers. They then measure and record. *Was your estimate accurate? Can you improve your estimate next time?* Where they have produced answers in litres and millilitres, ask them to express these in millilitres only as well. You can then see if they understand the relationship between litres and millilitres.

● Give children opportunities to solve problems using the four operations involving capacity, using the standard measures litre and millilitre.

Pints and gallons

● Talk to the children about pints. *Do we still use pints as a measure?* (Yes, for milk and beer). *Do you think the pint is larger or smaller than a litre?* Supply a collection of pint containers so the children can compare them with litres. Kitchen measuring jugs are useful as they often show both pints and litres. *Do you know what eight pints make? Ask your older brothers and sisters or parents if they remember when petrol was sold in gallons. If petrol is 68p* (quote the current price) *a litre now, can you work out roughly how much it would cost for a gallon?*

Volume

● The children should use the standard measure, a centimetre cube, cm^3, to measure volume. They can estimate and then find the volume of various cuboids by filling them with centimetre cubes. They record their estimates and actual measurements in cm^3.

● Ask the children to make models using centimetre cubes, count the number of blocks used and express the volume of the model in cm^3.

They can make several models, using a limited amount of cubes in each, and ask their friends to estimate the volume of the different models without counting the cubes.

Perimeter

● *What does perimeter mean? Who can find out?* (It means the distance all the way round the edge of something: the boundary.)

☼ List various large objects in the classroom (table top, blackboard, door and so on) and ask the class to estimate their perimeters and put them in order. They can then measure to check. *Who got the order right?*

☼ Ask children to find the perimeter of various shapes marked out on a geoboard.

● Ask the children to draw around shape tiles on to squared paper and estimate, then measure, the perimeter. Explain that whole squares count as one, half or more of a square counts as one, less than half a square does not count. They should record their answers in centimetres.

Area

● *What does 'area' mean?* Some of the class should be able to tell you that area means the amount of surface space an object has.

● Remind them about the square centimetre and how it is written as 1 sq. cm or 1cm^2.

☼ Ask the children to estimate the area in square centimetres of several objects in the classroom (book, table top, chair seat and so on) and order them.

They can then measure them to check. *Who got the order right?*

☼ The children can make shapes on a geoboard, calculate their area and record them in cm^2.

● The children can draw round shape tiles on squared paper and estimate, then count, the enclosed squares to find the area. Explain that whole squares count as one, half or more of a square counts as one and less than half a square does not count. They should record their answers in cm^2.

● Ask children to measure and calculate the area of rectangles and other simple shapes using counting methods and the standard units m^2, cm^2, mm^2.

Time

Revising time

If necessary, revise children's understanding of telling the time involving analogue and digital clocks. (O'clock, half past, quarter to, quarter past, to the nearest minute.)

● Re-introduce those children who need it to telling the time to the nearest minute, using digital and analogue clocks.

☼ Set a time on a clock hidden from the children, then give clues. For example, *The large hand is on the 5 and the small hand is just past the 7.* Children have to guess the time on the clock. They can repeat this activity in pairs.

Measuring time intervals

● Set an analogue or digital clock at 3:20. Write 3:45 on the board and ask: *How many minutes pass before the clock shows 3:45?* Say: *We can count in 5s, starting at 20.* Point and say *25* – hold up one finger, *30* – hold up two fingers, *35* – hold up three fingers, *40* – hold up four fingers, *45* – hold up five fingers. Pointing to the five fingers, count in 5s saying: *5, 10, 15, 20, 25. It takes 25 minutes to go from 20 past 3 to quarter to 4.* Repeat, if necessary, using other time intervals.

● Using an analogue clock, show children the time on the clock and write the time on the board. Show children another time on the clock and write that time on the board. Ask them to work out the time interval between the two. Repeat. Repeat again using digital time.

Give the children experience of working out time intervals using o'clock, half past, quarter to, quarter past and to the nearest minute.

24-hour clock and am and pm

● Re-introduce the children to the 24-hour clock and am and pm notation:

❱ show them a clock face displaying both the analogue and 24-hour clock together;

❱ count with them the hours from 1 to 12, on to 13, 14 and so on, to reach 24 hours or midnight;

❱ introduce them to the relationship between the 12-hour and 24-hour times, using the diagram below;

❱ show and tell the time to the children using am and pm notation for the 12-hour clock.

● Read, write and say the time using 24-hour time: *3.00 pm is 15:00 hours.*

● Ask individual children to tell the time using am and pm notation for the 12-hour clock and reading, writing and saying the time, using 24-hour time.

✿ Provide children with opportunities to use am and pm notation for the 12-hour clock and to read, write and say the time in 24-hour time.

✿ Using 12-hour and/or 24-hour and/or digital clocks, show the children times (o'clock, half past, quarter to, quarter past and to the nearest minute) and ask them to identify the time, using am and pm where appropriate.

✿ Working in pairs, the children shuffle together two, three or four different sets of time cards and play Snap or Pelmanism with them. The cards can show clock faces, writing in analogue words, writing using fractions, writing in digital time, writing in digital words, in 12-hour and 24-hour time.

● Give the children opportunities to:

❱ study bus, train, boat and air timetables to extract information;

❱ study this year's calendar to extract information;

❱ use the four operations to solve problems involving time using o'clock, half past, quarter past, quarter to and minute intervals.

Handling data

Look for opportunities to use science work for creating graphs.

Bar charts

Draw a blank bar chart on a large sheet of paper. An example, of marks in a test taken by Year 5, is shown opposite.

✿ Ask the children to collect, record, discuss and predict numerical data using a bar chart. They should collect their data using a tally. When the bar chart is completed ask questions that will enable them to interpret the graph.

● Repeat the above with the intervals increasing by intervals of 2s, 5s, 10s or 20s.

Pictograms

Draw a pictogram on a large sheet of paper. For example, of the number of occupants in passing cars.

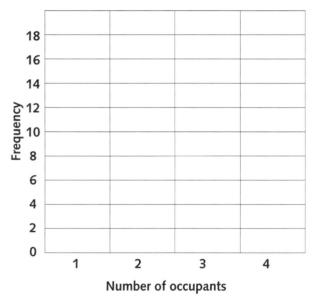

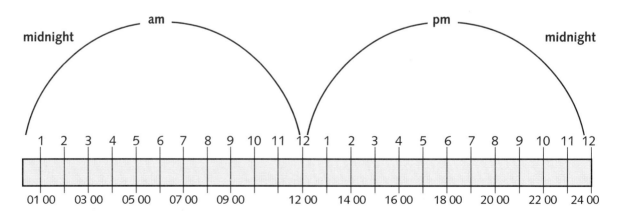

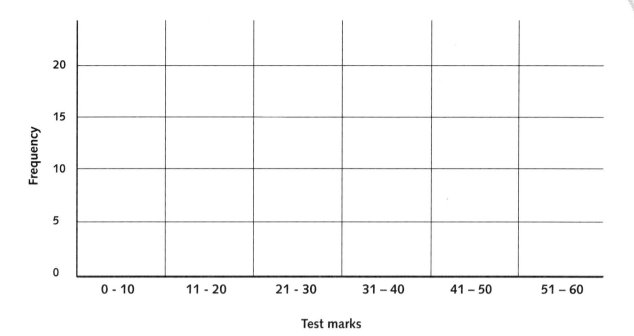

Test marks

○ Ask the children to collect, record, discuss and predict numerical data using a pictogram. When the pictogram is completed ask questions that will enable them to interpret the graph. Repeat, using intervals of 2s, 5s, 10s or 20s.

Line graphs

● Draw a line graph on a large sheet of paper. For example, of room temperature, as shown below.

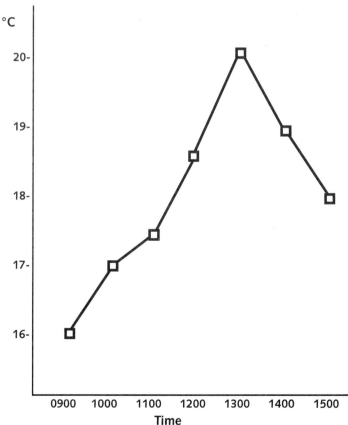

○ Ask the children to collect, record, discuss and predict numerical data using a line graph. When the line graph is completed, ask questions that will enable them to interpret the graph. Repeat, using intervals of 2s, 5s, 10s or 20s.

● Ask the children to interpret, discuss and make predictions from the data presented in a wide range of graphs, charts, lists and tables. For example, in a newspaper, bus timetable, or in computer data.

IT

The children create block graphs, pictographs and line graphs using a simple database package.

Mode

Do the children remember the term 'mode'? It is the value that occurs most often in a set of data. Find the mode using physical characteristics of the children, hair colour, eye colour, and so on.

Median

Ask the children if they remember the term 'median'. It is in the middle of a set of data once the data has been sorted in order to show clearly the full range. Find the median by asking a group of children to stand in height order. Find the child (or two children) who is/are the median average. Repeat for median average age.

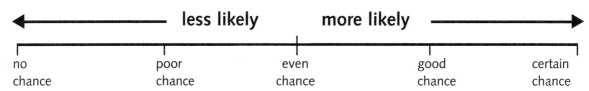

no chance	poor chance	even chance	good chance	certain chance

Mathematics

Groups of children can record their shoe sizes and then calculate the range of sizes.

✪ Children find the mode, median and range of data already collected, recorded and discussed in bar charts, pictograms, line graphs and other graphs.

Probability

⬤ Write PROBABILITY on the board with the headings *Certain*, *Likely*, *Unlikely*, *Impossible* underneath. Ask children to classify events, according to their degree of likelihood, under one of these headings.
You will watch television tonight.
The sun will rise in the morning.
You will have cereal for breakfast tomorrow.
You will see your favourite pop star on your way home from school today.
You will be 13 tomorrow.
A new baby will be a boy or a girl.
If I drop a coin it will land showing heads.
Encourage the children to contribute their own statements. Be prepared for heated arguments about the placing of statements.

⬤ Prepare cards with statements on them for the children to place on a scale, similar to that shown in the diagram above. (This could be a wall chart with envelopes for the cards.)

⬤ Children investigate how many heads and how many tails might turn up if a coin was tossed 10 times, 20 times, 30 times and so on. They predict first, then try it and record the results. *Did heads and tails come up the same number of times? What was the difference between heads and tails? Were the results different for the different numbers of tosses? Would the results be the same if you repeated the experiment? What do you think would happen if you tossed the coin 100 times?*

⬤ Children investigate whether the probability of throwing a 6 on a 1-to-6 dice is 1 in 6. They make a prediction first. *How many times will you throw it?*

⬤ Children investigate whether the probability of choosing a green cube out of a bag containing 1 red, 1 blue, 1 green and 1 yellow cube is 1 in 4. They make a prediction first and decide how many times they will try.

⬤ The children can record their investigations using a tally and can present their investigations in a bar chart or line graph.

Assessment

Children demonstrate the outcomes of their learning through speaking, writing, drawing and engaging in other activities.

A variety of assessment strategies is necessary if you are to have an understanding of where your children are in their learning and how best to further develop that learning. Whatever assessment strategies you use, it is important to ensure that tasks are appropriate to the individual child and that they are directly related to the learning objectives. Remember that those activities marked with an ✪ in the Practical ideas section are suitable for assessment.

The levels of expectation suggested at the beginning of this chapter under the *What should they be able to do?* heading provide a comprehensive checklist for assessing your children's learning.

Science

Although the National Curriculum specifies what science must be taught at Key Stage 2, each school has to decide in which order it should be taught and make some choices. The Orders for Key Stage 2 are divided up into 12 units of work to be taught over a 12-term period. It is not practical to deal here with every possible combination of units, so the following programme for Year 5 is suggested:

Autumn term	Spring term	Summer term
Unit 8 *Materials and their Properties* **3** Separating mixtures of materials	**Unit 12** *Physical Processes* **4** The Earth and beyond	**Unit 5** *Life Processes and Living Things* **5** Living things in their environment

(If your school has allocated the units differently, you may want to draw on the ideas in the other Key Stage 2 Yearbooks.)

The programme suggested for Key Stage 2 in the Yearbooks ensures that in each year every child will cover work within all three of the knowledge and understanding Attainment Targets.

Some units, such as Units 8, 10 and 12, are arguably more difficult to understand and so are included in Years 5 or 6. Similarly, units which are easier for young children to understand, such as Unit 11, Light and sound, have been placed earlier in Key Stage 2.

Units 3, 4 and 5 contain a heavy workload. They are about plant growth, variation and classification, and living things in their environment, and so have been planned for the summer term when outdoor work can be carried out most easily.

What should they be able to do?

The Statutory Orders for science are set down in four sections. When we examine these, it is easy to be lulled into believing that the three sections dealing with knowledge and understanding put the emphasis on the content of science rather than the process. This notion is soon dispelled by the realization that *Experimental and Investigative Science* (Sc1) is regarded as having roughly equal importance to the other three science sections combined. Although it offers no facts to be learned, Sc1 will only be achieved over a period of time, perhaps the whole of the primary school stage, or even longer. The aim is for children to develop an understanding of scientific phenomena through systematic and practical exploration and investigations.

The National Curriculum identifies three components within scientific investigations. They are: Planning experimental work, Obtaining evidence and Considering evidence.

Planning experimental work

Children have enquiring minds and are curious about everything around them. It comes naturally for them to try things out, to see how things work, to manipulate, to feel, to be curious, to ask questions and seek answers – exactly the attributes of a good scientist.

Planning includes asking questions and predicting. Provide plenty of opportunities for discussion between the children and between yourself and the children. Encourage them to ask questions of the *Who? What? Where? When? Why? How many? How much? How far?* variety. By Year 5, they should be identifying questions that can be investigated, and planning and carrying out their own investigations – considering how to make them fair. Some of their predictions will be based on science knowledge that is not directly related to their everyday experience but is related to the Programmes of Study for Key Stage 2 and even Key Stage 3.

In Year 5, the children should also be able to identify the key factors that affect what is being investigated. In the case of an investigation into plant growth, for example, they should be able to suggest that temperature, light, water or fertilizer concentration may affect growth.

Obtaining evidence

Most Year 5 children should be able to measure a limited number of quantities using instruments with fine divisions (for example, using a stopwatch to measure time in tenths of a second). They should recognize that it may be necessary to repeat observations. They should be recording their predictions and actual results using tables, charts, graphs, spreadsheets and datafiles.

Considering evidence

This includes interpreting the results of their investigations and evaluating the scientific evidence. Encourage your class to make comparisons, to look for patterns and to communicate their findings in a variety of ways. This gives them a great opportunity to share their thinking and to relate their understanding to scientific knowledge. In Year 5, the majority of the children should be able to draw conclusions based on the evidence and, using their scientific knowledge, be able to recognize and explain any data that do not fit the trend.

Knowledge and understanding

The three sections of the Programme of Study dealing with knowledge and understanding are: *Life Processes and Living Things* (Sc2); *Materials and their Properties* (Sc3); and *Physical Processes* (Sc4). These are instantly recognizable as the biology, chemistry and physics of secondary school days.

Is there an 'Sc0'?

There is a fifth area of the science curriculum which has no distinct title. Since it comes as an introduction to each key stage description, some people call this preliminary area 'Sc0'. This fifth area applies across the other four. It consists of five parts and, incidentally, highlights many important cross-curricular aspects of science.

1 **Systematic enquiry** includes giving opportunities for children to ask questions, use first-hand experience and simple secondary sources to obtain information, and also to use information technology.

2 **Science in everyday life** involves children relating their understanding of science to their own health and the environment.

3 **The nature of scientific ideas** is an opportunity to look at the work of great scientists, amongst other things.

4 **Communication** is concerned with the special ways we record and communicate scientific understanding.

5 **Health and safety** is concerned with children following simple instructions to control the risks to themselves and to recognize hazards and risks when working with living things and materials.

Practical ideas

Making a start

There are many ways of introducing the three units (5, 8 and 12) suggested for Year 5. The following are a few possibilities. Others are suggested in the Ideas bank on page 86.

Separating mixtures of materials

● When substances are mixed and not dissolved they can be separated fairly easily by methods such as sieving, straining or filtering. Mix together dry table salt and rice grains. *How can we separate them?* (Use a sieve or strainer, which will allow the small particles of salt to pass through but not the larger rice grains.)

● Prepare a mixture of iron filings and sand. *How can we separate these two materials?* The children may have to be reminded of work on magnetism before they suggest using a magnet, to which the iron filings will cling while the sand grains are unaffected. (To make cleaning the magnets easier, wrap them in clingfilm before carrying out this experiment. The film can then be removed from the magnets and the iron filings will drop off.)

The Earth and beyond

Safety: Warn the children never to look straight at the sun, even while wearing sunglasses, as this can damage the eyes or even lead to blindness. It is even more dangerous to look at the sun through binoculars or a telescope.

Shadows

● Stand a thin stick in a plastic bottle or plant pot of sand and put this device out on the playground early on a sunny morning. The children mark the end of the shadow cast by the stick with a pebble or chalk every hour. At the end of the day look at the changing position of the shadows. *What has caused the shadows to move? Is it the Earth that is moving or the sun?* (It is the Earth turning on its axis.)

● Ask the children to examine a sundial and try to tell the time by it.

● Record the temperatures in the playground in sunshine and shadows, to emphasize the point that we receive heat as well as light from the sun.

Living things in their environment

● Visit a zoo, wildlife park, botanical garden or the natural history section of a museum to give the children some indication of the many different habitats of the living things on the Earth today.

● Make a list of the habitats around the school. Make a collection of pictures of different kinds of habitat in this country and overseas. Display them and discuss and compare what the pictures show.

● Carry out a survey of the plants and animals seen by the children on their way to school.

Developing key areas
Separating mixtures of materials

Background

Everything in the universe, including all living organisms, is made up of materials.

Most of the materials around us are made up of several different substances and are either **mixtures** or **compounds**. Mixtures contain different substances mixed together without a chemical reaction. The ingredients can usually be separated quite easily.

Safety: It is good practice never to taste substances being investigated in science, even though the children may be handling substances they are familiar with at home. Avoid glass containers for liquids, and wherever possible use plastic. Take care that solvents, such as nail varnish remover, are not inhaled.

Filters

● Start by building on what the children know. *Who knows what a filter is? Has anyone seen coffee being filtered? What happens?* (The coarser parts of the coffee remain in the filter paper, while the water passes through the paper taking only the finest grounds, plus taste and colour.)

● *Why is a tea bag like a workman's face mask?* (They are both filters. The microscopically small particles of tea in solution can pass through the tiny holes in the tea bag, but the tea leaves are too big and are trapped on the inside of the tea bag. Similarly, a face mask allows the tiny molecules of gases in the air to pass through the minute holes in the filtering material, but larger particles of, say, dust and paint are too big and are trapped on the outside of the mask.)

Filter experiment

The children half-fill two jars with clean, warm water. They put a teaspoonful of sugar in one jar and stir it for two minutes. Then they put a teaspoon of sand in the other jar of water and stir it for two minutes.

They fold two filter papers or circles of blotting paper in half and then in half again and open out the triangle to produce a cone shape that will fit inside a funnel.

They then set up two funnels, filter papers and jars and carefully pour the sugar solution into one filter paper. (Warn them not to splash the liquid over the top of the paper.) They pour the sand and water

into the other filter paper and look in each of the jars under the two funnels. *What do you see? Look in the two filter papers. What do you see?*

The filter paper works as a kind of strainer. *Does a filter paper separate a substance which will not dissolve in water?* (Yes.) *Does a filter separate a substance which will dissolve in water?* (No. The sugar and the water molecules which form the solution are small enough to pass through the holes of any filter.)

Evaporation

Can you think of a way to get the sugar back from the water? (Some children may be able to suggest evaporation and be able to devise an experiment like the following one. Others can just follow the experiment without knowing what to expect.)

The children pour some of the sugar solution into clean saucers and stand the saucers in a warm place to be left for a day or so. Look at it from time to time. *What happens to the water in the saucer? Where has it gone? Look at the solid left in the saucer. What is it?* They can try this experiment with salt solution. *Does the same thing happen?* (Yes.)

(You can demonstrate this to the children much more quickly by heating the solution in a small foil cooking tray over a hot plate, so that the water evaporates quickly, leaving the sugar or salt behind.)

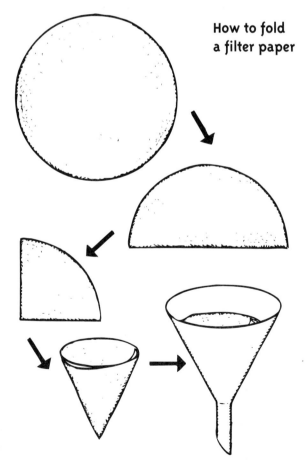

How to fold a filter paper

Nail varnish

*What happens when you paint your nails with nail varnish? (*Nail varnish consists of a solid lacquer dissolved in a special solvent. When the varnish is painted on a nail, the solvent evaporates, leaving a solid layer of lacquer on the fingernail.) *How can you clean it off again? How does nail varnish remover work? (*It is a solvent which dissolves the lacquer again.)

Separating cork and sand

Mix some small pieces of cork and sand together. *Who can think of a way to separate them? (*If no one can think of a way, talk about the properties of cork and how it floats.) Shake up the cork and sand mixture in water and then allow it to stand; the sand will sink to the bottom of the water, while the pieces of cork will float. The pieces of cork can simply be poured out of the jar or scooped out with a teaspoon or strainer. When the water has settled, the clear water can be decanted off, leaving the sand. Alternatively, the sand and water can be poured into a filter paper in a funnel – the sand will be retained in the filter paper.

Separating salt and sand

Mix some salt and sand together. *Who can find a way to separate them? (*A mixture of salt and sand can be separated by first stirring them into water. The salt will dissolve, while the insoluble sand collects at the bottom of the container. If the liquid is poured into a filter paper in a funnel, the sand collects in the filter paper. When the clear liquid is evaporated, either by heating to dryness or by leaving it to evaporate in a clean saucer near a radiator, the salt will be deposited.)

Cleaning water

● Before water comes to our homes, it has to be cleaned. *Where does the water come from?* Find out how your local water supply is cleaned. (Perhaps you could take the class to visit a water purification plant.)

● Investigate different ways of cleaning water. The children can make some muddy water by mixing soil and tap water and then try different ways of filtering it, such as through paper towels, tissues, filter paper, gravel, sand and cotton wool. They can put each of these things in turn in a funnel and pour the muddy water through. *Which method of filtering works best? Does all the filtered water look and smell the same? If it is clear and colourless does that mean that it is clean? (*No, it probably contains germs too small to see.)

Filtering dirty water

At the waterworks, sand and gravel filters are used to clean water before we use it. The children can make their own filters by cutting the bottom off a transparent plastic bottle, turning it upside down and wedging a piece of cotton wool in the neck. They can fix it upside down firmly inside a transparent jar, add a thick layer of clean, washed gravel on top of the cotton wool followed by a thick layer of clean washed sand on top of the gravel. They cut a circle of paper towel and lay it on top of the sand.

In another jar, they mix a little soil with water and slowly and carefully pour the muddy water through the filter. Some of the dirt will stick to the sand and gravel so that the water that comes out of the filter is cleaner than it was to start with. *Do you think this water is now fit to drink? (*No, the filter removes the particles of dirt but it does not remove bacteria and other germs that may have been in the soil to start with.)

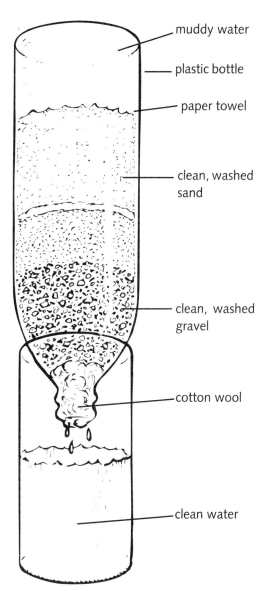

muddy water
plastic bottle
paper towel
clean, washed sand
clean, washed gravel
cotton wool
clean water

Food powders

Make a collection of food powders, such as flour, salt, cocoa, tea, instant coffee and powdered milk. The children can try dissolving each in equal amounts of water. *Shake or stir and then leave each one for an hour or so. Notice what happens. Is there anything left at the bottom of the jar? Is the water coloured? Is the water clear or cloudy? Filter the solution and see what comes through. Is it clear? Does the water look clean? Does it contain anything?* If there is time, they can try using water of different temperatures and see if it affects the results. They should prepare a table of their results.

Chromatography

Chromatography is a useful method of separating different coloured materials. It works because the particles of pigment are carried by water along an absorbent material at different speeds, according to their size, and so eventually form coloured bands. It is thus possible to identify the different pigments used to make up one colour.

● The children make a small ink blot in the centre of a filter paper and slowly and carefully add water, drop by drop, from a teat pipette to the middle of the blot. *What happens?* (The ink will spread out and, if it is made up of more than one pigment, these will form concentric circles on the filter paper.)

● They can try other colour solutions. For example, if they cover a Smartie with a few drops of water and leave it for a few minutes, a coloured solution will be produced. Using a pipette, they can drip this coloured solution drop by drop on to filter paper or blotting paper and watch the colours spread out. They can compare the solutions from different coloured Smarties. (Make sure the children label each paper as they work.)

● Try water-based felt-tipped pens. *Do they consist of a single colour ink?*
The children can write about these chromatography experiments and include the filter papers, which show the colours spreading, in their accounts.

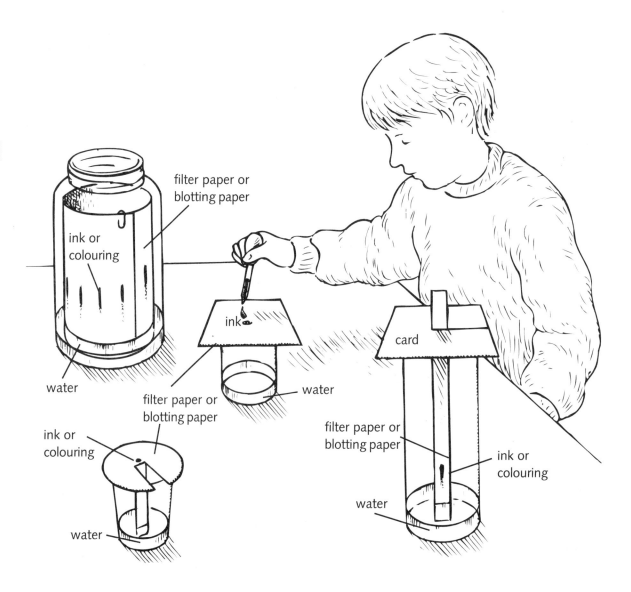

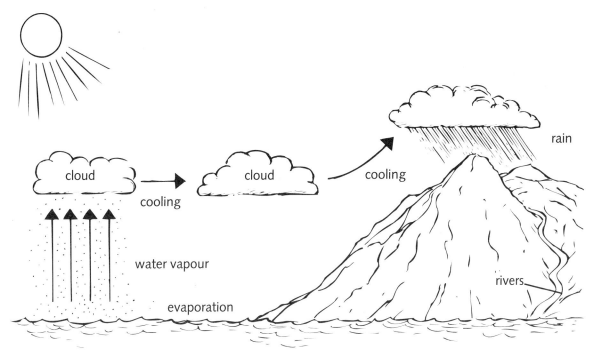

cloud

cooling

cloud

cooling

rain

water vapour

rivers

evaporation

oceans and seas

Distillation

● The process of evaporating a liquid and then collecting it by condensing the gas back to a liquid is called 'distilling' or 'distillation'. You can demonstrate the principles of the distillation of water by holding a long metal ladle, or a tablespoon tied to the end of a stick, in the steam coming from a kettle. The water vapour will condense on the cold ladle or spoon and water droplets will fall like rain so that they can be collected in a saucer or plate.

● A safer alternative method of demonstration is to put a dish of water in a plastic aquarium and cover the aquarium with cling film. Stand the aquarium in a hot place and examine the inside from time to time. Some of the water in the dish will evaporate and the water vapour will condense on the cold surface of the plastic.

● *Where does rain come from?* Talk to the children about the water cycle, the process whereby the finite amount of water on Earth is recirculated, allowing us to use the same water over and over again. It is really an example of distillation. During the water cycle, water evaporates from oceans, seas, lakes and other wet surfaces. Any salt and other impurities in the water are left behind.

High in the sky the water vapour cools, and condenses to form clouds from which rain falls. The rain water collects in rivers which eventually flow into the oceans, seas and lakes.

The Earth and beyond

Sun

Focusing the sun's rays

● Normally the sun's rays spread out as they reach the Earth's surface. You can demonstrate how the sun's rays move towards each other, or *converge*, by using a hand lens or magnifying glass.

On a sunny day, hold the lens a few centimetres above a sheet of scrap paper so that the upper surface of the lens is pointing towards the sun. Slowly raise or lower the lens until there is a small bright point of light on the paper. Hold the lens steady, and after a few seconds the sun's rays may burn a small hole in the paper.

This experiment demonstrates why it is dangerous to stare at the sun. The lens in each eye will focus the sun's rays onto the back of the eye, and burn the delicate tissue there, called the retina. Binoculars and telescopes will focus the sun's rays on the eyes in the same way.

● *How can you accidentally start a fire in the country by throwing a bottle away?* (The bottle acts as a lens and can start a fire by focusing the sun's rays on paper or dry grass.)

Moving shadows

The children work in pairs on the playground on a bright sunny morning. One child draws around the

other's feet with chalk, then round the shadow. They write their names and times in the outlines. At midday, they stand in their foot marks and their partners draw their shadows again. Then again in the afternoon. *Was your shadow the same size and in the same place on each of the three occasions? Why is this?*

Night and day

Demonstrate to the children why we have night and day. Take a globe and a powerful torch or a desk lamp to represent the sun. (Work in a dark corner, or draw the curtains, if possible.)

Shine the light from the lamp or torch onto the globe from the side. Turn the globe slowly in an anti-clockwise direction. *Can you see how each country gradually moves into the light. Where is it dawn/day/dusk/night?*

Stick a small piece of Plasticine or Blu-tack on the globe where the school is situated. Stand a pin or matchstick in the Plasticine or Blu-tack so the position is easy to see. Slowly turn the globe anti-clockwise. *When it is roughly midday at school, where else in the world would it be daytime? Where would it be midnight?*

The sun in the sky

On a sunny day ask the children to roll a piece of clay or Plasticine into a sausage shape and lay it on a sheet of card. They take their cards outside and stick a drinking straw in one end of the clay. They move the straw until it does not make a shadow. The straw is now pointing straight at the sun. Leave the experiment and return an hour later. They put another drinking straw in the clay and move the straw until it does not make a shadow. *Do the same thing every hour. What do you notice? Has the sun really moved?* (The drinking straws form a fan shape by the end of the day, showing how the sun seems to move across the sky. Remember, though, it is really the Earth that is turning, and not the sun.) (Link with work in Geography.)

Long and short shadows

Darken the room. Shine a torch onto a rod held upright in some Plasticine on a large white piece of paper. Ask the children to predict the length of the shadow cast on the paper as you change the angle between the torch and the rod. Ask them to predict what will happen to the shadow if you shine the beam directly above the rod. (There will be no shadow.)

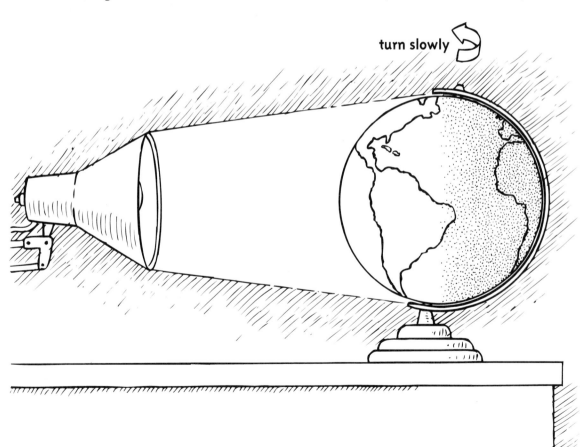

turn slowly

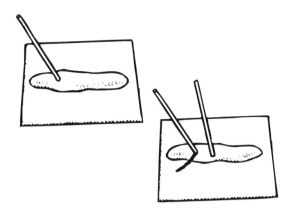

Sunset

The sun does not always set at the same time. *When does the sun set at this time of the year?* For one week, different people in the class can record at home the times when the sun sets and when the street lights come on. Next morning, they fill in a chart at school. *Is sunset getting earlier or later at this time of the year?* They could compare the chart with the one that some newspapers print.

Direct or slanting rays?

Sometimes the sun seems to be directly overhead, while at other times it seems to be low in the sky. *Does it matter whether we get direct rays or slanted rays from the sun?*

Lay a thermometer on a piece of black felt. *What temperature does the thermometer show?* Place a desk lamp so that it shines straight down on to the thermometer from about 30cm above it. Switch on the lamp and leave it on for about five minutes. *What temperature does the thermometer show now?*

Leave the lamp to cool down and the thermometer to return to room temperature, then move the lamp so it is directed at an angle towards the thermometer, but is still roughly the same distance away from it. *What temperature does the thermometer show?* Switch on the lamp and leave it on again for five minutes. *What temperature does the thermometer show now? Does the temperature rise more from the direct rays or from the slanted rays? Can you find places on the globe where the sun's rays are direct and others where they are slanted? Predict what kind of climate these places might have. Use reference books to see if you were right.* (The thermometer will show a higher temperature when the desk lamp is shining straight down than when it is slanted towards the thermometer. The sun's rays shine directly over the equator which, therefore, has higher temperatures. The sun's rays are quite slanted over the much colder polar regions.)

A model of the seasons

Put a table lamp without a shade in the middle of the floor. Tell the children that the lamp represents the sun. Darken the room and then carefully put a globe a little way away from the lamp. Stick a small piece of Blu-tack on the place on the globe where the school is situated. Put a pin in the Blu-tack. Move the globe round the lamp slowly in an anti-clockwise direction. *When our place is leaning towards the sun, it is summer. When our place is leaning away from the sun, it is winter. How long does the Earth take to go right round the sun? Name some countries where it is winter when it is summer where we live.* (When the northern hemisphere is tilted towards the sun, that part of the Earth has summer. Six months later, when the northern hemisphere is tilted away from the sun, it is winter. Spring and autumn are the in-between seasons.)

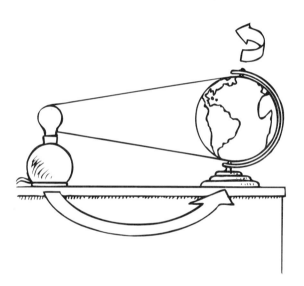

Moon

Activities involving observing the moon should obviously be done at a time of year when the moon will appear before the children's bedtime.

Light from the moon

Use this experiment to demonstrate to the children why the moon appears to shine. You need a bicycle reflector. Work in a darkened room. Point the torch at the bicycle reflector. *What do you see?* Turn the torch off. *What do you see?* Ask a volunteer to hold a large sheet of black paper between the torch and the reflector. Turn the torch on again and point it at the reflector. *What do you see? Why do you think you cannot see the moon on a cloudy night? Does it matter how far you hold the torch away from the bicycle reflector?* (The reflector only glows when the torch is on and when the rays have an uninterrupted path from the torch to the reflector.)

Record the moon's shape

Draw 30 squares, all the same, along a long, narrow sheet of paper or thin card. Inside each square draw a circle.

Ask the children to take it in turns to look for the moon at home each evening. They draw the moon's shape, and copy it into the appropriate circle the next day colouring the bright part of the moon yellow and writing the date underneath. There will, of course, be some evenings when clouds hide the moon. The circles should be left blank or shaded black on those evenings. When the chart is completed, the children will be able to see that the moon's shape changes in a regular way.

Changing shape of the moon

Take a small piece of card and trim it until it is 5cm x 5cm to fit in the slide frame of a 35mm projector. Poke a pencil through the centre of the card or use a hole punch to produce a small circular hole. Darken the room and use the slide projector to project a circular pool of light. Pass a small ball through the light, so the children can see how the illuminated part of the ball appears to change shape, just as the moon does in its various phases.

Moon in the night sky

At the time of a full moon, when it seems likely that there will be a clear night, ask the children to study the moon's position in the sky that evening. Suggest that they go into the garden or a bedroom and walk around until they are standing in the place where the moon seems to be touching the top of a tree, pole or television aerial. They should put something on the ground or floor to mark the spot where they were standing, and note the time. Ask them to return to the same place half an hour later, and stand exactly where they did before. *Is the moon still in the same place? Predict where the moon will be after another half an hour, and check to see if you are right.* Next day at school they can write about what they did and saw.

Craters on the moon

The surface of the moon is scarred with pits and craters. Scientists believe these were formed by meteorites crashing into the surface of the moon. Fill a strong wooden or cardboard box with loose sand. (This represents the surface of the moon.) The children take it in turns to stand on a chair and drop marbles, golf balls or pebbles on to the sand. They carefully remove the objects they dropped, examine and draw and, if possible, photograph the resulting craters. Compare the pictures with photographs of moon craters. *Which makes the largest crater, a large object or a small one?*

A living model

Make a living model of the sun and planets. Draw a diagram of the position of the sun and the planets on the board for the children to copy. Write 'sun' on a large piece of card and the names of the planets on nine other large cards and give them to ten children. Go into the hall and let the class, with the help of their diagrams, put the 'planets' in the correct position round the sun. (Make sure you have a master copy of the diagram yourself.) Now the planets have to spin round. At the same time they have to move around the sun in a circle, keeping the same distance away. They should take care not to bump into anyone else. *Which planet had to move the most/least?*

Average distance of the planets from the sun (in millions of miles)

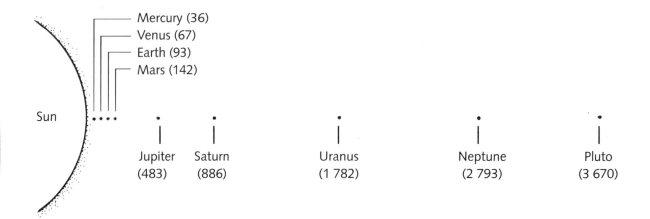

Living things in their environment

Background

The habitat of a plant or animal can be regarded as the address at which it lives. It is where the plant or animal finds food and shelter and raises its young.

All living things are interdependent. The basic reason for this is that the only living things which are able to make their own food are green plants. Animals, and plants which do not have the green substance, chlorophyll, have to rely on living green plants, or their dead and decaying remains, for their food and energy.

Data-logging

A data-logging package for use on the school computer will provide many opportunities to link scientific observations of habitats and information technology. A sensor can be used which will record temperature, humidity, light and even atmospheric pressure changes in a small part of a habitat throughout the day. Observations of the distribution and behaviour of the plants and animals can be linked and correlated to the recorded changes.

Animal addresses

First divide the school grounds into broad habitats, such as grassland, pavements, bushes and walls. Give small groups of children one main habitat to explore.

Are there variations within your habitat? They may have a wall with two sides, or sunny and shady areas of paving. There may be tall and short grasses, some of which are in the shade while others are in full sun. Ask the children to find animals and narrow their address down as far as possible, even to measuring height and distances. They should write an envelope for each animal they find. If they do not know the animal's name, they draw it and give it a temporary name until they have a chance to identify it later. After the hunt, they compare the animals found in the different areas. *Are there some special animals only found in one place? Is there another animal found everywhere? Write a home address for each animal on its envelope.* For a snail, for example, it might be:

Snail
Dark and Damp
Above Ground
Facing North

Homes

Discuss the idea of homes. *What are they? Why do humans and other animals have homes?* Give the children pictures of animals whose homes they are unlikely to know (giraffe, wolf, polar bear, porpoise). Ask them to design homes for these animals. They can make a list of the features of the home they would design for that particular species, then draw the house and label it. (For example, a high roof for a giraffe.)

A pond study

Safety: A pond is one of the most interesting habitats for children to study. Nevertheless, adequate supervision and great care are necessary to reduce possible safety and hygiene hazards to a minimum. You must make a preliminary visit to identify potential hazards (such as broken glass, brambles, nettles or areas of deep water) and decide how to tackle the work. Cover any cuts or abrasions with waterproof dressings before the children begin work, and make sure they wash their hands carefully when they have finished and before they handle food.

Discourage the children from making unsupervised visits to ponds, canals and rivers.

● Discuss with the children how they might begin a pond study. They might, for example, suggest making a map of the pond or, if it is reasonably shallow, making a cross-sectional diagram of it.

● Use nets or kitchen sieves tied to the end of stout sticks for the actual sampling. Put the catch in white dishes or ice-cream containers so that it can be seen clearly. Try to sample the surface, the middle depths and the bottom of the pond and keep the catch from these three levels in different trays or containers, but do not leave them in the sun. Encourage the children to use reference books to identify the catches from each of the three layers. *Are the animals living in the three different levels different? Do the water plants grow in distinct bands or zones? How are the animals and plants adapted to where they live? Can you construct some food chains for the pond you have studied?*

Carefully return the animals and plants to the pond when you have finished studying them.

A hedgerow survey

● Hedges are an endangered habitat in many parts of the country. Many hedges are extremely old and, generally speaking, the older the hedge the more wildlife is likely to be found living in or near it.

Scientists have found that, on average, it takes about 100 years for each new tree or shrub species to establish itself in a hedge. To estimate the age of

a hedge, mark off sections 30m long. Avoid the ends of the hedge. Record all the tree and shrub species growing along one side of each 30m section. Count wild roses, but exclude climbers such as brambles and honeysuckle. If the 30m section of a hedge contains five tree or shrub species, then it is approximately 500 years old. The more 30m lengths of a hedge you can check, the more accurate your results are likely to be.

● Record the birds, insects and other wildlife seen in or near the hedge in each of the four seasons. Notice the changes in the trees, shrubs and other plant life. *How do the animals living in the hedge depend upon the plants growing there? Why are hedges important to wild life? Why are so many hedges being cut down?* (The main reasons are to make fields larger, so that larger farm machines can be used, and because hedges are more expensive to maintain than, say, a barbed wire fence.)

Make a compost heap

Make a small compost heap in an out-of-the-way part of the school grounds. Collect grass cuttings, dead leaves and vegetable peelings. Pile these up in layers with a thin layer of soil between each. Wet the heap and then cover it with, say, an old piece of carpet or a sheet of plastic. Leave the heap to rot for several months, turning it from time to time to allow air into it. Take the temperature of the inside of the heap and compare it with the outside temperature. Wearing gloves, the children examine the heap to see what animals are living inside it.

Investigate a wall

Investigate a wall on the school premises. *What is it made from and how was it built? Are there any spaces for animals to live? What kinds of plants grow on or round the wall? Are the plants special in any way? How do you think they survive? Which animals live in the crevices? Do the same plants and animals live on both sides of the wall?*

Grassy areas

Use a hoop, or a square with sides of, say 30cm x 30cm, to sample a grassy area. The children record all the plants that occur within the hoop. Repeat the activity in different grassy areas such as a meadow, school playing field, or a lawn. Look at similarities and differences in the findings. *What effects do mowing or sunlight or shade have on plants which grow in grassy areas? Are grassy areas just grass?*

Grassland animals

What animals can be found in a tussock of grass? Mark out a square of turf measuring 30cm x 30cm and dig it up with a spade. Place the turf on newspaper and carefully take it apart. Count, and try to identify, the animals present. *How many animals are there? What kind are they? What colour are they? Are they camouflaged?* Let the animals go again where the turf was collected. If several samples are taken from, say, an area of the playing field, it may be possible to estimate approximately how many animals of each kind there are in the whole field at turf level.

Animal life on trees

Some trees have large numbers of insects and other small animals living on them. These animals often blend in with their surroundings. Their colour and shape make it difficult for predators to find and eat them.

● *How many of these small animals can you find on a tree in the school grounds or in a local park?* A hand lens will help the children to spot small animals. They should use paint brushes and pick the creatures up carefully and put them in clean pots. Tell them to look in cracks in the bark of the tree and search on both sides of the leaves. Lay a sheet of plastic under the tree. Knock a branch above the sheet with a stick. Look carefully at the sheet to see what has fallen into it. They can tie a plastic bag over a low branch and shake the branch, taking care not to break it. *How many small animals did you catch in the bag? Search through any rotting wood lying under the tree. Can you find any animals? What colour are the animals you found on the different parts of the tree? Do they blend in with their surroundings?*

● Have plenty of reference books available so the children can try to identify the animals they have found. *How many of the animals are herbivores? How many of the animals are carnivores? Can you write down some food chains for the tree you have studied?*

● When you have finished with the animals return them to where they were found. Search other trees. *Which kinds of trees have the most animal life?*

Keeping minibeasts

The children can search the school grounds for small animals such as spiders, woodlice and beetles and collect them in small plastic pots or tubes (Give them paint brushes and small plastic spoons so they can collect the animals without damaging them.) A layer of moist (not wet) soil and some stones, small tussocks of grass and moss, and a twig or two in an old aquarium or large plastic ice-cream carton will provide an environment as near natural as possible. A lid with several holes to allow circulation of air is important and a variety of vegetation will provide food for some animals. Return the animals to their natural environment as soon as possible after they have been studied for a few days.

Make a pitfall trap

This type of simple trap can teach the children much about the small invertebrate animals that live in different habitats. Many of these animals are active only at night and are rarely seen.

● Bury a smooth-sided plastic pot in a lawn, a flower bed, under a hedge, on waste ground or somewhere else where it will not be disturbed. The top of the container should be level with the surface of the ground. Bait the trap with small pieces of bread, vegetables, scraps of meat or dog food, and so on. Put two stones at opposite sides of the trap, and lay a piece of wood or tile over the top to keep out the rain. Leave the trap for several hours, or overnight.

Keep records of the kinds of animals you are able to trap in different parts of the school grounds or other study sites, and with different baits. *Do the numbers and kinds of animals caught differ*

according to the weather or the bait used? (Usually they do.)

Remember to dig up your traps as soon as they are finished with. If these traps are forgotten or left, large numbers of small animals may die.

Making a snail or woodlouse town

Go into the school grounds and find a piece of waste ground. Working in groups, the children design a small area (perhaps half a metre square) as a suitable place for snails or woodlice. *What kind of different facilities could you provide in your snail or woodlouse town?* (For example, a damp area, a leafy area, some food, some stones.) When they have made the 'town', they collect some snails or woodlice to put in it and see where these animals prefer to go. *Do all of the snails or woodlice choose the same places?*

Earthworms' favourite conditions

● Groups of children cover one half of the bottom of a small tray or sandwich box with damp paper towels and the other half of the tray or box with dry paper towels. They put two or three earthworms in the middle of the tray. They cover the tray with a sheet of black paper or black cloth then look at it again five minutes later. *Are the earthworms in the dry part of the tray or the damp part? Do the experiment two or three more times. Do you always get the same result?*

● Suggest the children do the experiment again but this time covering the whole of the bottom of the tray with damp paper. They then cover half of the top of the tray with black paper or black cloth, and cover the other half with transparent plastic. The worms are placed in the middle of the tray and left for five minutes. *Where do the earthworms go, to the dark part or the light part of the tray?*

Do this two or three more times. Do you always get the same result?

Which do the earthworms like best: wet or dry places, light or dark places? (Earthworms prefer dark, damp places.)

Light or dark preferences

The children can divide small boxes into a light half and a dark half and try with woodlice, millipedes, centipedes or slugs to see which half they prefer to be in. They can also do this with damp and dry conditions, and possibly warm versus cold conditions (using an ice-cube to create the latter).

Trampled plants

Find an area where there is grass with a path worn across it. Ask the children to look at the plants in the area. A survey is best done in groups of three or four, with children making a transect to see how the existence of a path has affected the type of plants growing on and near it. The children should place a line at right angles to the path and then

record which plants (or bare soil) are touched at 10cm intervals along the string. Having done this, they can present their results on a chart, perhaps drawn on graph paper. They should carry out their survey along the transect until they reach an area of grass which does not get frequent trampling.

When they present their results, they are likely to see the absence of grass near the path and an increase in plants such as plantain, daisies and dandelions which are more resistant to trampling. The children may also notice that the plants are shorter in the vicinity of the path. Let them examine the plants which are able to survive on the path to see how they compare with the plants in the untrampled area. They should, for example, appreciate the tough nature of the leaves of plantain. They may comment on the spreading nature of the leaves and this could be related to the amount of light that the plants are thus able to absorb.

Human activity

Take the children to an area which has been allowed to grow naturally, such as a wood. *You are detectives. Can you find any clues showing human influence?* (They could look for litter and footprints and evidence that trees have been cut or pruned. Encourage more careful observation, such as trees planted in rows, undergrowth cut down, ditches dug, and so on.)

Changed by humans?

Show the children a range of photographs of countryside scenery. Pictures showing such things as poppies in a cornfield, a field of large round straw bales, and neatly cut hedges are ideal. Distribute these to groups in the class. *List (in two columns) features that are natural and those that are caused by human activity.*

Studying a food chain

● Ladybirds are easy to catch and keep. House them in a large jar or plastic food container covered with a piece of muslin or tights.

Ladybirds are carnivores. They feed on aphids, small insects that are often called greenfly or blackfly. You can find aphids on the shoots of rose bushes, broad beans and other plants in summer.

● Put a plant shoot with aphids on it in a small bottle of water. Fix cotton wool around the top of the bottle to stop the insects falling in. Place the bottle with the plant shoot in a large transparent jar and put a ladybird on the plant shoot. Cover the container.

The children can watch carefully to see how the

aphids eat the plant shoot. They may need hand lenses for this. *How does the ladybird catch the aphids it eats? How does it eat them? Does it eat all of the aphids? If not, what parts are left?*

Finally, they can draw the food chain they have been studying.

Endangered habitats

Divide the class into groups, giving each group a different endangered habitat to work on – tropical rainforest, heathland, hedgerow, coral reef, native British woodland, pond, unimproved grassland and so on. Let them use the school and public libraries to find out why their particular habitat is under threat. *Is it home to any endangered animals? What are people doing to try to save that habitat?* A spokesperson for each group can report back to the whole class. *How shall we record what we have learned?*

Top predator

● Remind the children that all food chains begin with the sun. Ask them to suggest a plant or plant product which is reliant on the sun to make its food. Then ask them to name an animal which eats that plant. Continue in this way until they reach the top predator. As soon as one food chain is completed,

start another, jotting the chains down as you go for everyone to see. This will pinpoint the fact that living things are interdependent, and that everything ultimately leads back to the sun. It will also show that, no matter how hard you try, food chains are never very long.

● Once the idea of the food chain is grasped, the children can make paper chains as a model of the food chains they have worked out. They can write the plant or animal name on each link, and stick the links together in the correct sequence until the food chain is complete.

Ideas bank

Sea salt
Ask the children to devise an experiment to obtain salt from sea water. If needs be, give them home-made 'sea water' (salt solution) to experiment with. *Where does the sea salt you can buy in some supermarkets come from? How is salt obtained in some hot countries?*

If the sun went out
Ask the children to write a story describing what would happen 'if the sun went out'. *What does the sun give us? How would we survive?* (We wouldn't.)

Moon facts
Ask the children to consult reference books, newspapers and magazines for articles about the moon. They record each new discovery on a strip of paper, and add it to a chart under headings they devise themselves. A final decorative version of the chart can be created using word-processed labels and this could be part of a big display of work the class has done on the moon.

Matching pictures
Give the children a selection of pictures which include a range of different plants and animals, different habitats (such as a house, tree, wall,

compost heap, pasture, pond) and places such as woodland, coastal area, mountain and so on. (Use written labels as well if you can't collect enough pictures.) Ask them to match the plant and animal pictures (or labels) with the habitats. They should give reasons. They should recognize that the habitat must have particular features which make it possible for the plant or animal to survive there, such as a food source, shelter, somewhere to breed, etc.

Habitats in season
Give the children a picture of a habitat (or habitats). *At what time of the year do you think the picture was drawn/photographed? What will the picture look like in the next season of the year? Write down what plants or animals may live there, and what effect the change of season has on them.*

Habitat trail
Go on a habitat trail around the school. Map the different habitats you find, such as shrubs and bushes, lawn, compost heap, wall, flower bed, tarmac and so on. (Combine this with geographical work on maps.) Record where the different plants and animals live. *What is special about each of the habitats? Is it sheltered or exposed, wet or dry, shady or sunny?* Choose a way to measure and record these conditions.

Under bricks, concrete or wood
Make a survey of the animals that live under bricks, pieces of concrete or wood. Keep records of all the animals you find. Be sure to return the bricks, concrete or wood back exactly as you found them. *Are the kinds of animals found under bricks different from those that live under concrete?* (The animals most likely to be found are woodlice, slugs, snails, earthworms, centipedes, millipedes and spiders. It is unlikely that the animals living under bricks will differ from those living under concrete or wood. If there is a difference, it is due to the smaller size of bricks and the drier conditions under them than under large pieces of wood or concrete.)

Assessment

When you have finished the work with your Year 5 class, you will have a good idea as to whether the children enjoyed the topics and which style of teaching was most effective. You should also be able to judge how much the children have learned. Now is the time to evaluate each topic against the criteria with which you started.

What do they know?

There is no set list of facts they should know, but all the children should have gained something, even if that something varies from child to child. In Year 5 you might expect most nine- to ten-year-olds to know that:

- there is a wide variety of habitats (Sc2);
- any habitat contains a variety of plants and animals (Sc2);
- plants and animals are suited to the habitats in which they live (Sc2);
- the plants and animals in a habitat are linked by food chains (Sc2);
- food chains start with green plants (Sc2);
- we can change a habitat for better or worse (Sc2);
- when materials are mixed, changes may occur (Sc3);
- solid particles of different sizes can be separated by sieving (Sc3);
- some solids dissolve in water to produce solutions, while others do not (Sc3);
- insoluble solids can be separated from liquids by filtering (Sc3);
- dissolved solids can be recovered by evaporating the liquid from the solution (Sc3);
- there is a limit to the amount of solid that will dissolve in a given amount of water and that different solids dissolve to different extents (Sc3);
- the sun, Earth and moon are approximately spherical (Sc4);
- the Earth spins on its own axis, producing the changes we call night and day (Sc4);
- the Earth orbits the sun once each year, producing the seasons (Sc4);
- the moon takes approximately 28 days to orbit the Earth (Sc4).

What can they do?

Most Year 5 children should be able to:

- describe objects and materials, and things that happen;
- identify a number of questions which can be investigated, in familiar and less familiar situations;
- identify the key factors that affect what is being investigated;
- recognize the need for a fair test;
- change one factor and observe or measure the effect whilst keeping other factors the same, and know that this allows a fair test or comparison to be made;
- explain what a prediction is and how it differs from a guess;
- make predictions based upon relevant prior knowledge;
- suggest what observations should be made and suitable ways of measuring these;
- record their predictions and results;
- present their findings using charts, pictograms, bar charts, line graphs, spreadsheets and datafiles;
- provide explanations for observations and simple patterns in recorded measurements, and relate these to scientific knowledge;
- recognize and explain any data that do not fit the trend using their scientific knowledge;
- suggest improvements to investigations.

These capabilities all relate to Sc1.

Science

What have they experienced?

They should have:
- examined a variety of habitats;
- investigated how plants and animals are distributed in their habitats;
- investigated how plants and animals are suited to their environments;
- made a comparison of habitats;
- investigated a number of food chains;
- handled a variety of materials;
- investigated a variety of methods of separating mixtures of materials;
- investigated the way in which the Earth turns on its axis;
- investigated models of the Earth orbiting the sun;
- investigated the phases of the moon;
- carried out experiments under guidance;
- devised their own simple fair experiments;
- measured using fine divisions;
- recognized the need to repeat observations.

How have they made their knowledge public?

They should have discussed their work with others and displayed their work through drawings, models, charts, graphs and tables. They should also have produced clear, written accounts of their various observations, predictions, activities, discoveries and conclusions.

History

Year 5, the year before Key Stage 2 SATs take place, is a particularly critical one for the teaching of literacy. With the national spotlight on raising literacy standards, you will wish to do everything you can to give your children the best chance of acquiring a high level of competence in reading and writing.

If you need a new argument for teaching history in Year 5 this could be it, for not only does history add breadth to the curriculum, but it provides a potentially fascinating context for the demonstration and development of precisely those competencies that the SATs demand. Of course, history is also a worthwhile subject to study in its own right, and it provides the opportunity to do some exciting, enjoyable teaching.

Currently, primary teachers are expected to study history chosen from the National Curriculum 'study units' – although the compulsion to do so has been relaxed. For Key Stage 2 these are:
- Romans, Anglo-Saxons and Vikings in Britain
- Life in Tudor times
- Victorian Britain *or* Britain since 1930
- Ancient Greece
- Local history
- A past non-European society (Egyptians are the favourite choice)

You can study more history or different topics as well as these, but you will have to find the time to do it. Given that many schools opt to teach the units chronologically, you may well be asked to teach Victorian Britain in Year 5. Probably the most popular topic with teachers, Victorian Britain can appear more than once in the primary curriculum (it is a favourite with infant teachers) and, although it is an option, it is rarely missed out.

History skills and concepts cannot be separated from the content in which they are embedded, so the practical activities given in this chapter have been linked to teaching about the Victorians. If you have been assigned a different unit by your school, do not worry, general principles still apply; expectations and assessment will be exactly the same; and even the suggested activities will usually adapt to fit a different topic. (Check whether or not your particular history unit has been dealt with in one of the other Yearbooks.)

The programme of study for Victorian Britain says that children should be taught about the lives of men, women and children at different levels of society in Britain and the ways in which they were affected by changes in industry and transport:

a   steam power, factories and mass production,
b   the growth of railways,
c   people at work,
d   people at home,
e   people at leisure.
f   people at school.

(The National Curriculum, DFE, 1995)

Key elements

When studying any historical topic, children will have to tackle the essential elements of history itself, which are usefully defined in the National Curriculum as:
- Chronology
- Range and depth of historical understanding

- Interpretations of history
- Historical enquiry
- Organization and communication

Some of these elements will be taught during every topic and all of them will be taught over the key stage.

What should they be able to do?

Year 5s are alive to history. They know what it is, they read about it, watch films about it, ask questions about it and, most of all, enjoy it. Many people would argue that, at this age, you catch children at their best: they are enthusiastic, open to learning and unsullied by world-weariness. At ten they most closely correspond to adults' expectations in behaviour and are generally biddable. They also have foundations in history upon which you can build.

Individual differences do make nonsense of generalizations, but here is a guide as to what most Year 5 children will be able to do and understand in relation to history's key areas.

Key element: Chronology

Because of their increasing knowledge base, Year 5 children will place historic events and people in a broad chronological framework, although you must not expect precise dating. They will know, for example, that a Tudor house is older than a Victorian one and that a Roman villa is older than both.

Dates should now start to feature quite strongly in their vocabulary of time, a few key ones certainly (1066 and all that) and those remembered from other Key Stage 2 topics. Improving numeracy obviously helps here. 'Century', 'decade' (words describing the passage of time) 'ancient', 'modern', and, if they have been taught properly, even AD and BC can now be used correctly.

Key element: Range and depth of historical understanding

Children should be able to debate freely about straightforward differences between the lives of people within a period and across social classes as well as about basic differences between periods – 'then and then' as well as 'now and then'. Ideas and attitudes should now start to feature in these debates. *What were Victorian attitudes to the poor, the unemployed and the sick?* A Year 5's answers will not be hypothetical but will be rooted in fact: *They put the poor in horrible workhouses.* Or again: *They built huge hospitals for sick people.*

Giving reasons for past actions and drawing inferences from what people did is something that you can encourage your class to do. They need to be given lots of examples to follow. For example, laws about women and children at work showed that many people were worried about the working conditions in factories and mines. (These strategies are exactly the same as those required to extract meaning from text in Key Stage 2 English SATs.)

Year 5s are quite capable of giving reasons for their views and this is something that you must constantly ask them to do. The more able will make connections from the actions and attitudes of the past to actions and attitudes today. (The Victorians banned women from going down the mines. *How does that square with views on equality held today?* The Victorians built secure mental institutions which are now mostly closed. *What has changed?*)

Key element: Interpretations of history

Whether or not children will, or are able to, make judgements about the quality and honesty of the representations of the past that they meet is debatable. There is little research evidence to help us, but clearly the ability to make valid judgements will depend heavily on prior knowledge as well as intellectual maturity. Certainly, though, in Year 5 the questioning can begin.

The Victorian period is a particularly good one in which to start this process. It is easy to find 'dark satanic' representations of the period as well as warm romantic ones. Year 5 children can begin the questioning with visual representations, paintings, etchings and photographs. *Why was the scene shown in this way? What do you think the artist thought about the people and actions that he painted?* Year 5s will generally seek to resolve the issues in simple black and white terms. This is perfectly normal.

Key element: Historical enquiry

Historical enquiry is all about interrogating evidence. Given a good previous historical education, children of ten will be used to looking at evidence with a critical eye. In Year 5, the range of self-generated questions should begin to go beyond simple expressions of curiosity to more searching but appropriate questions. This is most apparent when they are presented with unknown objects or tools: they will ask questions about function, design and the effectiveness of the object to fulfil the task it was designed for.

Perhaps the real marker of ten-year-olds' growing historical skill is 'relevancy'. Most children will ask relevant questions, select relevant information and be less easily side-tracked by the insignificant or trivial.

Up until now, children will not have tackled much by way of written evidence. Now is the time to introduce it. Originals are by no means unapproachable but clearly printed transcripts and secondary sources are more accessible. Never underestimate children's ability to tease information from evidence, even if that evidence appears too difficult.

Key element: Organization and communication

Recollection, selection and organization are the three main demands that the communication of historical information makes of children at this stage. Year 5 children have more in the memory bank to call upon than before and it can be frustrating when they seem to have forgotten everything that they learned yesterday, although their memory generally responds well to a little jogging. Don't forget that recall depends upon children having been required to memorize information in the first place.

Children of this age are growing increasingly adept at selecting relevant information but may not be so good at organizing it coherently. This ability will grow rapidly with good teaching and practice.

They can present their knowledge in descriptive passages, structured narratives or imaginative stories. This is the age at which they can write quite convincingly as a soldier at the Charge of the Light Brigade or as a Victorian chimney sweep.

Practical ideas

Making a start

● Decide upon a few straightforward questions that you will try to answer with the class. From the questions, identify the direct teaching that you are going to do and the related activities that the children are going to do. (Some people prefer to start with the key elements and then go to the activities, but you will have a better chance of stimulating enthusiasm and motivating the children if you start from your teaching and their activities. When you have a clear idea of these, simply check what key elements are covered by them. If none, then you will need to change some of your activities.)

● Taking Life in Victorian Britain as our example, the key questions might be:

▶ *Who were the Victorians?*

▶ *What were the main events of the Victorian period?*

▶ *How has life changed in Britain since Victorian times?*

Even these basic questions are not so simple, and you may need to qualify them in order to have a chance of finding answers. For example, you may choose to identify some of the main events of the period according to selected criteria of relevance or importance. Again, you would have to consider the question of change in relation to a particular social class or category (leisure, work, travel, and so on). You cannot do everything.

● Divide your main questions into sub-questions which you might give to groups of children to investigate for themselves. For example:

▶ *What were the main events of the Victorian period?*

▶ *Were there any major wars?*

▶ *What events most affected the lives of ordinary people?*

▶ *What were the main events concerning royalty and government?*

▶ *What were the most important discoveries made? How did they affect people's lives?*

▶ *Who were the most important individuals of the period?*

and so on.

It is a good idea to involve the children in making the list of questions and in helping to select the ones to answer.

● How do you actually start the project when your planning is complete? There is no single way of doing this but you should certainly get stuck into something that grabs the children's attention – a story, a film, a picture, an object, a visit or a person. Avoid general introductions or rambling thumbnail historical sketches of the period. Start by making them sit up and take notice. To begin the project you might pick a significant event as the focus for your work. (A Victorian project can become a real mish-mash if it is not focused.) The following two activities are good examples.

● Use the poem 'The Charge of the Light Brigade' by Tennyson to kick-start a study of the Crimean War. The opportunities to develop and broaden the study are excellent. Compare evidence about the charge. (*Was it really 600?*) Study the photographs (*Were they posed?*) and newspaper reports. Follow these for possible lines of development: Florence Nightingale, nursing, newspapers, cardigans, balaclavas, photography, army reforms, public opinion, the Empire, local war memorials or street names.

● The Great Exhibition in 1851. This single event can provide an excellent anchor point to a more wide-ranging Victorian study. *Whose idea was it? Where was it held? Was it successful? What was it like to visit the Exhibition? How did people get there?* Modern issues have echoes in the exhibition

Questions about the Victorians

– the millennium dome, conservation (the campaign to save trees on the Hyde Park site), public transport (the beginnings of excursions). You can easily move on to study transport, dress, the Empire (many of the exhibits came from the Empire), architecture and industry.

The following ideas are presented in outline form and you can adopt the ones that appeal to you and then apply a little imagination to them. Most assume that the children will have been taught about or researched the events mentioned.

Developing key areas

Family life

Holidays

Compare a day out at the seaside in Victorian times with a holiday today. The painting *Ramsgate Sands* by Frith should be studied. *Where did the Victorians go on holiday? How did they get there? How did they enjoy themselves? What clothes did they wear? Did they change the places they visited?* Ask the same questions about today. Make a big 'today' picture to match that of *Ramsgate Sands* (which was painted in 1854 and bought by Queen Victoria).

Sing-song

Have a Victorian sing-song. Teach the children the songs first (make sure that they *are* Victorian) – any good music shop or library will provide collections. Invite parents to an in-costume concert (they dress up as well as the children). Provide suitable light refreshments.

Samplers

Get the children to make samplers. Base your designs on evidence (children can sometimes bring examples from home and the public library will be able to produce illustrated books). The constraints of time make the production of full-size samplers impossible so produce a simple version using designs transferred from squared paper to binca. Or do a complete drawn version on squared paper. Discuss the type of texts used: 'Honesty is the best policy' and so on.

Portrait photographs

Collect Victorian portrait photographs, study and discuss them (*Why no smiles?*) and then create your own. Model the setting on real examples. The children can dress themselves quite simply (or grandly if their parents want to take the trouble). It is very easy to create the Victorian look. Take the photographs in black and white using a good film and camera and in natural light. Watch out for reflections and unwanted modern intrusions. Have the films developed and printed by a good black and white developer (for example, the Jessops chain) and then get the children to turn them into sepia prints using the sepia chemical packs available from good photographers. Supervise properly. The results are like magic.

● Use the portraits you have taken to create Victorian framed pictures for an album or for display. Note how the Victorians sometimes decorated their albums with small decorative patterns and pictures.

Cards

Encourage the children to research (as always) and make Victorian Valentine cards or Christmas cards.

Food

Investigate the Victorian stomach. Look at rich and poor: remember Oliver as well as Mrs Beeton. Make a Victorian dish to sample – you have a wide choice from simple gruel to, perhaps, 'Bible Cake', for which you will need a to refer to Bible for the ingredients.

Ingredients for Bible Cake

a 225g of Jeremiah, chapter 6 verse 20

b 1 tablespoon of the first book of Samuel, chapter 14 verse 25

c 225g of Judges, chapter 5 verse 25 (end)

d 3 of Jeremiah, chapter 17 verse 11

e 225g of chopped Nahum, chapter 3 verse 12

f 50g blanched and chopped Numbers, chapter 17 verse 8

g 225g of first book of Samuel, chapter 30 verse 12

h A teaspoon of Amos, chapter 4 verse 5

i A pinch of Leviticus, chapter 2 verse 13

j Add second book of Chronicles, chapter 9 verse 9, to taste

k 450g of first book of Kings, chapter 4 verse 22

l 3 tablespoons of Judges, chapter 4 verse 19

(Note: leaven is baking powder)

illustration from:
Sara Crewe by F H Burnett (1888)

Children's books

Collect Victorian children's books for the class to read or for you to read to them, for example *The Secret Garden*, *Sara Crewe* (modern versions are called *The Little Princess*), *Little Lord Fauntleroy* (who was an egalitarian character and has a bad press largely because of his illustrator), *The Crown of Success* (which provides a fascinating introduction to allegory), *The Crofton Boys*, *The Fairchild Family*. Short stories by Maria Edgeworth are very accessible. (Try 'Waste Not want Not' and 'The Purple Jar' from *Early Lessons* and *The Parents' Assistant*.) As well as being riveting reads, the stories provide wonderful material for comparisons between then and now – in terms of family relationships, parental attitudes and children's lives. Good readers will enjoy comparing the books with children's books today and could report their conclusions, with extracts, to the rest of the class. (Ask the children's librarian at your library to help you track down some of these books.)

Board game

In groups of two or three, ask the children to invent a board game on a Victorian theme. (Let the creative be creative, but for those who need help suggest something on the lines of Snakes and Ladders.) Include instructions such as 'Wounded at Balaclava – go back to Scutari Hospital.' 'Argument with Turkish officer. Miss a turn.'

Gravestone record

If you have access to a local cemetery that has Victorian tombs, compile a gravestone record. Names, ages, dates of death, causes, styles of headstones – even the kind of 'words of remembrance' used. Consider the possibility of taking photographs as a record if the lettering is clear. Collate the data in class (use a data program such as *Junior Pinpoint*, Logotron). Lots of useful discussion and further research can follow. Who knows where it may lead?

Schooldays
Victorian day

Recreate a Victorian school day in your classroom. The 'Bible' for this is *The Victorian Schooldays – A Teacher's Manual* by W Frankum and J Lawrie (available through History in Evidence, TTS Ltd).

School stories

Read about Dotheboys Hall in Dickens' *Nicholas Nickleby* or about Rugby in *Tom Brown's Schooldays*. The children could dramatize and perform extracts.

Assembly

Hold a Victorian school assembly. Use only Victorian hymns and Victorian prayers. Make sure that the theme is appropriately moral.

Games

Until recent times, playground games had changed little since the nineteenth century. Have a playground games instruction week. Teach the children games they don't know. Iona and Peter Opie's *Children's Games in Street and Playground*, OUP, which should certainly be in the school library, will help but, better still, get a few spry great-grannies to come and join in.

Industry and architecture
Railways

● Find out all you can about the railways that existed near you in Victorian times. Map the lines. Find out about costs and timetables if you can. You may be able to see the Victorian legacy in the station buildings or disused tracks. *What has happened to the tracks today? Are they used for anything?*

● After studying paintings, photographs and descriptions of the railways in Victorian times, ask the children to write a letter to a friend describing a journey on a steam train. *Which class of carriage did you travel in?*

Trades and buildings

● Compare the Yellow Pages or Thomson's directories for your area with a Victorian directory of trades (Kelly is the most widely available – consult the reference library and photocopy sheets). *Do any of the Victorian companies survive to this day?* Look out for 'est. 1896' and similar signs on buildings, headed paper and advertisements. Have an 'Established in Victorian Times' board and pin evidence to it. Try placing selected businesses on an old map and on a new one. Compare yesterday with today. *What has changed and why? What has stayed the same?* Investigate the local businesses and industries that flourished in Victorian times but no longer exist (dairies, tailors, furriers, department

stores, blacksmiths, brickworks, glovemakers – the list alone is informative). The archives in the local library will provide information and elderly people may be able to tell stories passed down to them about life in nineteenth-century workplaces.

● Replicate Victorian tile-making (red clay tiles with slip-traced symmetrical patterns are the easiest). The Victorians had to rediscover how to make them and then they used them everywhere – the new Houses of Parliament, restored churches, public lavatories, fireplaces and so on. Use reference books but also check your locality (some splendid pictorial examples can be found in butchers' shops and old hospitals). Modern tile catalogues have many Victorian reproductions. Visit the tile works at Ironbridge if you can.

● Carry out an audit of Victorian buildings in your area. Use large-scale maps. Walk the area. Compare with old maps of the area. (Check for large-scale OS maps in the reference library. Urban areas were the first to be covered by large-scale maps.) Take photographs. Draw a map and display the photographs round the map with connections to the relevant locations. Small groups could do research on individual buildings and add their findings to the display.

Child labour

Use reference books to find out about child labour in Victorian times. Make this an opportunity to check that the children can use an index competently, then 'scan' the pages. Henry Mayhew's *London Labour and the London Poor* gives compelling evidence for your better readers (they can report back in their own words). Read aloud extracts from *Hedingham Harvest* by Geoffrey Robinson (National Trust Classics). The children can then use the knowledge they have acquired to design an advertisement against child labour.

Inventions

● Compile a catalogue of Victorian inventions (from postage stamps to washing machines). Ask children to write detailed entries for each one, saying what has happened to each invention since Victorian times, and illustrating them wherever possible.

● The Victorians invented most modern sporting events: Wimbledon, the Cup Final and so on. Choose a well-known event and compile a history. Alternatively, compile a history of a local club that dates from this period. You might also provide a pictorial history of technological change in sport – football, tennis and cycling have all undergone considerable changes in clothing and equipment.

Events and celebrations
Tape story

Make an audio tape of the story of the Charge of the Light Brigade. You could produce it as a docu-drama with interviews, eyewitness accounts, and extracts from the evidence. Use the poem as a linking motif with appropriate music and sound effects.

Memorials

Some areas are rich in memorials relating to Victorian wars: check local churches, graveyards, parks and town halls. Produce a guide to these memorials with notes about the events in which the soldiers died. (The Crimean and Boer wars are the most common, but you will find mention of soldiers who died of disease in distant corners of the Empire.) Find and mark these places on a map.

Jubilee celebration

Have a Royal Jubilee celebration. You may be lucky and have evidence (a log book?) of the celebrations carried out in your school/town/village at the time. Parades, banners, games and parties coupled with a singing of the National Anthem can make a memorable event. Do everything in costume and as authentically as you can. Invite the LEA drama adviser (if you have one) to join the celebrations in role as the local squire or policeman. This idea is not as difficult as it sounds and has been done successfully by many schools, so ask around and get advice from someone who has already done it.

Victorian Fair

The adventurous might consider holding a Victorian Fair. These are very popular as nostalgic community events and probably need the involvement of a community wider than the school, although there are certainly examples of good in-house fairs. The grander sort involve commercial craftsmen, artists and performers, everything from Punch and Judy displays to hot chestnut sellers. The best advice is to consult someone who has done it.

People
Drawing Victorians

What did the Victorians look like ? Take a specific event (again, the Charge of the Light Brigade, the Jubilee Parade, the 1851 Great Exhibition) and ask the children to draw people who took part in them. Use reference books to get the clothes right, and include ordinary people as well as important people. Cut out the pictures, mount them on card and display as standing figures. (You can cheat a little by photocopying Victorian faces pictured in books and sticking them on the drawings to give a touch of realism.)

Dictionary of biography

Compile a dictionary of biography about Victorian people – Elizabeth Garrett Anderson, Isambard Kingdom Brunel, Charles Darwin, Charles Dickens, W G Grace, Mary Kingston, William Morris, Florence Nightingale, Mary Seacole, Shaftesbury, Tennyson and so on. Include any local notables and people related to the areas you have been studying. Look at published dictionaries for ideas about format and the kind of information to include. Children can choose their own character to research and put the information into 'scaffolding' on the computer, which can then be spell checked, edited and sorted to put the entries in alphabetical order. If you have the technology, scan in pictures. Tell them that if they do a thorough, accurate job, the dictionary can be preserved in a more permanent form and go in the library for future classes to refer to.

Ideas bank
Resources

● Resources need to be considered from the start. You should have a pretty good idea of the ground that is likely to be covered and can therefore prepare the resources even before the detailed questions are agreed. To stimulate interest, try to turn a corner of your classroom into an Aladdin's cave of fascinating books, pictures, maps and artefacts. Make sure that at least part of your display demands some response on the part of the children. Invite them to try out some Victorian activities – playing with certain toys or games; finding out what it is like to beat carpets or put clothes through a mangle (no unsupervised finger crushing!); play a Victorian hymn on the recorder and so on. Displays can invite children to interrogate evidence – for example documents, maps and pictures, especially local ones. Old photographs are particularly useful because children

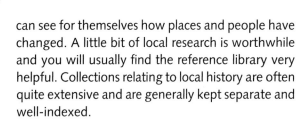

can see for themselves how places and people have changed. A little bit of local research is worthwhile and you will usually find the reference library very helpful. Collections relating to local history are often quite extensive and are generally kept separate and well-indexed.

● Layers and layers of history overlie almost every inch of this country so that, wherever your school is, you should find that walking around will reveal a great deal of evidence of the Victorian past. Your local environment is not, of course, a historical museum where all the exhibits are neatly separated into periods or categories, and a walk down the street throws at you a jumble of images from a number of different pasts. Getting to grips with this is part of learning what history is all about.

● Suitable books for children on the Victorian period abound, especially information books on popular topics such as childhood, transport and leisure. It is worth using sets of pupil books produced by publishers to service the needs of National Curriculum history (see especially Collins, Ginn and Longman).

● Use as much visual material as you can, especially old photographs and slides. Portraits are a splendid source for studies of the Victorians and many are available in slide form (from the National Portrait Gallery). Local newspapers sometimes have extensive archives of local pictures dating from the last century.

● Artefacts can usually be borrowed from your local museum or library as part of a schools loan service or can be handled in the museums themselves. Reproductions and facsimiles can be purchased via

suppliers such as History in Evidence and Past Times. But a topic so close in time to the present day can be mainly sourced with artefacts from the children's families, the school (especially if it is of old foundation), the staff and yourself. There is still a great deal of interesting material in general circulation. Ask, you may be surprised what you will turn up.

● Some historic sites and museums are particularly rich in Victorian material and, even if you are unable to take your children on a visit, they are worth contacting because they often have school resource packs, books and guides. The list is almost endless so here are just a few to whet your appetite: Beamish Museum; The Black Country Museum, Dudley; National Railway Museum, York; Museum of Science and Industry, Birmingham; St Fagan's Welsh Folk Museum, South Glamorgan; National Portrait Gallery, London; Museum of London; National Maritime Museum, Greenwich; The Army Museum, Chelsea; Osborne House, Isle of Wight; Linley Sambourne House, London; Ironbridge Gorge Museum (various sites at this heart of the industrial revolution – you must select and focus your visit; it is impossible and confusing to attempt it all); The National Waterways Museum, Gloucester; The Canal Museum, Stoke Bruerne, Towcester; The Museum of Childhood, Bethnal Green; The Museum of Childhood, Edinburgh.

If you can't visit a major museum or site, look for a relevant local visit.

● Education is a favourite topic in Victorian history, and there are many places where Victorian classrooms are recreated, often in genuine Victorian classrooms. If you make a few phone calls you will certainly be able to find a visit where the class can not only see but can enjoy the experience of being Victorian children for a day. Some examples are: Bishop Hooper's Schoolroom, The Folk Museum, Gloucester; Board Schoolroom, The Industrial Museum, Bradford; East Anglian Rural Life Museum, Stowmarket; Hartlebury Castle Schoolroom, Kidderminster; Herding's School Living History Centre, Sheffield; Judge's Lodgings Museum of Childhood, Lancaster; Katesgrove Schoolroom, Katesgrove Primary School, Reading; Sevington School, near Chippenham, Wiltshire.

● Victorian buildings are all around you. The local museum, the railway station and even the building you are in may be your best resource. Check to see if the local workhouse exists and what it is used for today. Old hospitals are often Victorian as are local parks, monuments, theatres, and town halls. Regimental museums have splendid displays on specific military events of the period. The Victorians built more churches than anyone since the Norman invasion so use your eyes; it is important that you do not miss what is right under your nose.

● Extracts from Victorian books, fiction and non-fiction, can be used for descriptive evidence. For example: *Lark Rise to Candleford* (Flora Thompson); *Kilvert's Diary 1870-1879* (Penguin); *Hedingham Harvest* (Victorian family life in rural England,

Geoffrey Robinson, National Trust); *Jane Eyre* (Charlotte Bronte); *Nicholas Nickleby* (Charles Dickens); *Tom Brown's Schooldays* (Thomas Hughes). Historical fiction is highly recommended as a way of capturing children's imaginations, but the stories must be good stories first, and a means of instruction second. The best way to use fiction is to read to the class, as some historical fiction poses reading difficulties for young children. Be selective. Examples are: *Ellen's Birthday* and *Ellen and the Queen* (Gillian Avery – there are a number of books set in this period by this author); *The Joshers* (H Carpenter); *Moondial* (Helen Cresswell); *Williver's Return* (A M Hadfield); *Fanny's Sister* (Penelope Lively); *Butty Boy* (Jill Paton-Walsh); *The Railway Children* (E Nesbit); *Jubilee* (B Willard); *The Lady from Scutari* (W Charles).

● Consider also music and videos. The best advice is to check the latest catalogues of leading suppliers as, like book lists, lists of these resources can date quite quickly. Examples worth seeking are: *The Illustrated Victorian Songbook* (Waters and Hunter, Michael Joseph); *The Victorians* (book and music cassette, A and M Bagenal, Longman); the *Landmarks* series (resource pack also available on the Victorians, BBC); *How We Used to Live* (Yorkshire TV).

● Computer software is sometimes produced to accompany TV series. Check the schedules and the catalogues. One of the most comprehensive software catalogues is produced by AVP, School Hill Centre, Chepstow, Gwent, NP6 5PH.

Assessment

You simply need to know that learning has taken place since the start of the project. There is no requirement to test against the level descriptors for history but they can be used as a guide.

The extent to which you record progress in history will be a matter of school policy, but you will check by observation, by questioning, by marking children's work and, in some cases, by testing whether learning has taken place.

Ask yourself: What do they know? What can they do? What have they experienced?

What do they know?

For this study unit you might check children's knowledge of:
● the main events and dates;
● major historical figures;
● the main changes within the period;
● changes and continuities to the present day.

Geography

During Key Stage 2 the children continue to learn about places, including their local area. They compare this with contrasting localities of a similar size, which might be within or beyond the UK, perhaps in Europe. They will also learn about more distant localities in less-developed countries.

Key Stage 2 children investigate aspects of their immediate and wider environment, including settlement, rivers, weather and environmental change, or other themes particularly appropriate to their school. These studies are about real places, near and far, large and small. Within these place and thematic studies the children extend their geographical skills, and particularly by using maps and pictures in context, by collecting and handling data, and developing their research skills as they access relevant geographical information from a range of sources including books and information technology.

Your school will have chosen the places and themes to be studied and decided how to locate them throughout the four years. Your geography curriculum model should provide opportunities for children to 'revisit' themes and localities, reinforcing and extending their geographical knowledge and understanding.

It is impracticable to deal here with every possible combination of topic, so the following content structure has been adopted. (You may want to draw on ideas from the other Yearbooks if your school has allocated topics differently.)

Year 3: Skills, enquiry
Place: Local (urban), Local (rural), Topical
Theme: Settlement (major), River (minor)

Year 4: Skills, enquiry
Place: Contrast (UK), Less developed country (urban), Topical
Theme: River (major), Weather (minor)

Year 5: Skills, enquiry
Place: Contrast (EU), Less developed country (rural), Topical
Theme: Weather (major), Environmental Change (minor)

Year 6: Skills, enquiry
Place: Local (revisit), Less developed country (contrast), Topical
Theme: Environmental Change (major), Settlement (minor)

Whichever model your school has chosen, there are four fundamental key areas of geography in which your children should be progressing:

- Ability to undertake geographical enquiry and use geographical skills.
- Knowledge and understanding of places.
- Knowledge and understanding of geographical patterns and processes.
- Knowledge and understanding of environmental relationships and issues.

What should they be able to do?

Year 5 children should continue to make progress in the four key areas of geography. To facilitate this continuing progress, you should provide opportunities for the children to observe, describe, compare and explain human and physical features, identify patterns, processes and relationships, and investigate issues with a geographical dimension in a variety of locations. These activities may either be in designated lessons or in topic or thematic work in which the geography is explicitly identified and planned.

Key area: Geographical enquiry and the use of skills

Children should develop and extend their ability to:
* understand and use appropriate geographical terminology;
* recognize geographical aspects of topical events;
* ask and seek answers to their own geographical questions, drawing on their own observations;
* make, record, communicate and compare their own observations about places and environments from experiences, and secondary sources including the Internet;
* collect, record and present information or measurements pictorially and geographically, including the use of IT, and begin to analyse or explain it;
* carry out teacher-planned and their own enquiries, using an increasing range of skills;
* undertake fieldwork tasks and activities, using different kinds of equipment and resources you provide, for example, make measurements and observations and record on a large-scale map;
* begin to identify and find the resources they need for an enquiry, including accessing the World Wide Web.

Key area: Places: features, characteristics, contrasts and relationships

(Illustrative examples are given in brackets.) Year 5 children should recognize, describe, compare and express views about and record:
* the main physical (landscape, vegetation) and human (industries, transport networks) features of their local area and other localities studied, using appropriate geographical terminology;
* how combinations of human and physical features give a place its character (a National Park);
* that places change on a range of time scales (commercial activity);
* that buildings and land are used for a variety of purposes (for education, public institutions);
* the significance of location – why features are where they are, why things happened where they do (hill farming determined by an area's landscape and weather);
* similarities and differences between the places they study, beginning to explain them in terms of their wider geographical setting (urban and rural localities in a less-developed country);
* the 'nested' relationships of places (farm, village, county, country, continent).

Key area: Patterns and physical and human processes

The children should make observations and respond to questions about:
* where things are (siting of a new school or a recreational facility in or near a settlement);
* physical (natural) and human processes: explaining why things are as they are (erosion and deposition in a river channel);
* the pattern of how things change (the effect or pattern of change following the closure of a factory).

Key area: Environmental relationships and issues

The children should:
* identify the different views people hold about the physical and/or human features of their environment (the views of workers and local residents about a proposed quarry expansion);
* recognize that their environment changes and that people affect it (deforestation);
* recognize and describe how the quality of the environment can be managed and improved (by strategies of landscaping a land-fill site).

These aspects are looked at in more detail in the Practical ideas section, although the focus is on geographical skills and enquiry, the tools of geography.

Practical ideas

Developing key areas

Geographical vocabulary

Practise and extend children's geographical vocabulary, introducing specialist terminology for the features, patterns and processes met with in place and thematic studies.

● Make word lists, for example, features associated with weather, environmental change and rural localities in less-developed countries, then use the words to label photographs.

● Make word lists from topical, place or theme pictures, and group the words into categories.

● Make alphabet lists, selecting a theme – say, countries – and encourage children to name one for each letter of the alphabet: Austria, Bulgaria, Canada and so on. They can increase their locational knowledge by finding them on a globe and marking them on an appropriate map.

Maps and photographs

Field sketching

Field sketching is an important geographical skill which can be learned in the classroom before being used outdoors. Children should make field sketches from photographs initially by tracing, then freehand, identifying the key features. Encourage them to make field sketches, label features, land-use and landscape, and annotate as required. From this activity, which encourages children to view the whole picture, you discover what they notice when they look at photographs – whether or not they see and recognize what you intend. Extend this skill by asking them to sketch and annotate the view from a suitable window or tall building.

Questioning pictures

● When looking at photographs, ask the children different types of question: *concrete, descriptive, speculative, reasoning, evaluative and problem-solving.*

● Encourage the children to write their own geographical questions around a photograph, and to seek answers. Encourage their visualization by asking them to extend a photograph, drawing what is beyond its limits, or to complete a photograph in which you have blocked out the centre.

Aerial photographs

● Ask the children to identify the human and physical features in aerial photographs, using correct geographical vocabulary. They can make a sketch from the photograph (see Field sketching above).

● Ask them to match the aerial photograph to an appropriate map, orientating the latter appropriately; ask them to identify landmarks on the aerial photograph and plan a route to visit them, marking the route on the map.

● They can compare oblique and vertical aerial photographs, perhaps of the school or local area. *What is similar/different about them?* Then they can compare each photograph with a map and mark what each shows on the map. *Do they cover the same area?*

● The children can each make a map from an aerial photograph, marking those features they consider important. Use the completed maps to discuss the inclusion/exclusion of information on maps. *Who decides what to include in published maps? Are they 'right', accurate or too selective?*

Using maps

● Use a wide range of plans, maps, atlases and globes, sketch maps, pictorial maps, different scales, road and world atlases, political and physical globes whenever appropriate and in as many contexts as possible. In addition to using larger-scale Ordnance Survey maps (1:1,250, 1:2,500), increasingly use 1:25,000 and 1:50,000 maps. Use maps to:

▶ locate places being studied (identifying place, county or state, country, continent) or in the news (have a topical event map on the wall, with newspaper cuttings and photographs);

▶ locate places to be, or that have been, visited (identify the 'shape', distance and direction of the route relative to school);

▶ relate to photographs of places;

▶ help answer questions. *How will/could/did we get to X? How many different ways could we get from A to B? How long will it take? How much will it cost?* (use with timetables);

▶ carry out geographical enquiries.

Use atlases to develop research skills (such as using an index) and globes to recognize continents, countries, seas and oceans, equator and Tropics of Cancer and Capricorn, latitude and longitude. Begin to explain seasons, climate and vegetation.

Making maps

● Provide opportunities for groups of children to make large-scale maps or representations, and for individual children to draw free-hand maps for representations of localities being studied, of journeys undertaken within the local area or further afield, of journeys in stories (this requires visualization of the location of a story).

● Encourage the children to make their own sketch map for recording data, rather than providing them with one. Photocopy the 'best' map(s) for the rest of the class to use.

● Year 5 children can make maps or plans for Key Stage 1 children to use. These could perhaps be a large-scale plan of the school and/or its grounds or a map of the village or the local shopping arcade, and could be the basis for a wall display.

Topical geography

Regularly find an item in the national or local media that has a geographical flavour, such as an earthquake or volcanic eruption, an environmental threat or a political event. Use it as text for Literacy Hour, for discussion, and to develop geographical general knowledge, interest and understanding. If appropriate, use it for a small-scale geographical enquiry (it doesn't need to be a half-term's topic!).

Geographical facts

Introduce some new geographical facts each week, for example, the names of the ten highest mountains, ten longest rivers, ten biggest conurbations. Encourage the children to find them in an atlas, to name their countries, and to find additional information about them. You could develop this into your own version of Geographical Trivial Pursuits, developing children's geographical general knowledge while introducing or reinforcing geographical vocabulary.

IT

Use appropriate geographical software, including CD-ROMs, and encourage children to use the Internet and other electronic sources, including the exchange of ideas and information with other schools at home and abroad through fax, e-mail and telephone.

Places

EU contrasting locality enquiry

Many teachers have visited Europe and, with the increased flexibility in the National Curriculum, might choose to use this experience for a contrasting locality study in Key Stage 2.

● Rather than carry out an encyclopaedic study of one place, select a focus for the study (for example, economic activity, tourism, settlement or environmental change) which will give it depth, rather than breadth, and enable you to reinforce

and extend geographical skills and enquiry in a new context. The children should compare the EU locality with their own local area, identifying and offering explanations for similarities and differences, and identify connections and interdependence, becoming increasingly aware of the position of the UK in an expanding Europe.

● Provide opportunities to consider both cognitive aspects (human and physical features and so on) and affective aspects (preferences, feelings, experiences, memories and so on) of the locality which, collectively, contribute to a 'sense of place'.

● In Year 5, increasingly encourage the children to ask and seek answers to their own geographical questions, rather than yours. Before beginning, and possibly using a picture as a stimulus, ask the children *What do you already know about this place* and *What are you interested in finding out about it?* Respect and use their answers to the latter to give structure to your study, and extra motivation to the children. Help them to consider how they can find out, and how to set up an enquiry.

A question framework

In studying an EU contrasting locality (and other places) you could select from the question framework introduced in earlier Yearbooks. It is not sequential, for example, you might like to start with *What do you think it would be like to visit/live in/ work in X?* Progression is achieved through the depth of the children's geographical understanding and thinking. (It is inappropriate to require the same type of geographical work, and same level of geographical thinking as previously, but in a different locality!)

Local enquiry area

In studying the local area (and other places) you could use the following question framework:

Question and skill or concept	Response
What is it? What is it like? Observation, description.	Identify the main human and physical features, describe the morphology of the contrasting locality.
Where is it? Location, distance, direction.	The 'address' of the locality; its relationship to the children's local area (distance, direction), and to major physical and human features (motorways, rivers, cities, hills and mountains, coast).
What sort of place is it? Categorization, classification.	How the features give it a specific identity as, for example, an Alpine village, a Mediterranean resort, an Eastern European capital city, a Greek island.
Is it like any other places you know? Comparison, similarity and difference.	Compare it explicitly with the children's local area and other localities they have studied or know.
How could we get there? Communications, time, cost.	Find and describe (using maps, timetables, pictures and words) routes to the locality, including distance, time, cost. Encourage the children to plan a visit to the locality.
Why is it like it is? Hypothesis, speculation.	Begin to consider how and why a place develops in a certain way and at a certain pace, for example, as a resort, an industrial town or capital city.

If you know a place well and can call upon other people who have visited or lived there, and have suitable resources or evidence, you could ask the children to consider the following questions:.

Is this place changing? How? Continuity and change, dynamics, time, spatial process, development.	Recognize that places change, they are dynamic. Find out about recent or proposed changes (on TV, in the press). Are these changes unique to this place?
Are these changes unique to this place? Cause and consequence, power (economic, social, political) in the source of who or what has the power to sanction or cause change.	Begin to look for explanations.
Why do you think it is changing? Recognize outcomes of changes.	Recognize who or what has the power to sanction or cause change.
What effects might proposed changes have?	Recognize that the environment might be changed; that some, but not all, changes are improvements; that some, but not all people benefit from changes.

Encourage the children to consider, while comparing with their own locality:

What do you feel about it? *Do you like it?* Opinions, values, attitude.	Recognize particular likes and dislikes, and give reasons for these preferences.
What would it be like to live or work here? Empathy.	Give opinions and justify them.
What gives this place its character? Generalisation.	Develop the idea that places have a character of their own, and what it is for this particular locality, compared with their own.
What's special about this place?	

Geography

These are challenging questions, but by Year 5 children can meet the challenge at their own level. The questions make cognitive and affective demands on the children, who will be learning about the morphology (the features, shape, form, structure) of a place, and also developing a 'sense of place'. This is about their own, unique, experience or interpretation of the place. They will be learning that everyone experiences and thinks about a place differently – there is not one 'right' answer or opinion. This will be further developed as you introduce children to controversial geographical issues. (Later they will learn about consensus and decision-making processes.)

Hypothesis testing

As an alternative to this question framework approach to enquiry, you may prefer to test an hypothesis, for example, *A is a better place to live/ work than B (our local area)*, with the children defining 'better'. Or you may like to post one key question to investigate, for example, *Why is C the capital city of D?* or *Why is E a popular ski resort?* The hypothesis or question could be identified by you or the children.

A postcard from ...

Whichever approach you use, this postcard activity is useful. At the start of the study, describe a postcard view of the locality to the children. Give them a postcard-sized piece of cardboard on which to draw the view, making their own 'Postcard from X'. At the end of the study, return to the postcard and invite the children to write the postcard home, telling the recipient the most important things about the place. This provides you with quick feedback about what the children have found most interesting about the study, what they have learned and their misconceptions, and also gives you some informal assessment evidence.

Less-developed country: rural enquiry

Children's study of a rural locality in a less-developed country carries the danger of reinforcing negative ideas and what might be described as 'mud hut' stereotypes. Children often believe that all people in less developed countries suffer from disease, drought, war, famine and so on. It is important to foster positive images as much as possible, to consider positive things about what it is like to live in this locality, to recognize the similarities with their own lives, the same basic needs of food, water, clothing, shelter, education and work. Encourage children to think about what the place is like for the local people, to begin to move away from a Eurocentric perspective which can be unnecessarily judgmental.

Remember that in your rural locality study you are saying 'this is what it is like for these people to live in this place, now'. You are not making generalizations about the country, and certainly not – in the case of a locality in an African country – about the continent.

Resource packs

● There are some good resource packs to support a rural locality study, especially from the development education centres (for example Birmingham DEC). You may like to choose one that has a complementary urban pack for comparison. Examples include Action Aid's India (for example, Chembakolli and Bangalore) and Kenya (for example, Kapsokwony and Nairobi) packs – but there are others.

It is important to avoid exoticism or tokenism and to study the ordinary, everyday life experiences and environment of the local people – children are always interested in people!

Use the teachers' notes in the resource packs, a selection from the cognitive and affective 'place' questions given above, the children's questions, a role play focused on a local issue (with the children carrying out the preparatory research). Use artefacts and visitors – people from, and people who have been to, the locality – to enrich work from the photopacks. Identify the key question(s) to structure the enquiry. Integrate the use of maps, photographs and secondary sources (including books and IT) to develop and reinforce geographical skills.

Geographical patterns and processes

As children observe, describe, record, compare and explain their observations, you will be developing the idea of geographical pattern and process. Encourage them to observe, and begin to explain, the importance of location, such as how (and, later, why) the vegetation in tropical areas differs from the vegetation of the UK, and how animals are used for work in less-developed rural areas. Encourage them to recognize the distribution (spatial) patterns made by individual human and physical features and the associations between them, such as why a town grew up at a river crossing, how and why lowland agriculture differs from upland or highland agriculture.

On appropriate scale maps colour in, for example, different types of amenities, different types of land-use, land above a certain height, motorways, railways and cities. Encourage the children to describe the distribution patterns and explain 'why things are like that'.

Use topical and local events. Encourage children to identify and explain changes or short-duration events, for example, how and why a hurricane (or cyclone) affected a locality; how a new theme park affected a locality; how building a new bypass has changed traffic patterns on nearby roads; how winter storms affect the coast; how the creation of local cycle-ways could make the local area safer.

Environmental relationships and issues

Developing from their studies of an increasing range of localities, encourage children to reconsider how they feel about and value their own locality, what's good/not so good about it, and to reappraise its aesthetics and people's responsibilities within it. Help

them to justify their opinions and to appreciate other children's views, which might be different from their own. Help them to consider other people's opinions in the wider community too, for example, they might not like to walk to school, but other people do not like all the extra traffic the schools generate.

Environmental change study (introductory)

Using local newspapers, identify environmental issues that involve change in the locality. These might include the expansion of a quarry, the diversion of a river, building a wind farm, creating a one-way traffic system, changing land use from agriculture to theme park. The advantage of starting 'local' is that information and opinion should be readily available. Encourage children to identify the individuals or groups interested in the issue, and discuss what their opinions might be – *what 'side' are they on?* Consider why they might think this way – *what influences their perspective?* Some people will agree and others disagree, so begin to develop the key ideas of conflict and consensus. This forms a useful introduction to the democracy element of Citizenship.

You may find the following questions useful.
What is the issue? Why is it an issue? Why is it important locally?
What are its geographical aspects?
Where is the issue taking place? How will/could we get there?
What are the background factors to the issue? (historical, political, economic, environmental)
What groups or individuals are involved? (identify the 'interested parties')
What views do they hold? Why?
What alternative solutions are there? (routes, locations, time scales)
What are their advantages and disadvantages? (from the different interested parties' perspectives)
What are your feelings about the issue?
How will a decision be made? On the basis of what information or criteria?
Who will make it? Are they elected/appointed? (introduction to democracy)
What do you think the decision should be, and why? (Encourage the children to have, express and justify an opinion; more preparation for Citizenship.)

Role play

This approach lends itself very well to a role play. Children working in threes can create a character

(one of the interested parties), present their views and argue the issue in a simulated council or public meeting. Provide them with documentation (press releases, newspaper articles and follow-up letters to the press), TV news clips, maps and illustrations and a proforma on which to record their points for and against the proposed change, to summarize their views, and to record their vote.

Geographical thinking

At the Year 5 stage, geographical thinking is more sophisticated: the children begin to realize that different people have different views; that changes don't just happen but that someone or a group of people have the power to allow or cause things to happen; that decisions are made, based on evidence or criteria; that not everybody agrees with the decisions. You may consider that, to some extent, the factual basis for the evidence the children present can be considered less important – that this can be improved with experience in Year 6 and beyond, as the children understand the need for accurate information and good quality data and as they appreciate that anecdote, assertion or faction (not quite fiction) are insufficient.

By focusing on issues, the different key areas of geography are drawn together naturally. Children develop and use their geographical skills to investigate real places where physical and human processes are affecting the environment.

Weather study

An introductory or small-scale weather study was described in the Year 4 book in the series. It was centred on the immediate vicinity of the school. Through it children will have learned:

▶ how site conditions influence the weather;
▶ to use weather measuring equipment;
▶ to record weather information;
▶ about the variability of weather, in the short term (during one day), the medium term (during a week or month) and the longer term (during the year);
▶ of the relationships between aspects of weather (for example, between cloud types and rain, sunshine and temperature).

In Year 5 they will be ready to learn more about seasonal weather patterns and about weather conditions in different parts of the world, about how weather influences way of life and to be introduced to ideas about climate.

Using weather reports

● Look out in the local press for articles on issues associated with weather and climate, and use these to initiate an enquiry. There are often articles about flooding, freak weather (uncharacteristically hot, dry, wet, cold, windy), climate change, and so on. Use clips from TV programmes, including weather forecasts. The children can locate the incidents on a world map and look for patterns.

● Collect national weather reports from national newspapers. These include data for towns and cities throughout the British Isles.
Ask the children to:
▶ find the places in an atlas;
▶ extract the data, graph it by hand or using IT;
▶ locate the towns and cities on a wall map, position the graphed data appropriately around the map;
▶ compare the weather in the north, south, east and west;
▶ compare the published data with the TV weather forecasts.
Repeat this regularly, over a term or preferably a year. Look for patterns.
Ask questions such as: *Which is the hottest, wettest, sunniest place?*

● Collect worldwide weather reports from national newspapers. These include data from towns and cities in all five continents. The children, working in pairs or small groups, should select two contrasted localities from those listed – different continents and latitudes – and keep a weather record for them. They can plot the data graphically over a period of time, by hand or using IT, and position the graphs appropriately around a wall-display world map. It is important that the children look for and identify patterns – temperature change from polar to tropical, rainfall highs and lows – otherwise this is a not-very-geographical 'so what' activity! Relate the patterns to the world model or globe. Look for explanations.

● Encourage the children to research the places for which they are collecting weather data, using secondary sources like *Encarta*, the Internet, videos and books. Encourage them to make links between the weather and the housing, clothing, vegetation, economic activity and way of life in these places. (This work introduces ideas which later lead to knowledge and understanding of world climate zones.)

● Set up a class 'Book of Weather Records' – for example, record the hottest, coldest, wettest place each week/month, and relate the records to the globe.

● If you are travelling abroad, collect weather forecasts from overseas newspapers, including those available on flights. Many have excellent colour forecast maps, especially from North America and Scandinavia. Encourage children to interpret the

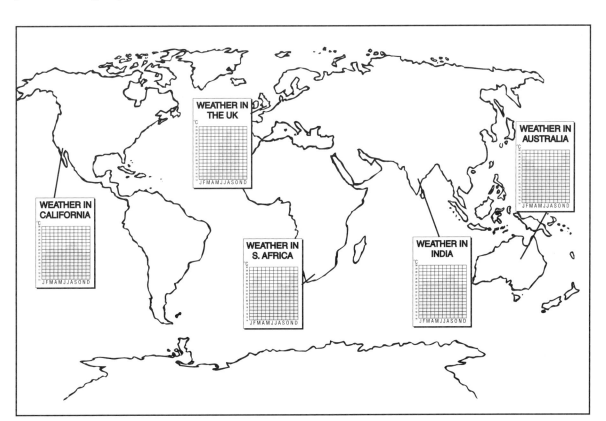

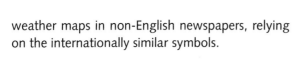
weather maps in non-English newspapers, relying on the internationally similar symbols.

● In the Science chapter, you will find work on globe position, seasons and so on which relates directly to this Geography work.

● Look in detail at the weather in the place chosen for your distant locality study. Look for evidence in photographs, extract the data for the nearest place listed in newspaper reports and consider how the weather influences the way of life in the place. Is weather information for the country available on the Internet? Ask *Why is the weather like this here?*

– look for explanations in terms of the position of the place on the globe.

● If you have chosen a tropical locality with hot/dry and hot/wet seasons, it is probable that the photopack you are using only illustrates one of these. Try to obtain photographs to illustrate the other. Ask: *What's the difference between the two seasons – how do they affect everyday life?* Compare the two-season locality with our four-season pattern (It is important for the children to appreciate that not all the world has spring, summer, autumn and winter) and begin to look for an explanation related to global position.

Assessment

In Year 5 you will want to keep a simple record of the progress children are making, against the Expectations (QCA 1998).

What do they know?

Evidence will include their:
● accurate use of geographical vocabulary to talk and write about the places and themes studied;
● understanding of maps and geographical pictures;
● increasing geographical general knowledge.

What can they do?

Evidence will include their:
● use of geographical skills;
● ability to ask and respond to geographical questions;
● ability to find information from resources, give opinions, make comparisons and offer explanations.

What have they experienced?

Place and thematic studies, geographical skills introduced, activities, fieldwork (experiences outside the classroom).

Music

By the time the children have arrived at Year 5, following a full, carefully planned, developing music curriculum, they should be growing musically competent. They will have discovered the elements of music and be combining these elements in their compositions. They should be actively involved in listening, composing, performing and appraising. The National Curriculum suggests that they should be able to 'perform accurately and confidently' and should be 'showing an awareness of other performers'.

In their own compositions they will be expected to 'select, and combine appropriate resources' in identified structures using the musical elements. As they listen, they should be 'identifying changes in the character and mood' of the music of other composers and be 'recognizing how musical elements are used to communicate moods and ideas'. During the year, the children should be able to discuss in more depth their own work and that of others and 'be able to describe and compose music from different traditions, using a musical vocabulary'.

At all times music should be seen as a part of the whole curriculum, integrating with other subjects where possible, while still having an identity of its own.

Key areas : Listening, Composing, Performing, Appraising

A curriculum for music-making will always ask for sounds to be explored through listening, composing, performing and appraising and at times it is useful to look at the areas separately. However, in a successful music session, all four areas are in action at the same time. A music-maker will listen to sounds, discuss them, choose appropriate ones to place together in some order, move them around and then perform them. This is as true at Year 5 as it is at university, and should be encouraged at all times. These skills are involved in all the activities suggested here. The activities will explore all the elements of music as suggested in the National Curriculum. These are: pitch, duration, dynamics, tempo, timbre, texture and structure.

What should they be able to do?
Key element: Pitch

Year 5 children will already have spent a great deal of time exploring pitch in previous years and should have discovered that music cannot only be high and low, but can also slide up and down, move in steps and move in leaps. They should now be encouraged to create music using these ideas, with instructions such as *Try to write a short piece that has an ascending tune.*

They should be singing a wide variety of songs in many different styles, and should be made aware of diction, as well as where to take breaths, as suggested by the phrasing. Some easy songs in two parts should be tried, as well as rounds in many parts.

Most children should be beginning to know the letter names of the notes (C D E F G A B) and where these notes are on the tuned instruments. Those children who are learning the tonic sol-fa sounds and signs will have used soh, meh, lah and will now move towards the home note of doh.

Most of the music the children will be singing, playing and creating involves the use of pitch and there should be a growing awareness of this.

Key element: Duration

Year 4 should have introduced the children to a more formal recognition of the longness and shortness of notes through the signs and symbols used to represent lengths of time (♪, ♩, ♫). They should be noticing how composers (themselves and others) use these symbols . To the three most-used notes you could now add the longer note of a semibreve (o) and also have a look at the signs used for rests (𝄽, ▬, ▬), with the importance of silences in music being discussed. The children should already be grouping music in 2s, 3s and 4s and be using bar lines, but they should also be experimenting with the less usual grouping of 5s. They should be creating for themselves simple rhythms and be extending them.

Key element: Dynamics

Dynamics will have been thoroughly explored by Year 5 with the children having a working knowledge of *p, f, pp, ff, < >, mp, mf*. The majority of them should be able to identify the signs, know their musical names and be able to hear when these dynamics are being used both in their own music and others'. During the year, you could add the accented note, which is played a little more strongly than the others and usually comes at the beginning of the bar or a group of beats.

Key element: Tempo

Music moves at different speeds and the children should have graduated from knowing that tempo is just fast and slow, to understanding that some pieces will move faster or slower than others. They should be using these changing tempos to create effects and be listening to how well-known composers use tempo to suggest a special mood. A very slow tempo will often give a sombre feel to the music while a quicker, livelier tempo suggests life and jollity. The tempo of background music for poetry and stories will at once tell something about the content of the piece and this is something to be explored during this year.

Key element: Timbre

There should be a greater awareness by Year 5 of special sounds of voices and instruments. During the previous year, orchestral instruments might have been listened to and you should develop this interest by giving the children many opportunities to appreciate the wonderful sounds the various instruments can make. The listening should move forward from hearing families of instruments (strings, brass, woodwind, percussion) to more careful listening to the individual instruments. If some of the children in your class play orchestral instruments, encourage them to perform to everyone, but you should also let the children hear recordings of expert instrumentalists. Year 5 could be a year for discovering how the instruments work, how the timbres are made and why they sound different from each other. Encourage the children to try to remember sounds they have enjoyed, possibly the musical sounds they might associate with a holiday abroad – you could discuss how this timbre is typical of that country.

Key element: Texture

By Year 5, the children should be aware of the many ways in which musical pieces can be put together to create different textures. They should have collected sounds from the environment at an earlier stage and placed them one after the other, should have used one rhythm with another, added accompaniments to songs and should be making tunes weave round each other. All of these ideas create interesting textures and you should encourage them. To these could be added the use of chords (more than one note being played at the same time) as accompaniments to songs. Accompaniments should also include more than one part and you should encourage those children who play guitars and recorders to join in, creating a wider variety of textures with their rhythms and sounds.

Key element: Structure

As the children grow more used to the elements of music and how one can use them, encourage them to choose from a wide variety of structures in their compositions. They should already be familiar with the use of repetition and the sandwich structure (ABA), and most of them should be able to pick out and play an ostinato (repeating tune) with their vocal and instrumental music. Questions and answers will have been explored both with the voice and on the instruments. All of these structures should be explored and developed during the year. More work with the phrasing of music could be included and short phrases (four bars) can be extended to longer phrases (eight bars). New combinations of repeating tunes, such as AABB or ABCBA, can be tried in small group compositions. The children might enjoy writing their own verse and chorus, adding tunes to the words or background music. At all times, encourage the children to discuss with you the structure of their piece to avoid time wasting with rambling tunes. Sometimes all that is needed is a simple instruction such as 'Begin and end on the same note' for a successful composition.

Practical ideas

Music-making can often look and sound very disorganized. In fact, the best results will always come from very careful organization, even if the preparation is very noisy. Decide just what it is you would like to achieve in a session, or group of sessions, and make a plan of linked starting activities and main group activities, always giving time at the end for performances to one another. Some music-making will be in small groups so plan your space well. Check on the availability of instruments, that they are complete and, if appropriate, have beaters. If you are expecting the children to record their music, have paper available for both graphic and traditional notation as well as a tape recorder for the final results.

Time your sessions and keep stopping and starting small group work, inviting children to perform. Ask *How much have you done?* to check that progress is being made. Visit the groups, giving a helping hand when required, but generally stand back and watch as leaders emerge, instruments are chosen and creations develop. Encourage the children to discover for themselves, to make decisions, to create, to work in a team and then to perform.

Making a start

Ask the children to sit in a circle and listen as you clap three, think three, clap three, think three. Can they fit words into the three spaces ('bubble gum', 'lemonade')? You all clap three and the person to your right fits in a word, saying and clapping. Move this round the circle, filling the three-beat gaps. Change to clapping four and thinking four. *Which words will fit in now?* ('Coca-Cola', 'double decker'). Try the same using five beats ('toast and marmalade', 'sand at the seaside').

Singing

● Play 'Copy me' by singing any four notes to the class. The children then copy you. Once this is working, point to different children who should answer you with four different notes or the same ones in a different order. This could also be tried with tuned percussion and recorders.

● Sing 'In the Quartermaster's Store' (*Ta-ra-ra Boom-de-ay*, A&C Black) as a class but ask different children to make up new verses about their school life.

● Introduce improvised singing with this chant (or you might be able to fit a tune to the words):

Call:	Response:
I woke up this morning	*I woke up this morning*
My head felt like lead	*My head felt like lead*
All I could think of	*All I could think of*
Was to go back to bed.	*Was to go back to bed.*

Invite someone else to become the caller and to change the words.

● Take one of the songs the children know best and sing it all together. Once you are sure everyone is taking part, ask each child to sing a note each. Always put the whole song together again at the end.

● Add whistling to your sound bank. Some children find it hard to whistle while others find it very easy. Try the song 'Whenever I feel afraid' from *The King and I* and whistle the chorus.

● Using the voice or a tuned instrument, begin on a given note, play a very short tune and return to the same note. *Who can copy me?*

Body percussion

● Use body percussion to make up longer rhythm patterns. For example, the leader claps – all clap. Leader: clap, click – all: clap, click. Leader: clap, clap, click, stamp – all: clap, clap, click, stamp. This continues until no-one can remember the pattern. Then change the leader.

● Ask the class to give you the names of their favourite football teams. Write them on the board, then clap the patterns of the words. Choose four with different-sounding patterns. Divide the class into four and give each group a sound pattern. (If you have real football fanatics, you may save trouble by ensuring that they are in the group of the appropriate team.) Point to group one who say, clap or play their football team.

Once this is going well add another, then the others. Suggest that names can sound effective spoken quietly as well as shouted. Ask them to move from soft to loud to soft in response to the conductor's hand signals.

Manchester United
Chelsea   Arsenal
Leeds United

Introducing key elements

Long and short

Give small groups of children, working with a variety of instruments, a limited number of notes to work with. Invite them to use only quick notes to create a piece of music. On another occasion, ask them to use only longer notes. On another day, ask them to try to make up a contrasting piece using both short and long notes in contrast. They could use the structure ABA or questions and answers.

Tonic sol-fa

If you are happy to use the tonic sol-fa, then add to your note bank the home note of doh. The children will enjoy using doh because it is familiar to them, since much music begins and ends on doh. Take the words of any well-known limerick (or better still, make up a new one to link with your project or school life) and sing the limerick to sol-fa notes.

There once was a class singing sol-fa
s   s   m   m   s   l l   l s

Whose children progressed very far
s   s   m   m   s   l l s

They could sing soh, me, doh
s   s   l   s   m   d

They knew where to go
s   l   s   s   m

So the teacher gave them a gold star
m   m   s   s   l   s   m   m   d

Mood music

Use scenic pictures from old calendars, cards and so on and discuss, as you look at them with the children, how many sounds you might hear if you were inside the scene (waving trees, wind blowing, train whistle, river flowing, cuckoo, footsteps). Give one picture to each small group and ask them to choose their instruments after discussion about the mood of the picture. The tempo of their music might also help the mood. Some groups will want to place the sounds in random order in their music, while others might like to use the picture as a score, reading it from left to right, adding sounds as they occur.

Class song

Take a short, simple poem or rhyme. It could be something the children have written. Clap the word rhythms together as a class. Place a xylophone by you and take off the Fs and the Bs (leaving the pentatonic scale). Ask one child to play the word pattern on the remaining notes for the first line. Do the class like the sound? Can they sing it? If not, invite a second child to try. Once everyone has agreed on the best tune, move on to the next lines and compose tunes for each of them. Make sure someone in the class writes down the letter names of the notes to help everyone remember the tune. Try to include as many people as possible in the composition. Play it through a few times and enjoy singing a home-made class song.

Making a storm

Ask the children to sit in a circle. Pass storm sounds around the circle, first using finger tapping, then hand clapping, knee slapping and then foot stamping for the thunder. Make sure the sounds begin quietly and gradually get louder. Give everyone an instrument. The instruments should stay on the floor until you are ready to begin. Using their instrument in the best way possible to create storm music, the children should respond to a conductor who points to one person. This child plays softly, the next joins in until, by the end of the circle, everyone is playing at the height of the storm. Continue a second time round the circle as players drop out and the storm abates. You could also listen to Beethoven's 'Storm' from *Pastoral Symphony No 6*.

Musical pairs

Create with the children a game of musical matching pairs using dynamic and duration signs. Some flash cards show symbols (*p*, *f*, *mp*, *ff*, *pp*, <, >, ♪, 𝅗𝅥, ♩, o) and others the names (*piano, forte, mezzo piano, fortissimo, pianissimo, crescendo, diminuendo, quaver, crotchet, minim, semibreve*). Working in small groups, the children play Snap with the cards. They could make the cards for their group, thus helping them to remember this musical language.

Introducing chords

Introduce chords (more than one note being played at the same time) to the children by playing two notes together and asking if the sound is pleasing or not. If the answer is 'No' then place other notes together and ask the same question. You should find that the notes C and E, A and C$^\#$, D and F$^\#$, E and G played together will gain a favourable response. Many songbooks give suggested chords for accompanying singing (for example, *Flying a Round*, A&C Black) and tell the children which notes to play as well as where to play them.

Holiday sounds

Invite the children to tell you about their holidays. *Did you hear any different-sounding instruments?* Today's children travel far and wide so you may hear about the tabla, tambura and sitar in India, the cimbalon in Hungary and the Czech Republic, the kalimba and talking drums in Africa, steel drums in the Caribbean, as well as castanets and guitars in Spain. Develop this by asking the children to try to recreate the sounds they hear in other countries by using the available sound bank in the classroom. (Pentatonic music sounds very Chinese and upturned buckets as well as drums can be used to send messages to friends in a neighbouring village.)

Developing key elements

Just two notes

Play and sing 'Michael Finnegan' and 'Ten in the Bed' to an accompaniment of two notes, D and A. Ask the children to make up a pattern using some of the words (first line) and to play them in a rhythm that fits in with the song using just D and A. These two notes could also be used as a chord by playing them together. D is the starting note for the singers.

Magic music

Listen to Dukas' 'Sorcerer's Apprentice', or watch the Disney video of the same name, to hear how the composer effectively uses sounds to make magic music. Once inspired by Dukas' work, the children can make up the words of a spell and sing it or play background sounds while a small group chants the words.

Left and right

Divide the class into two groups. Using sol-fa signs ask the children to respond to your hand signs: left hand for the group on the left, right hand for the group on the right. Begin with both hands in the

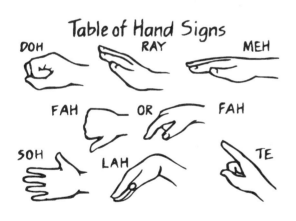

Table of Hand Signs

soh position. All sing soh. Change the left hand to meh; the left group changes while the right group sings soh again. Return to everyone singing soh. Keep changing the hand signs but return often to everyone singing the same. This can produce some lovely combinations of sounds. Ask a child to become the conductor.

Songs of the nation

Find songs and recordings that accentuate the character of each of the countries in the British Isles. There are many folk songs to be sung, each telling a little of the life of the country, and the recordings will show the timbres of instruments that are typical of that area. (Ireland: *Riverdance* music, Celtic harp, Irish pipes, 'Cockles and Mussels', 'The Minstrel Boy'. Scotland: Highland fling, Scottish bagpipes, 'Eriskay Love Lilt', 'Charlie is my Darling', 'The Campbells are Coming', 'Skye Boat Song'. Wales: 'The Welsh Harp', 'Men of Harlech', 'All Through the Night'. England: Morris dancing, English country dances, English recorder music, 'Lincolnshire Poacher', 'Widdecombe Fair'.) Investigating music from the British Isles makes a fascinating project and could provide a great deal of practical work which could be shown and played to the school as an assembly.

Two different songs

It is great fun and can be quite difficult to sing more than one song at the same time. Each song will have its own rhythms and notes, but some fit neatly together. Try singing the war songs 'Pack up Your Troubles' and 'It's a Long Way to Tipperary', first separately and then in two groups together. *Ta-ra-ra Boom-de-ay* (A&C Black) has other suggestions.

Stress

Give the children a well-known phrase to look at. 'She sells sea shells on the sea shore' would be a good one. Explain that in music, as in the spoken word, if the composer or writer expects a stronger sound to be placed on any word or note they need to use an accent. In music this is shown as <. Use your chosen phrase and place accents on different words to change the meaning of the phrase. Do the same with a well-known song. You could use the National Anthem:

instead of singing

     <   <
God save our gracious Queen

sing

       <   <
God save our gracious Queen

Whistle codes

Sheep dogs have an amazing ear for recognizing the whistle of their master as a signal to move in a certain direction. (In sheep-farming areas, some of your children will know about this and other children may have seen sheepdog trials on TV.) Ask the children, working in pairs, to make up a code of whistles or recorder/pipe sounds to direct their partner. Sliding up might mean move forward, short sounds might mean move backwards, a long sound could mean stop. *Can you use these whistles to move your partner around the playground or playing field?*

Ideas bank

● Play part of Mendelssohn's *Fingal's Cave* as a starting point for the class for art work linked with the sea. Discuss the mood of the music and how it might make everyone feel. *Does it make you want to go to the cave?* Link this listening with any projects about water, the sea, caves, exploration, wrecks, storms or the weather.

● Create pieces of music with the children called 'Take Five'. Instead of encouraging them to use patterns of two, three or four beats, ask them to try patterns of fives. These could be on tuned or untuned percussion instruments, recorders, pentatonic instruments. (The main beat will be on every fifth beat.)

● How many songs can the class think of that have a verse and a chorus? Many folk songs and hymns, as well as old time music hall songs and pop songs, will come into this category.

● Make a tape recording or use a pre-recorded tape with a selection of music that has clearly identified tunes with different number beats in the bar (two, three, four). Can the children work out how many beats by trying to conduct in time to the music ? Is it two beats ? three beats? four beats?

● Divide the class into groups of three. Give each group any three instruments. They must decide who is A and B and C. Ask each of the children to make up either a rhythm or a tune on their instrument. They then play them in a given order – A B C B A or AA BB CC AA. Ask the rest of the class if they think the order is successful or if the sounds would be better moved around.

● Play the 'No Laugh Race' song from *Okki-Tokki-Onga* (A&C Black). In pairs, children face each other, sing the song and try not to laugh.

Assessment

The most important outcome of music-making with all children is that they should have enjoyed it. This should be extremely obvious at the end of a session since the children will be animated about what they have been doing, as they move on to their next activity.

However, there are many other observations to be made to help in your evaluation of the work they have done. You should:
- encourage them to listen to sounds around them and the sounds they and others make on the instruments;
- ask them to give their opinion on all the music they hear;
- give them many opportunities to be creative in their music-making;
- let them perform as often as possible.

What can they do?

The children should be able to:
- listen attentively and collect sounds;
- recognize differences in sounds and recreate them;
- use sounds in a structured way and discuss them;
- respond to sounds through dance/drama and movement;
- sing a wide variety of songs in different styles;
- play pieces on tuned and untuned instruments;
- play accompaniments that are independent of songs;
- have a greater awareness of pulse/beat;
- listen to longer pieces of music;
- use a growing music vocabulary in their discussions;
- use a form of graphic and traditional notation;
- use the letter names of notes to record music;
- use a pentatonic scale in compositions and accompaniments;
- use a wide variety of structures and be able to identify them;
- describe and compare music from different traditions.

Can they perform?

Your music-making should be shared as much as possible with other children in the school, parents and friends. Everyone, not just the specialist performer, should be given a chance to perform. Look for abilities rather than disabilities – everyone can do something. Encourage those children who are having specialist lessons to demonstrate their skills to others by joining in whenever it is appropriate. School assemblies and school concerts should become a place for sharing successful activities.

Keeping a record

By Year 5 the children could be keeping a record of their own achievements in music, which will certainly help you in your evaluations and discussions with parents at the end of the year. One easy-to-write, quick-to-look-at record could be on a postcard or index file card, one for each child, with children writing about their explorations, compositions, performances and achievements whenever appropriate.

Art

This year builds on the things which the children have explored and experienced in Year 4.

Experiences should cover the development of visual perception and the skills that are needed for investigation and making. The children should:

- record what has been experienced and imagined, expressing ideas with increasing confidence and represent chosen features of the world around them with developing accuracy;
- gather and use resources and materials and experiment with ideas in response to these;
- experiment, showing increasing control, using a range of tools, materials and techniques;
- reflect on and adapt work.

Introduce the class to a range of work by various artists, designers and craftspeople. The children should be:

- recognizing the work of some artists, craftspeople and designers;
- looking at the intention and purpose behind works of art;
- understanding something of the historical and cultural context of works of art;
- responding to and evaluating their own art, craft and design and the art, craft and design of others, relating it to their own work.

What should they be able to do?

In Year 5 children should be more capable of developing ideas from resource material and sustaining the work over a longer period of time. They should have increased knowledge of tools and materials and control over their use. You will, therefore, be able to introduce new techniques and materials such as Mod-Roc, which require more control. You can also introduce work on a larger scale. Children in Year 5 can be expected to take on increasing responsibility for organizing their own work, making decisions about how the work can be developed, locating appropriate tools and materials and clearing up afterwards.

You can hope that most children will have:

- experienced a range of graphic materials;
- experienced thick paint and watercolour;
- made prints, using found objects, press print, and possibly other methods;
- worked with a range of collage materials;
- worked with textiles and threads;
- experienced transfer crayons;
- modelled and constructed with a range of materials in three dimensions;
- been introduced to the work of a number of artists, craftspeople and designers from Western and non-Western cultures;
- reflected on and made changes to their work.

Looking at the work of others

In Year 5, children will be aware of reactions to their work from peers and adults. You should offer them a range of source material and an increasing element of personal choice. It also helps to show them work by a number of different artists and craftspeople which will enable them to see that, in art, there are many ways of responding besides producing an accurate representation. Encourage them to recognize the *elements of art* in the work of others and apply this knowledge to their own work, for example, looking at colour and line in artists' work and responding by using it vigorously to express feelings. In Year 5, most children can begin to analyse aspects of artists' work, compare and contrast materials, techniques and imagery, and relate it to their own work.

Encourage them to describe a variety of images and artefacts, to voice likes and dislikes and to make choices about which they like best. This can take place through whole-class discussions, group work or spontaneously on an individual basis.

Experiences in Year 5

Experiences in Year 5 should include:

- developing the use of familiar tools and materials, and the introduction of new or more complex ways of working;
- continued work in the visual elements which are the building blocks of art: pattern, texture, colour, line, tone, shape, form, space;
- visual communication and expression, using personal ideas and work from the imagination stimulated by visits, events, stories, music and so on;
- a range of developing skills relating to the techniques of drawing, painting, printing, collage, fabric work and work in three dimensions;
- working from memory and imagination;
- introduction to imaginative and abstract images in the work of other artists, craftspeople and designers, including at least one example from a non-Western culture;
- opportunities to develop a vocabulary in art by talking about their own work and the work of others.

Experimenting with new or unfamiliar tools and materials is still of great importance and you should help children to make connections between this exploratory work and the finished product. However, remember that progression doesn't always mean the introduction of new techniques. Some development will be through more complex use of techniques already learned.

Practical ideas

Making a start
The learning environment

The whole classroom environment, from the pictures on the walls to the way in which the tools and materials are arranged and cared for, is part of the display and is a statement about the way in which children's work is viewed and valued. This, in fact, is a significant part of the teaching, and in Year 5 children should help to maintain the art area. They should also help to organize and maintain a lively and rich learning environment where they, as well as you, bring in collections of visually exciting and tactile objects. Written comments can usefully accompany the displays, particularly if they are presented in the form of a task or challenge. This will stimulate curiosity and encourage an interest in, and response to, the world around them. Items for still-life drawing can be bought cheaply in car boot sales and junk shops.

Tools and materials

Provide good quality tools and materials and remind children of the need to care for them. In Year 5, the children should assume greater responsibility for organizing and maintaining the tools and materials which they need. For example, they can look after their own watercolour box, watercolour brush and packet of crayons, storing them in their drawer. In the long term, this is more economical as the materials are much better cared for if children feel ownership of them and the class should be able to take their materials with them into Year 6.

Other equipment and materials should be stored appropriately. Paint pots, collage materials and so on can be quite an attractive feature if they are organized neatly.

Developing visual skills and ideas

Working through the senses is of vital importance through all the stages. Develop the children's visual and tactile skills through:
- observation of real and interesting things brought into the classroom;
- going to places of visual or historical interest locally or farther afield.

Ask open-ended questions and discuss what they have seen and discovered to stimulate interest and provide ideas and starting points which can be followed up in sketchbooks and developed into a sequence of work.

Work can be further enriched and informed through researching images and ideas from related books, videos and the computer. Also give them the opportunity to study the work of a range of related artists. Starting points should sometimes be initiated by the children, coming from their own ideas, triggered by something they have read or imagined or an experience they have had.

Images and artefacts

As well as encouraging the children to bring interesting objects into the classroom, you can borrow collections of interesting items and artefacts from museums or your LEA. These may relate specifically to a topic or theme you are working on in another area of the curriculum, but can also be useful for extending the children's art experience.

If it is a picture, discuss the colours, the way the artist has worked, the mood and what is happening. If it is an artefact, ask the children to look at the shape, colour and pattern and to consider and discuss the country of origin. If it is not valuable, allow them to handle the object and encourage them to describe the design, shape, use and so on. They can record their initial responses in a sketchbook using words and drawings.

Choices and experiments

Using the knowledge and experience which they gained in Year 4, children in Year 5 should be able to make choices and decisions about materials and the way in which they will respond to a challenge in two or three dimensions. Provide opportunities for working both on individual projects and collaboratively or as a whole class.

Software

Continue to use graphics and painting computer software as another means of drawing, creating and changing patterns and exploring alternative combinations of colour by moving and dragging, cutting, copying and pasting. Children can produce their own drawings. Introduce scaling the picture to fit. Suitable software includes *RM Colour Magic*, *Advance*, *The Big Picture* and *Paintbrush*.

Themes

These themes offer potential for this age group.

● **Travel:** You could use some of the bus, train and cruise ship posters from the art deco period. The London Transport Museum is a good source of these. The London Underground map, one of the most famous pieces of transport design, could also be a source of ideas. Children could design their own travel poster or map.

● There are many paintings to choose from, depicting various kinds of transport, which will also stimulate discussion about changes in modes of travel over the years. You could look at Constable's *The Haywain*, Turner's *Steamer in a Snowstorm* and *Rain, Steam and Speed* and paintings from the futurist artists (for example, Severini) who were fascinated by the new inventions of the machine age. There are paintings by artists who depicted distant and imagined places, for example Rousseau, who produced paintings of forests with exotic plants and animals. The colourful paintings of Tahiti by Gauguin would also be a good starting point for the theme of travel to distant places.

● **Mood:** This theme could include feelings and pictures such as Munch's *The Scream*, and Picasso's *Weeping Woman* and *Guernica*. *Unexpected Reply* by the surrealist artist Magritte could provide an interesting starting point, as could work by the expressionists. Paintings from Picasso's Blue and Pink periods contain some very poignant images, for example, from the Blue period, *Beggar playing a Guitar*.

The following sections will refer to these themes and offer suggestions for working with them.

▶ Developing key areas

Expressive work

In Year 5, the children should be doing expressive work based on real or imagined experiences and working from memory and imagination. Stories, music and drama are all still good starting points and individual responses and ideas should be encouraged and shared.

Observational drawings

Observational work should be continued from natural forms such as pebbles, shells, feathers, plants and flowers; and forms from the made environment – machine parts, car parts and so on. Linked to the theme of Travel, children could also bring in models of cars, trains and planes and make observational drawings from them. As their skill increases, you should see these drawings become more detailed and accurate.

Exploring materials

Exploration to find out what art tools and materials will do (sometimes through trial and error, and sometimes through guided discovery), combining materials and overlaying them, is an essential part of all stages in children's development. You will also need to continue to teach specific techniques.

Techniques
Drawing

● In Year 4 children should have had experience of the range of marks made with soft drawing pencils, charcoal, oil pastels, coloured pencils and chalks. In Year 5, you can consolidate and extend the experience by encouraging children to combine materials. Provide a range of materials and let the children choose, or restrict the choice yourself, for example, by providing only biros and pencils. Bring in a variety of house plants with large or interesting leaves and ask the children to make drawings of different leaf shapes in their sketchbooks.

● Provide drawing boards, paper and black felt-tipped pens. Introduce the jungle paintings of Rousseau. At first, focus on the leaf shapes again. *How many different leaf shapes can you see? How does Rousseau combine leaf shapes to make a jungle? Look at the shapes between the leaves.* When the children are familiar with the shapes, combine the living plants to make a 'jungle' in the classroom. The children can then use the classroom 'jungle' to give them ideas for their own jungle. A similar session could take place using model animals.

Painting

By Year 5, children should have had experiences of colour mixing and of different consistencies of paint. Building on these experiences, continue from the work outlined above, by exploring colours and a range of paint consistency for an imaginary jungle picture. Promote discussion about the range of greens which can be seen in the Rousseau jungle paintings. The children can experiment with mixing colours to match some of these. They can do this in a sketchbook adding notes on how they made each green. This provides future reference. They can go on to explore bright colours and colours for the animals. You could make a display of the plant jungle, the animals and the Rousseau reproductions and any other plant paintings as a continuing stimulus and these, together with the children's experiments, can provide the material for a further painting – either an observed or an imaginative response.

Printing

● The leaf drawings will provide useful shapes for printing. The children can go back to their sketchbooks and combine two or more leaf shapes to make a repeat print. They can also rotate these shapes, consolidating work on rotation in

mathematics. The initial print can be over-printed, starting with light colours and adding darker ones.

● The children can make string blocks by coating a piece of cardboard with PVA glue and adding the string in the required design. They can then coat

the block with PVA and allow it to dry before using it for printing.

● They can mix plaster of Paris with PVA glue and pour it into a rectangular mould, for example, a large matchbox. Before it is dry, they can make marks into it and, when dry, use it as a printing block.

(Drying and storage space for prints can be provided by buying commercial drying racks. Alternatively, 'washing lines' of string can be used with pegs.)

Collage

● Cover the tables with newspaper. Provide paper, scissors, glue and spreaders. Show the children a reproduction of, for example, *The Snail* by Matisse. Discuss the way in which Matisse made his own coloured collage pieces for this picture. The 'jungle' idea could be developed by their adding collage to their existing work for things in the foreground, exploring the notion of visual depth.

● Linked to the theme of Mood, the children could make a series of small collages each representing a different mood. Provide a range of colourful collage material including fabric and paper. This activity

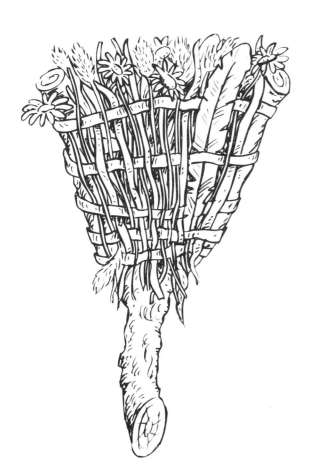

could take place in pairs to encourage discussion about choice of materials. The colours could be based on an analysis of a painting, for example, from Picasso's Blue or Pink periods. The texture and shape to best express the chosen mood should also be considered.

● One of the collages could be selected to develop into a mood weaving. It is not necessary to use expensive commercial looms – card looms or looms made from small branches are equally effective.

Modelling

● Working from the figure is a suitable starting point for Year 5s. Linked to the theme of Travel, children could make models of a small family group relaxing on the beach. You could look at Stanley Spencer's painting *Figures on a Beach* and Victorian and modern photos of people on holiday at the seaside. Children can pose for each other and model figures from clay. (If you don't have a kiln, fibre-reinforced clay which does not require firing can be used. This clay dries in the air and can then be painted with readymix paint and varnished.) Arrange the finished figures on a 'beach' which can be created on a piece of stiff card. Paint the sea on one end and use real sand at the other.

● Another travel challenge could be to model a figure on a motorbike travelling fast or someone riding on an animal. This should all be pulled out from one piece of clay.

● Introduce the work of Elizabeth Frink, a twentieth-century sculptor who represented humans and animals using powerful forms. Contrast her work with the gaunt forms of Alberto Giacometti and the semi-abstract figures of Henry Moore.

Vocabulary

● Continue to build on previously learned vocabulary. A good vocabulary of art-related words is increasingly important for sharing ideas. Encourage the use of words to describe, discuss, analyse, compare and contrast. Generate opportunities to relate this, and previously learned vocabulary, to the work of artists, craftspeople and designers. Encourage the children to express their feelings and support their views with reasons.

● Introduce the vocabulary relating to techniques (for example, printing – *roller, inking-up, over-print, rotate*) and an extended range of art and design forms (for example, work in three dimensions – *construction, sculpture, modelling, firing, glazing,*

three-dimensional). This vocabulary work can be incorporated in the Literacy Hour.

Sketchbooks

By Year 5, children should have developed a number of strategies for using sketchbooks and be aware of a number of purposes, including experimenting with different tools and materials, recording observations, and developing ideas or designs. They should be using them as a research tool to gather material from which to develop ideas. For more information about how to make a variety of sketchbooks and use them effectively as a tool for learning, look at *Sketchbooks Explore and Store* by G Robinson (Hodder & Stoughton).

The elements of art

Give your class opportunities for experimentation with all the elements of art: line, colour, shape, pattern, texture, form. It is seldom that a work of art has only one element in its make up and children will usually be involved in working with several of the elements in one challenge or project. A response to the Mood theme, for example, could incorporate many of the elements.

Reviewing

Spend time sitting alongside children so that they can talk about and evaluate their own work, finding something positive to say about it. From opportunities to discuss their work, children will learn to reflect on it, to modify it and suggest new ideas. It also provides an opportunity for you to reinforce vocabulary related, for example, to new experiences, elements, tools or techniques. Reviewing should not just occur at the end of a process, it is formative in the interim stages.

Resources

● In addition to monographs of individual artists, the following books are helpful as a general reference to get some idea of the range of artists' work available:
The Art Book, *The Modern Art Book* and *The Pop Art Book* (all published by Phaidon). *The Art Book* is now available cheaply in a small format volume. Other useful books include those published by Thames and Hudson, particularly *The Arts of Man*, *From Giotto to Cezanne* and *A History of 20th Century Art*. If your school library is short of art books (and try to rectify this) try the public library (usually the oversize section).

● The Education Departments of the main galleries in London are very helpful if you are planning a visit or want information about artists relating to a specific theme. This can help you introduce children to a range of different artists and to three-dimensional forms. These can be in the form of postcard reproductions, collected in a photograph album. If you know a lively artist, willing to come into the classroom, this would be a great stimulus.

Ideas bank

Recording what has been experienced, observed and imagined

Tell the children that they are not going to make exact copies of what they see. They are to look intently and notice things which they had not noticed before. Children feel threatened at this stage by an insistence on exact representation and need opportunities to make non-representational responses, for example, imaginative or abstract imagery. However, looking is still a vital skill and should be encouraged.

● Bring in some car parts or items of new technology for observational or imaginative drawing. Look at the work of futurist artists of the early part of the twentieth century: Boccinini, Severini, Wyndham Lewis. These artists were fascinated by the new machines and technology which were developing around them.

● Ask them to draw head and shoulders portraits of two elderly twins standing close together. One is a happy person and one is bad tempered. The children work in pairs with mirrors to explore expressions before drawing.

● *You are in a strange land and coming towards you is a creature or vehicle such as you have never seen before. The colours are strange and the whole experience is frightening. Paint a picture.*

● Ask the children to close their eyes and take them on an imaginary journey. You could use pre-recorded sounds. Talk about sights and sounds, scents and feelings. Then children express what they have heard in any way they choose.

Look for:
▶ an ability to concentrate and observe carefully;
▶ an awareness of ways in which the elements of art can be exploited to create expression and mood;
▶ an ability to use colour appropriately;

▶ a developing ability to extend and develop exploratory work from the sketchbook;
▶ an ability to select and make decisions.

Images and artefacts

● Make a collection of textiles from another country. Maybe a friend or member of staff could lend an Eastern rug. Talk about a magic/flying carpet. Children could design their own and create a story around it. You could read the story of Aladdin. The stories of the *Arabian Nights* might be worth investigating too.

● Fill a suitcase with articles and clothes of an imaginary traveller. Unpack the suitcase in front of the class. Ask them to imagine who might have packed the items and to describe the character and the travels. *Which countries might he/she have visited? How did he/she travel? What was he/she doing there?* Children can make observational drawings of the suitcase and its contents and paint imaginary pictures based on the character's adventures. Read current adventure stories to provide more ideas.

● Look at Picasso's *Weeping Woman*, Munch's *The Scream* and portraits by Goya. Discuss the ways in which the artist achieved a particular mood. Children

can make their own version of these paintings.

Look for:
▶ interest and motivation;
▶ a personal response;
▶ visual and tactile awareness;
▶ an ability to use descriptive vocabulary;
▶ inventiveness;
▶ an ability to use initial stimulus to generate ideas.

Tools, materials, techniques

In Year 5, projects will tend to be fewer but will take longer and involve extension, development and work in a variety of media.

● Bring in some pieces of rock. Talk about mountaineers and rock climbers. Show pictures and photographs of rocks/mountains/climbers. Ask the children to imagine that they are about an inch high and climbing. *What would you see? How would the surface of the rock feel?* Make this a starting point for work on texture, colour and form. Offer pencils, crayons and chalk pastels which will give very different effects. Encourage experimentation in their sketchbooks and allow them to choose which of the three materials they would prefer to use. Discussion afterwards could include questions such as *What are the differences among the different pictures? Why do you think this is? Which effect do you like best and why?*

● Develop the drawing into a simple weaving on a loom made from a basic rectangular frame with smooth string for the warp (wool tends to break rather easily). You will need an interesting 'bit box' which contains strips of torn fabric of all kinds – ribbon, braid, tinsel, dried grasses, small bendy twigs, in fact anything which can be threaded into the warp. The weaving could be based closely on the colour and textures in the drawing or the children could change the colour mood entirely. The result should be a small hanging rather than a woven 'scarf'.

● Design and make a puppet which expresses a particular mood or feeling. An example is shown on page 128. The toe of old tights makes a good head if stuffed with toy filler. (Old, clean, quilted material can be taken apart and the filling used again.) To economize on the filling material, start with a ball of newspaper and wrap the filler around it. Push this into the toe of the tights and secure with an elastic band. The 'head' can then be pinched and sewn in place. Features and hair can be added from the 'bit box' to create a character.

many examples but the following can all be found in *A Concise History of Modern Painting,* H Read (Thames & Hudson): two paintings by Picasso, *Woman in a Blue Dress* and *Seated Woman*; Kokoschka's *Woman in Blue*; Tamayo's *The Singer*; Soutine's *The Madwoman*; Modigliani's *The Italian Woman*; Matisse's *Lady in Blue* and *Portrait of Madame Matisse.* Non-figurative examples of colour and mood are conveniently in the same book, for example: Rothko's *Number 10*; Santomaso's *Reds and Yellows of Harvest Time*; Manessier's *Night* and many others. You could also use paintings from Picasso's Blue and Pink periods. If you photocopy and laminate the reproductions, you can use this 'gallery' in a number of ways as a starting point for activities.

● Involve the children in discussion about the moods of different pictures. Talk about colour and mood – angry/sad colours and about lines and shapes which convey a particular mood. *Which lines make you feel calm/angry/sad ?*

● Get the children to make :
▶ some annotated experiments in sketchbook.
▶ a series of drawings using mirrors to see their face being angry, sad, happy, and so on. (This could precede the 'twins' activity above.) Draw parts of the face in the sketchbook.

● They can also try:
▶ a large piece of work using coloured chalks;
▶ a portrait of a person, quite large scale (about half lifesize to lifesize), based on the style of one of the pictures in the 'gallery'.

Look for:
▶ an ability to use an appropriate vocabulary to describe and compare;
▶ evidence of a considered personal response;
▶ an ability to choose from a range of possible tools and materials;
▶ a willingness to experiment;
▶ confidence to work on a larger scale;
▶ increasing knowledge of the work of a range of artists and craftspeople;
▶ an ability to apply the knowledge to make links with their own work.

Look for:
▶ willingness to experiment with tools and techniques;
▶ an ability to make choices and give reasons;
▶ an ability to build on previous experience and develop an idea;
▶ a personal response and use of imagination to evoke mood and feeling;
▶ involvement and concentration;
▶ manual dexterity in the manipulation of materials and threads;
▶ use of appropriate descriptive and critical vocabulary;
▶ an ability to reflect on work done and make appropriate changes.

Artists, craftspeople and designers

Linked to the theme of Mood, put up a 'gallery' of paintings by artists who have depicted a character in a particular mood or frame of mind. There are

Responding and describing

● Look again at paintings relating to travel and modes of transport, for example Constable's *The Haywain* and Turner's *Steamer in a Snowstorm* and *Rain, Steam and Speed.* You could also look at paintings of unusual modes of transport. *I Spy Transport,* which is available in the National Gallery shop and also through ordinary bookshops, has a large number of paintings of a variety of types of transport, including paintings from other cultures where there are more unusual modes of travel.

● *Can you see the means of transport in this picture? Can you describe it? How would it feel to travel by camel or elephant?* Some children may have done so and can describe the sensation to the rest of the class. Design the decoration for a ceremonial elephant.

● *Design and invent your own unusual transport.* This could be started off in their sketchbooks and develop into a drawing and/or a painting where the context can be imagined as well. Some children could extend this project into three dimensions using card and/or Mod-Roc. A useful book which describes a range of appropriate 3-D challenges and explains the use of Mod-Roc is *Three-dimensional Experience* by Norman Manners (Hodder & Stoughton).

Look for:
▮ an ability to experiment with tools and materials;
▮ an enthusiasm to try new materials and techniques;
▮ an ability to respond imaginatively;
▮ communication skills and art vocabulary;
▮ personal motivation and response;
▮ independent thinking.

Special occasions
Greeting cards
● Suggest to the children that they might use a piece of work done previously or base the card on their work on transport, jungles and colour. Allow the children a free choice of tools and materials but discuss possible choices with them:
▮ *Would it be more effective to use a few colours only? Which colours would you choose?*
▮ *What size will your card be? What about an envelope? Will you choose a size that fits a ready-made envelope or will you choose an unusual size and make your own envelope?*

▮ *What will you use to decorate your card – collage, painting, drawing, print?*
▮ *Do you think you could make a pop-up card? Or a card with a shape linked to the subject?*
▮ *What sort of message will you write? Will it be poetry? Will you write it in pen? Crayon? On the computer?*

● The children can print their own wrapping paper and design gift tags.

Decorations
Ask the children to make hangings, either painted or woven, based on a colour theme which describes the mood of the special occasion. Children can work in groups on a large piece.

Display
Display is one of the ways in which we evaluate children's work.

● Try to involve the children as much as possible in making decisions about the way their work is displayed. Encourage the children to mount their own work and to think about what backing will display it to its best advantage. They can use the computer to make simple labels. Try to include everybody's work in the display and make sure some displays are of work in three dimensions. Whenever possible, include the source material in the display to give a context and inform others coming into the classroom about the starting point for the work. Year 5 children should sometimes have full responsibility for designing and putting up displays.

● Sometimes a 'pavement show', laying out the work on the hall floor, for example, or pinning it up quickly so that it can be celebrated and talked about immediately is a valuable way of building on the children's experiences and making teaching points while the experience is still fresh in their minds. Involve the children in making positive observations about each other's work at this time. This helps them to identify developing skills and to use art-based vocabulary to describe them.

Assessment

In Year 5, children will be increasingly concerned about their drawings looking representational. You will need to take this into account when evaluating their work. It is important to respond sensitively to the questions they ask, the things they say, what they do and what they give you, whatever stage they are at. However, it is also important to discuss with them ways in which their work might develop using other methods and materials, for example using print and textiles.

With the greater use of sketchbooks at this stage, you should make time to sit down with individuals and talk about their experiments, as this provides a valuable opportunity to use art-related language and to see how they have handled process as well as product. A vital consideration in any evaluation is respect for personal and cultural identity, particularly as art should be instrumental in developing self-confidence. Develop positive attitudes to art through praise, help and encouragement. Encourage peer group evaluation, emphasizing, as always, the importance of positive comments. For example, *I like the way in which this piece of work has developed into a three-dimensional piece.*

It is possible to evaluate some of the following aspects of the children's art endeavours at this stage:

- How have they used what you have given them?
- What have they done and what they are they trying to do?
- What evidence do you see of independent thinking and personal ideas?
- Have they begun to look for their own reference and resource materials?
- Have they been willing to experiment?
- Are they developing an increasing knowledge of how tools and materials behave?
- Have the materials been used in an imaginative way?
- Have they built on previous experience of colour mixing?
- Have they learned a new skill/technique?
- Are they beginning to experiment with combining techniques?
- Are they becoming more aware of art, artists, galleries?
- Have they learned about art from another country/culture/period?
- Are they growing more confident ?
- Can they make a personal response?
- Are they motivated and involved?
- Can they work independently/co-operatively?
- Can they talk about their own and each other's work, using appropriate vocabulary?

Physical Education

By the time children join your class in Year 5 they will have had a wide variety of movement experiences. Some will have done little activity outside their PE lessons, while others may have been involved outside school in a number of activities and will need to be challenged to extend their capabilities. Most children will want to use and enjoy their rapidly growing movement confidence and competence and will need opportunities to participate in physical activity on a regular basis in school. In most schools, however, PE is timetabled only two or three times a week so you will need to decide when the six activity areas of PE are taught and for how long. You have to ensure that you teach a balance of the three core activities of gymnastics, games and dance throughout the year. The length of each PE lesson may vary but you should expect a minimum of 30 minutes' activity for each session. Here it is assumed that one unit of work (for approximately half a term) for athletics, and outdoor and adventurous activities will be included in Year 5, although swimming may also be one of the activities included.

Whatever their previous experience of PE, the majority of children will be keen and eager to please, but they will require a consistent, firm but supportive environment in order to use their energies in purposeful and positive ways. You will still need to explain and establish your own special routine and arrangements at the start of the year. A mention in the school brochure and a notice on the classroom door will help to remind your class what clothes to bring.

Ensure that children are involved in the processes of planning, performing and evaluating their work. Find opportunities to develop other aspects of their learning (language, mathematics, personal and social development) through the practical physical activities that follow.

What should they be able to do?

There will be vast differences in experience, interest, physique, temperament, attitude and effort when the children come into your class. Be very sensitive to the differing chronological stages at which children enter the adolescent growth spurt and the effect which early or late maturation may have on their performance. Whatever their previous experience, some may still need reminders and lots of encouragement to participate fully in physical education.

Throughout the year, all children should demonstrate their developing body management when performing basic actions in the different areas of activity. Many will be agile and energetic and have a wide range of actions which they can perform successfully. Most will enjoy the challenge of learning new skills, but some will be able to control their bodies more easily and with greater awareness than others. They should be developing their ability to clarify or refine their own actions, working individually or with a partner or within a small group. Watch for children who need particular encouragement and those who need additional challenges. Most children will be able to combine actions, some more fluently and easily than others.

They should be able to discuss the reasons for changing into suitable clothing for each activity, get ready quickly and independently and help others prepare for activity. They will be able to make links between PE and work in the classroom on the heart and 'my body' and understand more about how their body reacts to exercise. As the year progresses you will notice that many will be able to sustain energetic activity for longer periods, although this will vary tremendously

with each individual and differences between children will widen.

Although the sequence of progression through the stages of motor development is similar for most children, they do not progress at the same rate or at an even rate and so there will always be a wide range of differences in the ways children in your class achieve various actions/ movements. This is natural as every child is unique. Observe and enjoy the actions of each child, continue to create an atmosphere of success, fun and satisfaction and support.

Key area: Dance

Depending on their previous experiences, most children will show a variety of expressive qualities and increasing sensitivity in their movements. Often physical changes in the body associated with approaching puberty can inhibit physical and emotional responses but, with sensitive encouragement, they will be able to incorporate contrasts in movement exaggerating and refining their actions by varying shape, size, direction, level and speed. Most children should be able to use individual parts of the body more precisely as they gesture, travel or clarify body positions in time with different forms of accompaniment, recognizing and responding to changes in rhythm and phrasing and adjusting their movements accordingly. There will be great variations in the ways that they do this, some demonstrating more improvement in timing and rhythm than others.

Most children will enjoy dancing and will be able to move confidently with increasing co-ordination, while some will still need encouragement to create and clarify motifs or phrases of movement and to link them into a sequence, individually, with a partner or in a small group. You will notice their increasing awareness of group and partner relationships and their developing observation skills as they comment on how a pattern or phrase of movement was performed.

Develop links with other areas of the curriculum and encourage them to use their imagination. A clear stimulus or focus (for example, portraying characters and narratives from stories they have been reading) will help them to focus on important movement qualities, discuss and clarify their ideas and extend their imagination. They should be able to capture moods or qualities with increasing precision and clarity as they interpret words, music or ideas in their actions and gestures.

Watch for their ideas; develop and use some of them to feed in new suggestions to others in the class. Most children will show an increasing ability to observe and repeat phrases of movement but they will do this with varying degrees of accuracy and fluency. Their body awareness when performing a variety of travelling, turning and jumping actions is developing and they should be able to include other actions like ambling, gyrating or sagging as their movement vocabulary increases. Encourage them to make up their own step patterns and to learn steps (for example, a simple line dance or side step with change of direction leading to the polka). With practice, most of them will be able to do this rhythmically and continuously with different types of music. They should be developing their ability to use the space thoughtfully and well, use a variety of pathways, and show increasing awareness of their own personal space (behind them as well as in front). They should be increasingly able to collaborate with others, describing their actions and appreciating their movements, explaining what they liked or found interesting. They will be able to discuss ideas and make simple judgements which will enable them to work on improving the quality and precision of their dancing.

Key area: Gymnastics

Year 5s should be able to demonstrate their developing ability to perform and refine the quality of a range of jumping, leaping and stepping actions (also cat spring). Encourage them to work on the quality of these actions by improving the clarity of the shapes they make in the air. Insist on safe, controlled, resilient landings. Provide time to practise these in the warm-up part of the lesson, both individually and in pairs (matching, follow-my-leader). Most children will be agile and adventurous and keen to participate in gymnastics, although some may still need encouragement and others may need reminders to be more cautious and aware of others. They will need time to practise and refine their gymnastic actions in different situations on the floor and to show inventiveness as they try them on different parts of the large apparatus.

Children will be increasingly able to move about the floor and apparatus in a variety of ways using their feet, hands and feet and other body parts. Help and expect them to show increasing control and awareness. Encourage them to be inventive and imaginative in response to tasks and suggestions. They should be able to balance with increasing confidence and control in a variety of positions holding still, clear shapes using different parts of their bodies (shoulders, seat, one foot, or two hands). Children will develop strength in their upper bodies if you give regular opportunities within each theme to take their weight on their hands, for example, travelling on two hands and two feet (bunny jump, cat spring, cartwheel), travelling on two hands and one foot, trying different balances near the ground on two hands and one foot or just two hands, or climbing, hanging and pushing away from or pulling along or up the apparatus.

Most children will be able to share the space and apparatus with others in the group considerately, but some will still need help and reminders so that they do not dominate parts of the apparatus. Many will use the large apparatus confidently but should be encouraged to keep to the movement tasks set and work on the quality of their actions. Expect them to develop a greater awareness of what they are doing as they learn to improve their performance through observation, demonstration, review and practice. They will be able to link several actions (for example, jump, roll and balance) into a sequence with increasing fluency and be beginning to understand how they might do this more smoothly (the end of one movement becoming the beginning of another), with clear starting and finishing positions.

Teach, then check, that all children have the opportunity to use all pieces of apparatus over a series of lessons and share the responsibility of setting it out and putting it away. Insist that children lift and carry equipment efficiently and safely.

Key area: Games

Most children will be energetic and keen to participate in games, although some may need more motivating than others. They should be aware of the space and others as they play, but they will still need reminders to use the space well. Chasing and dodging games will provide opportunities for them to practise and improve their ability to stop, start and change direction quickly. Take care how you group children so some do not become disheartened and others bored or unchallenged. Use different groupings (mixed or same ability) at different times.

They will be able to roll, tap, bounce, throw, or kick a ball accurately towards a variety of targets (between skittles, into a hoop, to a partner, or between markings on the floor or wall), both stationary and on the move. Challenge them to try in more difficult circumstances (a smaller target, from further away, moving more quickly). When passing a ball to a partner (using hands and feet) encourage signalling and passing ahead into the space. All children should be able to catch, stop or trap a ball in different ways (high, low; moving to the sides) fed by a partner, and many will be able to do this in small-sided games. Many will be able to anticipate and run into the space to receive the ball and pass to a team-mate avoiding the opposition. The majority will also be able to bounce a ball (large, medium or small) and dribble it with one hand while moving in different directions, at different levels and at varying speeds to avoid the opposition.

Many will be able to use a bat with increasing consistency and success. Give them lots of opportunities to co-operate in small groups (pairs, threes or fours) to make up their own games. They will show an increasing ability to negotiate, plan and discuss ideas with others and to invent simple rules for their games (take turns to start the game, decide how to score). Many will be able to work at the consistency and accuracy of their skills and most should be able to identify what can be done to improve their performance.

Practical ideas

Making a start

Dance

Starting the lesson

Try different ways to start your dance lessons:

▶ moving, shaking, bending, stretching different parts of the body (raising awareness of the different ways this can be done);

▶ practising and refining different steps and travelling actions (skipping, side-stepping, creeping, striding) with various forms of accompaniment (percussion, music or voice);

▶ using popular music to develop step patterns individually, or follow-my-leader or matching sequences in pairs or small groups to encourage response to rhythm and raise the heart rate (you could use a group sequence or a partner dance devised in previous lessons as a warm-up activity);

During the lesson

Work with the children to build motifs or phrases of movement and to enlarge or refine their actions individually, in pairs or in small groups. Encourage them to vary the level, (high, medium, low), shape and direction (sideways, diagonally, up and down) of their actions and to vary their pathways (straight, curving, roundabout, zigzag). They should be able to choose their own starting and finishing positions to help them compose and perform simple dances with clear beginnings, middles and ends.

Ending the lesson

Encourage relaxation and a cool down by using calm music (the 'Skye Boat Song', for example) for slow stepping or stretching or swaying at the end of every lesson.

Gymnastics

Encourage and help children to think carefully about their actions by selecting a focus or theme for their attention (symmetry, for instance). Try out ideas in the floorwork part of the lesson and then try them on the apparatus.

Organization of apparatus

Whatever the theme, emphasize the correct and careful handling of the apparatus, and check the children's awareness of the safety factors:

▶ divide the class into five or six groups (to ensure all children have a range of experiences and to help spacing);

▶ give each group responsibility for handling the same apparatus each lesson (change over each half term);

▶ make a plan of the apparatus to be used which will support the theme;

▶ establish a fair and logical pattern of rotation of groups (for example, zigzag, clockwise, or a straight swap if there are groups with similar apparatus) so that over a period of several lessons, the children can explore fully each group of apparatus in turn (have a maximum of two apparatus changes in one lesson);

▶ remind each group how to get out their apparatus (positioning to carry apparatus, bending knees not backs, all looking in the direction of carrying the apparatus) and where to put it (use apparatus cards to indicate the positioning of it);

- check apparatus fixings and placement before it is used;
- establish 'ground rules' (for example, working quietly and considerately, using the space well);
- insist on a quiet working atmosphere, but discuss with the children why this is necessary;
- encourage and help the children to share space and equipment (using the floor space around the apparatus), particularly when there is limited apparatus;
- establish a consistent routine for stopping, coming down and sitting away from the apparatus.

Children will enjoy the responsibility of lifting and carrying the apparatus and co-operating with their group to make sure it is carefully and safely placed and checked by you and them.

Developing key areas

Dance

Themes

Volcanoes

Groups may be able to compose their own music for this theme, using drums, cymbals and other percussion instruments, or you can use part of 'Mars' from Holst's *The Planets* suite. Select key action words either from poems ('The Volcano' by E M Stokes or 'Volcano' by R Kent) or from observation of video extracts (for example, smouldering, rumbling, trembling, shaking, exploding, bubbling, oozing, spreading). Encourage the children to explore each word in movement, developing motifs and building action phrases individually, then in groups.

Sporting actions

For music, use the *Match of the Day* theme (or *Ski Sunday* for winter sports) from the BBC tape *Sporting Themes*. Choose one sport (tennis, in this example – children can choose their own later):

- begin with jogging to the music, encouraging exaggerated actions, in slow motion or speeded up; do some stretching, and then ask the children to clarify details of position(s) individually, then with a partner, guessing and refining each other's actions;
- choose three different action statues (freeze frames) for the sport (bounce ball, service, forehand drive) and encourage the children to develop them into a phrase (jogging, bouncing ball – freeze – preparing to serve – freeze – follow through and move

from side to side ready for forehand drive – freeze and repeat sequence);
- extend the mimed actions into dance by developing a motif which can be repeated in different ways to create a phrase of action in time to the music. Refine, clarify then extend this by adding a travelling action such as: side-step, side-step and backhand; ask the children to exaggerate each phrase making their movements larger than life. This can be developed by repeating the sequence with a different side of the body or at a different level. Action/reaction sequences in pairs (hitting a tennis ball backwards and forwards) can then be introduced, which can be elaborated by adding a jump or turn;
- suggest a Mexican wave and/or a cheerleader-type sequence for everyone to finish.

Dances from other countries

Music from Tchaikovsky's *Nutcracker Suite* can be used to explore dance from different countries. For example:
- Chinese dance: shuffling footsteps, leading, following, making curving patterns on the floor, bowing, opening gestures;
- Arabian dance: focus on rising and sinking, slow, continuous, light, flowing movement with particular emphasis on the tummy!;
- Russian dance: strong, energetic actions with lots of stamps, jumps, leaps and turns (Cossack step, scissor kicks);

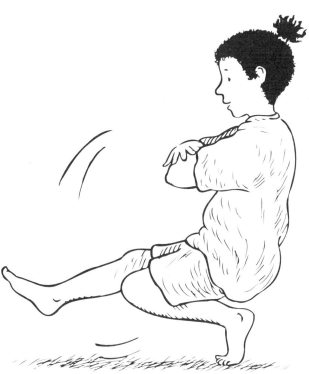

others include Spanish dancing using maracas, Greek line dancing, Indian dancing or any other form which might be familiar to some members of the class or staff.

Gymnastics

Flight with shape

Ensure that landings from jumps on the floor are resilient before developing flight.

Encourage a spring-like action of the legs and the use of arms on take-off to assist elevation, then develop and clarify shapes in the air (stretched, symmetrical, tucked, twisted); consolidate two feet to two feet jumps and then develop other combinations of take-off and landing (one foot to two feet, one foot to other foot, two feet to one foot or with a turn in the air).

Practise jumping from hands to feet (donkey kick), feet to hands (cat spring) and also try knees to feet.

Using apparatus, start with low benches, boxes and trestle tables and gradually vary the height – emphasizing 'look before you leap'! Try different ways of jumping off and on apparatus considering change of direction, shape, and using hands and feet, and encourage cartwheels over benches (the hands go on the bench one after the other, the legs are wide, and there is a 1, 2, 3, 4 rhythm).

Matching and mirroring

Children can choose individual movements or an action phrase (balance, travel, balance) which they have practised to show a partner. Together they can select actions and work on a short sequence matching each other's movements. They can try this both on the floor and on apparatus. Ask them to focus on timing and shape. You can also encourage them to try different positions together (side by side, following). Later explore the different concept of mirroring, in which pairs work on actions as if their partner is a mirror image.

Travelling – changes in speed

Take care when introducing changes of speed. Encourage the children to experiment carefully with basic actions such as jumping, hopping, rolling and bunny jumping, trying each one a little more slowly or a little more quickly. Ask them then to put together a sequence of action (slow, slow, quick, quick, slow) which highlights the contrast in speed.

Symmetry and asymmetry

Encourage the children to explore thoroughly symmetrical travelling actions and balances on different parts of their bodies. Make sure they understand that both sides of the body should be matching, doing the same thing at the same time. When they have explored symmetry on the floor and apparatus introduce them to asymmetrical

actions and balances in the same way. Finish the unit of work with the composition of a sequence which includes two symmetrical actions and two asymmetrical ones. You can also explore rotational symmetry in movement, and relate it to mathematical work.

Holes and barriers

Ask the class to explore in pairs possible balance actions on different parts of their bodies which form a shape which their partner can then go through, under or over (jumping over a still shape, leap frog).

Games

It is not possible to offer every game within the curriculum, therefore schools need to select examples of different game forms (invasion, over the net, striking and fielding) to introduce to Years 5 and 6. Adapt and modify the games to enable all children to participate fully; use small-sided and simplified versions of recognized games in preference to full-sided adult versions. For fuller details see Val Sabin's *Primary School Games* or *Teaching Children to Play Games 5-11*, B Read and R Edwards (BCPE/NCF/Sports Council).

Small-sided invasion games

Select and play an invasion game such as new image rugby, netball, or five-a-side soccer.

▶ After lots of individual and pairs practice of throwing/catching/kicking, play 2v2 and 3v3 games using grids or sections of the netball court.

▶ Establish rules: at least two passes must be made before touching down/kicking/shooting at goal (use skittles); ways of restarting the game; pass behind/ahead for partners to run on to the ball.

▶ Encourage players to keep defenders guessing by varying the type of pass (long/short), to use all the players and to get in a space to receive the ball.

Over-the-net games

Examples of these are short tennis and padder tennis.

▶ After individual practice with bats and balls (or using the hand as a bat), introduce co-operative passing in pairs (high or low, side to side, hitting on forehand and backhand) letting the ball bounce once or twice before returning it over the line (a chalk mark or a low 'net' made of skittles and cane).

▶ Set a challenge with a beat-your-own-record activity: *How many continuous/side-to-side passes can you make with your partner?*

▶ Encourage children to make up their own across-

Physical education

the-net games: *How much space do you need? Who starts the game? How do you score? Who restarts the game if the ball goes out of play?*

Fielding/striking games

Play, for example, cricket. Using tennis balls to begin with, get the children to practise basic skills individually and in pairs:

▶ bowling and wicket-keeping (use underarm first, and practise without a batter; encourage movement behind the direction of the ball);

▶ bowling and batting (stand sideways to the wicket);

▶ throwing and fielding (getting behind the direction of the ball; being ready to move in any direction).

After practising these skills, play:

▶ French cricket, with three fielders and one batter: the fielders try to hit the batter's legs below the knee; the batter uses the bat to shield his/her legs;

▶ non-stop cricket and stool ball in small groups (3v3), with a bowler, batter, wicket-keeper and three fielders: each player has a turn in each position; if batter hits the ball he/she runs round a stump/post and back to the batting mark; fielders retrieve the ball and return it to the bowler who can bowl again whether or not the batter has returned; the batter can only be bowled or caught out.

Athletics

Hurdling

Stress running, rather than jumping over the hurdles. Use ropes on the floor to start with, then introduce low hurdles – skittles and canes, plastic poles – or triangular soft hurdles from the athletics kit. Set them up with equal spacing between the hurdles, but change the distance to suit groups of children with different leg lengths.

▶ Establish children's lead leg (favoured leg to cross the hurdle first), and emphasize maintaining a rhythm of 1-2-3 over, 1-2-3 over.

▶ Practise individually, in pairs or in a relay situation (three or four in a group). In pairs, one child can sprint alongside the other who is hurdling, to encourage running at speed over hurdles.

Throwing for distance

Emphasize safety when throwing – everyone throws, then everyone collects.

▶ Use a variety of balls (airflow, foam, tennis, cricket, rounders or sometimes a large ball). To give children an idea of how far they throw, it is helpful to have lines five metres apart marked on the playground or grass. Practise overarm throwing, then work on specialist throws.

Pulling action

This is a javelin-type throw.

Get the children to practise, from sitting, kneeling and then standing, overhead throws with two hands: they should take the ball back, high over the head, with flexed elbows. When standing, they should step one foot forward, throw and follow through.

Then encourage them to use one hand to take the ball back high behind the shoulder and to pull it

forward over the shoulder, keeping it high as they do so; then to try this with two running steps. If available, give them soft javelins to practise with.

Pushing action

This is a shot-put-type throw.

From sitting, kneeling then standing, ask the children to practise a two-handed chest pass, following the ball through with their arms and fingers.

Then, get them to hold a small ball under the chin with one hand, keeping the elbow high and the opposite leg forward. They put their weight on their back foot, flex their legs and rotate their shoulders to face away from the direction of the throw. They then push the ball from back to front, transferring their weight to the front leg and following through in the direction of throw (up and out).

Measuring and timing

How far can you run/hurdle in 10 seconds, 20 seconds, 1 minute? What is the farthest you can throw? Set time or distance challenges for groups of children to practise, giving them the opportunity to make lots of attempts to beat the record. They can record scores individually or total them as a group score. Have them run relays, with each team trying to beat their own record rather than beat each other.

Outdoor and adventurous activities

Orienteering

Compass run

(This is part of the 10-step Award.) With a compass in the centre, mark north, south, east and west with a cone or bean bag, each ten metres from the centre. Replace the compass with a cone. Starting at north, each runner is timed running to the centre and to each of the points of the compass in turn, returning to the centre after each and touching each cone, and finishing again at north. Try this several times, varying the order in which the points of the compass are visited.

Points of the compass

Use the hall or playground (the more space the more exercise!). Place nine cones, marked with numbers or symbols, in a rectangle. Identify north and south cones, and allocate the start cone – the west cone, say. Starting at short intervals, pairs of children follow a set route going to one cone at a time (walking,

jogging, hopping and so on) as indicated on the task sheet. Each pair records the symbols or numbers attached to each cone and then checks the master result sheet. Pairs can then make up new courses for other pairs.

Star exercise

Make copies of a map of the playground with the key features marked. Starting from you at the centre, pairs of children orientate their map and visit different landmarks represented by symbols or letters (gate, door, netball post, tree and so on). They go to the landmark and must complete a task or punch the control before returning to you to be given another landmark to visit.

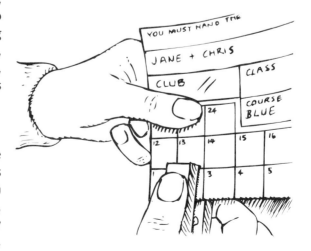

Problem solving

Shuffle the pack: seven or eight children stand on one gymnastic bench. Once they are in position, ask them to arrange themselves in alphabetical order of names, or height order, without falling off or touching the ground. This is not a race!

Swimming

Swimming is important for safety, survival, confidence, fitness and recreation and it is a National Curriculum requirement that children are taught to swim. However, it is very unlikely (unless your school has its own pool) that classes will be taken swimming for more than a short time during their primary schooling. Teaching swimming, therefore, will be unique to each school and dependent upon facilities available, authority guidelines, staffing and expertise available, previous experience of the children, timetabling, transport, funds and other factors.

If you are accompanying your class to a pool, these guidelines may help you.

▶ Prepare the children well before the lessons take place: tell them what to expect (depth of water, changing rooms and toilets, fire exit), what to bring (bag for wet clothing, swimming cap), how to take care of dry clothes (use of lockers). Discuss safety (pool code of practice: walk don't run, no shouting, jumping or pushing and so on) and consider hygiene requirements (visiting toilets, blowing noses, foot check, foot bath).

▶ Some children will be confident and competent swimmers while others may be quite fearful of the water and find the pool a daunting experience. You and/or the instructor will need to consider carefully how the children should be grouped.

▶ Alert the instructor to any medical conditions (ear infections, asthma) and discuss any special arrangements.

▶ Insist that the children listen and watch attentively and establish a routine for waiting (sitting) until they are told to get into the pool.

▶ Check the procedure for stopping the class (for example with a whistle, voice, a hand signal).

▶ Be in a position where you can see *all* the children and observe their efforts and responses.

▶ Encourage and support children with your interest in their progress.

(Safety in different environments and hygiene are important parts of the cross-curricular theme of health and relate particularly to children's welfare.)

Ideas bank

● Identify local opportunities for children to be able to participate in games or other physical activities outside school. Where possible, try to establish links with the local sports/leisure centre or local clubs (swimming, gymnastics, dance) and encourage children to join. Give particular encouragement to those children whose parents are least likely to arrange these activities for them or to be aware of holiday activity clubs and so on.

● At school, children of this age will enjoy the challenge of gymnastics, athletics, dance or games activities if these can be run as after-school or lunchtime clubs.

Assessment

Because of the fleeting nature of physical actions, detailed observation of a class of children constantly on the move is difficult. However, it is a good idea for you to get a general impression or overall feel for the class response before looking more specifically at the movement of individual children. Consider questions such as:

● How do the children respond and listen to your instructions/suggestions?
● How well do they use their initiative/follow others/do a bit of both?
● How well do they use the space? How well do they use different directions? Are they aware of others when they do so? What could you say that might help them?
● How well do they sustain energetic activity?
● Are there other observations you need to make?

Then try to watch how individual children respond and move. Continual review with a focus on a few children at a time is recommended. There will be times when you note achievement which is particularly significant for a child or the class, or look for specific actions or responses.

● Do they use the whole of the body when required? Which parts could they make more use of? How controlled are their movements? In which ways could they refine their movements? (For example, the fluency of the action – is it easy or awkward?) .
● Can they notice, talk about and discuss their ideas and actions in PE?

Dance

● How well do they respond to your voice, the rhythm, sounds or music? How imaginative/ creative are they?
● Are they achieving the qualities required? When? If not, why not? What might help?
● How well can they isolate and use individual body parts? Do they use some parts more fully than others?
● Do they use different levels, directions or speeds effectively?
● How well do they remember a phrase or sequence of movements?
● Can they use appropriate and inventive starting and finishing positions?
● Can they follow their partners' pathways or match their actions?

Gymnastics

● How well do they use the apparatus? Are there pieces of apparatus which you need to encourage them to use? How inventive are their actions?
● Can they hold balanced shapes on different parts of their bodies? How confidently can they take their weight on their hands (bunny jumps, cat jumps, cartwheels)?
● Can they choose, repeat and refine their favourite movements and select appropriate actions? Can they remember several actions and perform them one after the other with a starting and finishing position?

Games

● How well do they move about the space in different directions and in different ways?
● Can they stop, start and dodge in and out of each other?
● Can they use the equipment imaginatively and confidently in a variety of ways?
● How accurately can they roll or throw towards a stationary or moving target?
● Can they make up and play a variety of simple games?

At all times take care to stress the positive aspects of children's movement and to enjoy and encourage their attempts. There will be as many different responses as there are children.

Information Technology

A feature of progression within IT in the primary school is children's increasing independence in their use of software. By Year 5, the majority of children should be able to operate a computer quite effectively without assistance. The focus of this year's work should be on extending the range of software features which children can use confidently and providing opportunities for children to decide for themselves that a particular task would be best undertaken using a specific computer package.

What should they be able to do?

Key area: Communicating and handling information

The majority of your children should now be very familiar with word-processing packages and be using them as a matter of course in many areas of the curriculum. They should be combining different types of information, including clip-art, pictures, other graphic elements and tables, into their work. They should have a good awareness of their audience, thinking about text size, language used and the overall look of the finished document, including decisions about page orientation and the number of folds in the paper. All children should now be using more sophisticated editing techniques, such as search and replace, and they should also be introduced to some of the more advanced features associated with desktop publishing such as moving and shaping blocks of text and pictures to achieve particular effects.

Children should already be familiar with the idea of a database for storing and retrieving information, and they should be encouraged to use this as a method of collecting and analysing information in many areas of the curriculum. Many children will probably still need the basic format of the database provided with field names and some examples included although, by now, the most able children should be encouraged to edit existing databases to make them more appropriate for a specific need. They should be confident in their use of databases, sorting lists of data both numerically and alphabetically, and presenting this information in an increasing range of useful graphical formats. They should also be familiar with CD-ROM databases, such as *Encarta*, and, increasingly, the Internet (by 2002 all schools should have at least one Internet link). Teach strategies to enable them to search effectively for information.

Key area: Controlling, monitoring and modelling

Children should be aware of the power of spreadsheets and some of their everyday applications. In particular, the use of the *What if I changed this?* type question can be very useful in emphasizing how a spreadsheet can model a real situation. Most of them should be able to enter simple formulas into spreadsheets and to use a spreadsheet for practical purposes.

Year 5s should already have worked with programs such as LOGO and be familiar with programming structures such as REPEAT. Now they can take their first steps in using a computer to control lights using a similar programming approach. Most of them should now be able to test and modify procedures which they write themselves.

They should look at the first stages of monitoring the environment using a data logger to collect data, graphically displaying the information, and making attempts to interpret the results.

Practical ideas

Making a start

Interesting titles

All children should be familiar with a word processor and its basic elements. They should feel confident to use a word processor for any of their written work, particularly if it is going to be used for display purposes. Many packages have the facility to produce headings using different shapes, and children should be able to explore these possibilities. They should use these features to produce titles at the top of their more traditionally word-processed work.

IT in the real world

A visit to a large supermarket for a 'behind the scenes' look at the computer systems in use will provide children with a good opportunity to see how computers can be really useful in speeding up the checkout and keeping good control over the stock. Some supermarkets have hand-held bar scanners for customer use. This can lead on to discussions about the future of shopping. *Will you be able to browse through 'virtual' shops, clicking a pointer on the television screen to make your selection, and then having the goods delivered? What changes to people's lives would this make? Would there be disadvantages as well as advantages?*

Introducing new key areas

Producing a newspaper

Children should be able to manipulate text and pictures by now, so a newspaper project will give them many opportunities to give more detailed consideration to layout (number of columns, size of headlines, placing of graphics and so on) as well as thinking about the audience for their publication. The paper could be sold in the school. Small groups of children can be responsible for each page, although there should be some co-ordination between the groups to ensure a range of stories. As well as the technical skills that will need to be developed, this is a good activity for highlighting the importance of drafting, redrafting and proof-reading material.

This project can be allied to history work and a Victorian, 1920s or 30s, or Second World War newspaper can be produced. The children can look at contemporary newspapers to identify appropriate layout and font styles and the content can be directly related to the particular work on the period that they are doing. They will need to find illustrations (from resource packs, reference books or elderly relatives), which can be scanned into their publication. There are some clip-art collections which have appropriate images.

Brightness of light

As part of science work on light, children can use a light sensor connected to a computer to investigate the amount of light given off by a range of different candles. They would need to ensure that the experiment was conducted in a fair way: for example, that the distance from the candle to the sensor was always the same and that the ambient light level in the room remained the same. The results would be recorded graphically using the sensing software and the children could then integrate this into their word-processed account of the experiment. They could look at whether the amount of light given off depended on features such as the height, the thickness or the colour of the candle, or the original length of the wick and so on.

 Reinforcing key areas

Decorative borders

To extend the children's work in LOGO, ask them to produce a regular border around sheets of paper on which they are producing project work. Regular repeating patterns can easily be developed using repeating procedures, but there is also opportunity for extension material when it comes to rotating the pattern at the corners of the page.

Decorative logo

This activity can be linked with many activities, particularly those related to designing and making a product in design and technology or creating an identity for a team of children engaged in a group activity. It requires children to make use of a simple drawing package and incorporate some text as well. At this level it is probably appropriate that children do not use clip-art unless they are able to edit it extensively by ungrouping and further manipulation.

Tuck shop profit

Children should be able to construct their own spreadsheet, in most cases selecting their own fields. In this case the fields might include *Name of item*, *Buying cost*, *Selling cost*, *Number sold*, *Number in stock*, *Total money taken*, and *Total profit*. Encourage them to predict what might happen, before the data is typed into the spreadsheet, and to look for patterns in this data. Ask them then to look at ways of increasing the profit. *Is it better to keep the profit small and sell more products, or increase the profit margin on the most popular*

items? Children can use the spreadsheet as a model, and can investigate the model by asking questions of the type *What happens to the profit if I ...?* This activity could also be related to the operation of stalls for a school fair.

Traffic lights

Children should extend their use of LOGO from drawing to controlling external events. A simple traffic light set-up using three LEDs connected to the output of a control box can be controlled. (Output A ON; WAIT 3 seconds; Output A OFF; Output B ON; WAIT 3 seconds and so on.) Once they have written a program for a single set of traffic lights, they could combine it with a second set that would control the traffic in the other direction across the crossroads. This activity could be developed still further so that the traffic on the model road produces an input to the control box, which starts the traffic light sequence off. Encourage them to produce flow diagrams to provide a model of the system.

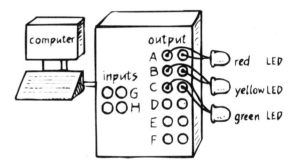

Ideas bank

Wallpaper design

The main feature of a wallpaper design is that it is repeated. This activity is ideal to give children the opportunity to use a drawing package to create a relatively simple design and then to use copy, cut and paste to produce a wallpaper design using repeating patterns. In order to make the pattern regular they can also be introduced to the 'align' command found on many drawing packages.

Children who are familiar and competent with these commands can then be introduced to 'rotate' and 'mirror' in order to create more sophisticated designs. (Link this to work in Mathematics, see page 41.)

Designing a Tudor house

It is a very time-consuming process to use a drawing package to draw an accurate plan of a house which children can then build. However, a number of framework programs exist (*My Word*, for example) which have the components of a house

already drawn, so that the components just have to be assembled. A typical example would be a Tudor house design. The outcome would be a completed net of a house, which can be printed on to card and then constructed. The disadvantage of such an approach is that you are very much limited to the designs and sizes which the package provides. There are no opportunities to edit the components. However, it does provide a basic structure and a good foundation on which to base further open-ended work using a proper drawing package.

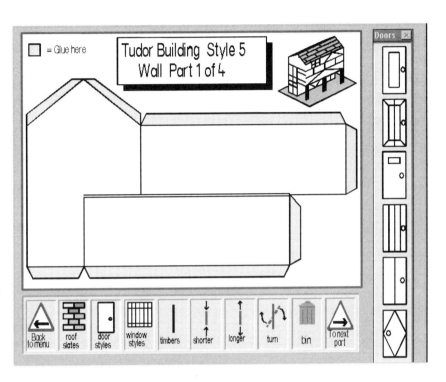

Assessment

By the end of Year 5 you would expect most children to be able to save, load and print independently and use a spell checker and dictionary. Most children should have:

● used IT as part of their work in a number of curriculum areas;

● produced a piece of work in its entirety on a word processor or desktop publishing system, including an illustrative heading, making use of cut, copy, paste and formatting commands such as justification, rulers, margins and tabs;

● produced some artwork making use of the cut, copy, paste and flip commands of an art package;

● imported images into an art package and edited them using basic tools;

● developed a database of their own, having been given the basic structure and answered questions about the data;

● written a LOGO program that will control a simple sequence of lights connected to the computer, making use of SWITCHON, SWITCHOFF and REPEAT commands;

● used a sensor connected to a computer to monitor features of the environment and presented that information in a graphical format.

Design and Technology

Designing and making need to be practised in Year 5 in a variety of contexts and with a range of materials. The aim is to develop design and technology capability as a combination of know-how and know-what. The National Curriculum suggests some areas of knowledge and understanding but design and technology draws on others, such as scientific and mathematical concepts. Examples you might use with Year 5 children are described below. You can use these examples directly, adapt them or use them as models for activities which suit your particular teaching needs.

Some design and technology activities in Year 5 develop knowledge and understanding. For instance, a case study of a solution to a practical problem may be used to extend knowledge of design, making, vocabulary, control and structures. A product might be examined, mentally disassembled, parts named and their function explained. Case studies can also cover the human component, placing a solution in a geographical and historical context. A focused practical task may be used to develop and practise a designing or making skill or to develop knowledge and understanding by direct experience. A designing and making task brings together a variety of knowledge, skills and mental processes. It gives the children a chance to practise these together and gives you an opportunity to gauge the coherence of their design and technology capabilities.

It is important that there is progression in design and technology capability. In Year 5, capability of 'standard' ways of solving certain practical problems is extended. Designing and making skills and knowledge should become progressively more interrelated. Children of different capabilities can often attempt the same task (essentially differentiation by outcome). While you may tune a task to particular children's capabilities by the amount of support you provide and the reserve you show in intervening, there may be some children who need a slightly different provision where particular knowledge and skills are deficient.

Year 5 children should continue to develop facility in using hand tools. Plan for safe working. Consider the safety of the child using the tool, the safety of others and also of yourself. Check tools regularly and withdraw any from use that could be unsafe and repair or replace them. Store them securely when not in use. The place where the children use the tools should be in view. Year 5 children should be expected to take increasing responsibility for safe practices, for organizing the workspace, for recognizing hazards and risks and for taking action to avoid them.

What should they be able to do?

The children should already have practised and consolidated some designing and making skills and have studied some manufactured products.

This is expanded by:

- extending their understanding of aspects of manufacturing, products and their quality;
- making explicit what counts as design and technology capability, giving some prominence to the integration of designing and making skills;
- extending the range of contexts experienced;
- widening and deepening designing and making skills;
- increasing technological knowledge and understanding.

Key area: Contexts

If design and technology activities are related to work in other areas of the curriculum they can help to integrate and make concrete fairly abstract ideas. It may mean, however, that some aspects of the design and technology curriculum may receive insufficient attention. You should make good any deficiencies through separate design and technology projects. Such contexts and activities may extend beyond the familiar to novel situations.

Key area: Designing skills

Children should draw on a variety of information sources (books, videos, pictures, software, interviews) and practise generating and clarifying ideas, taking into account the users and the purposes of a product. Designs should be explored and developed through, for instance, thought, discussion and diagrams which show alternative viewpoints and models. Children can practise reviewing a design to see if improvements can be made. Encourage them to look for a new idea if the favoured one shows itself to be impractical. They should consider the appearance, function, reliability and safety of the product while designing it. They should give thought to the sequence of actions and division of labour, when appropriate. You will have to teach some technological knowledge and know-how directly (conveyor belt action, for instance).

Key area: Making skills

By the end of the year, the majority of the children should be able to:
- construct a plan of action for realizing their designs and be willing to adapt it;
- select and use tools appropriately;
- measure, mark out, and prepare the materials with some precision, avoiding waste;
- join and combine materials in appropriate ways and with some care;
- choose, justify and apply finishes which suit aesthetic and functional needs;
- test and evaluate products and identify some of their strengths and weaknesses;
- improve a product, when appropriate, based on their evaluation.

Key area : Knowledge and understanding
Materials and components
Remind children of the properties of materials they have used before they renew their experience of them. They should explore the properties and forms of materials and take these into account when designing and making. They should have some experience of the way properties change when materials are mixed and combined (for example, blockboard and fibreboard).

Mechanisms and control
In Year 5, the children's knowledge of mechanisms may be extended to include conveyor action, ways of powering moving things, and the bringing together of prior knowledge and know-how such as return mechanisms and levers.

Structures
The children should extend their knowledge to learn how objects may be supported (for example, suspension cables in bridges) and how they may be made durable (various ways of binding sheets in a book, for instance).

Products and applications
Whenever possible, present products which illustrate in simple ways the mechanisms and structures

the children will make. These should be at least mentally disassembled to find out how they work. On occasions, there could be case studies of situations in which some mechanism or structure was applied. The children can consider the problems or needs that these were intended to satisfy and the views of users.

Quality

Emphasize that the function, reliability, appearance and feel (sometimes smell , sound and taste) of products are important. Sometimes you may have to ask a child to remake a component rather than accept one that was very badly made. Children should begin to be aware of the difference between a good design badly made (*It would probably have worked well if that wheel wasn't so loose*) and a bad design which has been well made (*It looks good but doesn't work well*). They should begin to recognize instances of wasteful manufacture in what they make.

Health and safety

Develop a conscious concern in the children to avoid injury to themselves and others (for example, they identify hazards in pictures and the design and technology workplace and show others how to use tools safely). This should include some consideration of the safety of people who might use their products and may be used to introduce an awareness that they, as consumers, should consider such matters.

Vocabulary

Communication, thinking and learning are all enhanced by knowing the right words. Case studies, in particular, provide opportunities for extending children's technological vocabulary (machines and mechanisms found in factories, for instance).

Working at higher or lower levels with the key areas

Working at other levels is sometimes achieved by altering the degree of support you provide. While it is always possible to provide simpler tasks with different contexts, this can make a child's inadequacies, real or otherwise, apparent to all. Instead, you might use a context which allows a variety of possible products or materials (a collaborative project on railways, perhaps). You might then allocate tasks to ensure that each child is working at an appropriate level. If, however, there are children whose special needs make a particular task impossible, you will have to provide other activities to develop their knowledge and skills.

Children with well-developed design and technology capabilities can be stretched by your withholding some support, expecting more know-how in their products and providing practical extension tasks, find-out-about tasks and case studies. These activities are intended to broaden and deepen technological knowledge. They may be structured research tasks in which, for example, the child might find out about the life and work of Isambard Kingdom Brunel or construct a chronological sequence of communication devices. Make sure you have the relevant books or software which are needed for research tasks like these.

Practical ideas

Making a start

Cross-curricular themes and subject-specific topics can lead to design and technology activity. Something to catch the children's interest can arise from a recent event in school, a local event in the community, or a situation from farther afield. These provide the background for a practical problem to solve.

Help the children to clarify their design ideas by responding to *What? Why? When? How? How else? What if?* questions and by explaining and justifying their intentions. While making, they should order the tasks and evaluate as they proceed.

Developing key areas

Providing contexts

Children may have some intrinsic interest in solving a problem but they should also see purpose in what they do. The feeling of relevance comes from some obvious need that a task satisfies. As in other areas of the curriculum, prior knowledge and know-how will also have to be brought out and related to the task in hand. Some strategies follow.

Events

These may be happenings in the school, home, neighbourhood, or farther afield which are potentially of interest to the children and which can be turned into problems to solve in the classroom. Some situations (such as local house building) last over a number of years and so may be used regularly.

Visits and visitors

Planned visits which relate to other areas of the curriculum can often have a design and technology element, even on the journey itself. For instance, a trip to a railway station might be included on the way to an event. You can also use a television programme to provide a 'visit' where it is not otherwise feasible. In lieu of a visit to a railway station, for instance, a video about the history of the railways might be used. However, these alternatives are not of equal value and, when direct experience is remote, other experience must supplement it. Reading *The Railway Children*, E Nesbit (Puffin), for instance, might achieve this end.

Challenges

In a sense all design and technology tasks are challenges, but a task may be presented explicitly in that form. *Can you make something to carry this [delicate object] from one side of the school hall to the other side?*

Supporting designing

Designing is not a linear process. An idea may develop, be abandoned, picked up again, changed and adapted. There is a degree of toying with possibilities and moving towards a solution, but the path is often erratic. Develop some awareness of this in the children so that they accept that dropping or adapting an idea is not failure.

Exploring the task

Ensure that the children know what the task means and what it encompasses. Ask questions to stimulate the recall of relevant prior knowledge and check on vocabulary. Supplement this knowledge so that the task is meaningful. Year 5 children should contribute to the preparation for a task by using a variety of sources of information.

Stimulating ideas and focusing

To help children generate ideas, state the problem and ask for responses. Review these in turn and have the children consider what is feasible in the classroom and what has most chance of success. Be explicit about the vague bits of a design. Group work in which the children explore the questions, *What? Why? When? How? How else? What if?* together and report back to you can be helpful and it also offers practice in collaborative skills.

Developing new knowledge

Additional knowledge may be needed at this point. Related artefacts can be useful for this, particularly if they are everyday objects with visible components. The children should examine them and explain how they work or were made. Some things might safely be dismantled and reassembled. Pictures of artefacts may be used in the absence of the real things.

Supporting making

Avoid making all the decisions yourself and oblige

the children to think for themselves. There will be times when you will know that the product might have been better if you had given specific instructions, but the aim is to encourage independence of thought and action.

Choosing materials

When feasible, materials can be in a variety of forms and sizes. Expect children to do their own marking out and discourage waste by, for instance, giving the children a fixed budget to 'spend' on resources.

Modelling

Consolidate the habit of trying things loosely before fixing them permanently. Some products may be modelled in card and difficulties overcome before using other materials. Mechanisms can often be explored and tested with construction kits such as LEGO Technic.

Quality

The purpose of the exercise is not simply to make a product which works or satisfies a need. Children can become lax about the quality of the product. Be explicit about what counts as quality.

Introducing new ideas

Contexts for designing and making

In the following examples, (a) sets the scene, (b) is a focused practical task, (c) is a designing and making task and (d) are other tasks. They may be used as they are, adapted, or may serve as models for other activities. Note that, in Year 5, activities may often move directly to problem solving and that a number of materials may be used in a product.

The factory

Mixed materials, conveyor belt.

(a) When raising the children's awareness of mass production in factories, tell them about the function of a conveyor belt. (A story to accompany it is *Charlie and the Chocolate Factory* by Roald Dahl.)

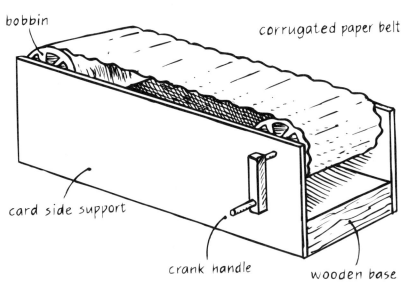

bobbin

corrugated paper belt

card side support

crank handle

wooden base

(b) The children design and make a model conveyor belt. (Bobbins can be used as pulleys and corrugated packaging paper may be used for the belt. A crank handle is used to turn one of the pulleys and make the belt move.)

(c) A tracked vehicle is essentially a conveyor-belt-machine turned upside down. As an extension, children can examine some examples of toy tracked vehicles and then design and make one.

Help the aged

Mixed materials, various mechanisms.

(a) Discuss the problems experienced by old people who cannot bend easily. *What could we make to help them pick things up from the floor?*

(b) The children model potential solutions using a kit or stiff card. They test modifications and improvements.

(c) They finalize, make and test their designs.

(d) The product is tested by one or two adults who give sensitive feedback.

Keeping cool

Recycled materials, person- and other-powered.

(a) In warm weather, discuss the need to keep cool and show a simple fan made from card. The children make one. Discuss modern fans.

(b) Show the children how to make a hand-operated fan. Card blades are fixed to a wheel. The wheel is fitted to a length of dowel. The dowel is pushed through holes at one end of a card tube. The other end of the tube is held in one hand and the card blades pointed towards the face. The other hand is used to spin the protruding axle.

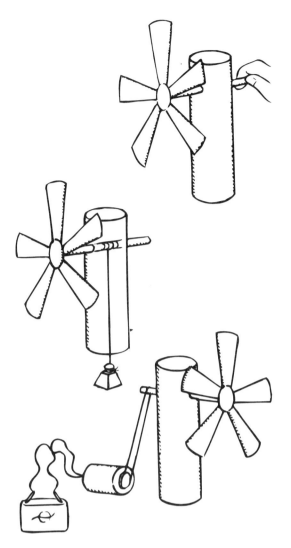

(c) *Can you make it spin by itself?* One solution is to attach a thread to the axle, wind it on to the axle, attach a weight to the other end, and allow it to fall to the floor. As it does so, it turns the fan. Another would be to use a battery-powered electric motor and a belt drive (elastic band) from the spindle to the fan axle.

Bridges

Wood and recycled materials.

(a) Look at pictures of a variety of bridges, including suspension bridges, and talk about them.

(b) Set the children a 'Bridge this gap' problem. They are to do so using their new knowledge of suspension bridges.

(c) Extend the task or make it more difficult by introducing the need to make a bridge which lets river traffic through.

The railway

Mixed materials, a variety of structures, made to a standard size.

(a) In a Transport topic, link work to the railway station or the Channel Tunnel, for instance. Describe the standard gauge of railways.

(b) As a class task, each group or person designs and makes an item for the railway. They can use reclaimed boxes for vehicle bodies, but you should emphasize the need for everyone to work to a standard gauge. You can do this by setting up two strips of wood which are the 'rails'. Any product made must fit these rails.

(c) Extend the work by having the children recall how to make shock-absorbing shapes and hence add bumpers to their vehicles. A station and/or tunnel will also be needed. There may be a need for bridges over railway lines. (See also the Victorian case study on page 152.)

Ideas bank

The book business

Children can do some research on the early days of printing and the ways in which books are made. They could print something themselves using the small kits of rubber or plastic type that are available and develop this further in word-processing practice. They might also take an old book apart and draw its components and a design plan. Explain the need for a small brochure which describes the school for parents and supply a range of small brochures for the children to examine. *Which look the most interesting and are easy to read?* Ask the children to design and make a small information brochure for parents, with the help of a word processor, if possible. Make several copies.

Planning for a school trip

Discuss what is needed on a school trip (particular clothing, footwear, bag, food, drink). Focus on each and discuss the constraints of the situation (for example, the food package must not be too heavy, it should not contain food which will deteriorate quickly, it needs to be well wrapped to keep the food clean and keep out insects). The children then design a meal with something to drink; and research the items to determine the overall size of the package. This can be extended to clothing, and other items.

A game for a long journey

Ask the children to design and make a game for a long journey. *Why is a game useful on a long journey? What should it be like: large or small; complicated or simple; a lot of small bits or a few large ones? What kind of box should it be in?*

Freewheeling vehicles

Keep a scrap box for small pieces of wood. When

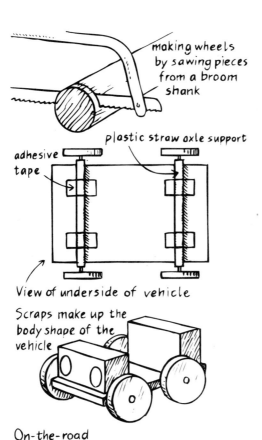

making wheels by sawing pieces from a broom shank

plastic straw axle support

adhesive tape

View of underside of vehicle

Scraps make up the body shape of the vehicle

On-the-road

enough has been collected, the children can turn the scraps into small vehicles with wheels which turn. A small piece of wood, roughly 5cm by 3cm, serves as the base (chassis). Small lengths of plastic straw will make axle supports. Dowel or toothpicks make axles. Wheels are cut from thick dowel and glued to the ends of the axles. Scraps of wood are cut and shaped to make a variety of vehicles. The activity practises the cutting, shaping and fixing of wood and some manipulative skills.

A plan for a walk

Describe an overgrown and unattractive path or disused railway line. Visit such a site, if possible. The challenge is: *Design an attractive and safe walk for the people who live nearby.* Ask the children to consider what people might like, carry out a survey, draw a plan and make a table-top model to show their proposal in three dimensions. The children should then describe their model systematically to others. You could videotape the presentation and discuss how it could be improved.

Pneumatic mechanisms

Show the action of plastic syringes (without needles) connected by tubes. Make a simple device using syringes to obtain movement (such as a cuckoo that comes out of a 'clock' face; Pinocchio with a nose that grows; a lorry that tips). Challenge the children to design and make something different which uses syringes for movement.

Fabrics in the kitchen

Design and make oven gloves. Design and make a cover for a cake or a bowl of sugar.

Case study: the Victorians

A topic on Transport or the Victorians gives an opportunity to study some engineering achievements. In particular, there is the development of the railways and the work of the Stephensons and Brunel. (Brunel also built bridges, tunnels and ships; his 'broad' gauge railway was wider than that which is now the norm in the UK). Make these research topics for the children. Point out that in Victorian times it was difficult for a woman to be an engineer or inventor, but that that has changed today.

Case study: the umbrella/parasol

An umbrella has a push–pull rod which ends in a handle. The collar is slid up the rod to push hinged struts into place. These support a framework which holds the open umbrella taut. A catch holds the collar in place when the umbrella is open. This catch also has a return mechanism attached to it. *How does it work? What parts can you name?* The children might compare the umbrella and a bats' wing.

Case study: litter bins (product design)

No doubt an occasion will present itself when the children have left litter around the classroom. Discuss the need to keep the room tidy and examine and evaluate a variety of litter bins (flap topped, pedal bins, swing tops). The children design, make and display posters which remind others to use litter bins and keep the place tidy.

Assessment

In design and technology both knowledge and skills are assessed. While a product can provide some evidence of skills, it cannot tell you everything. In particular, you need to know about designing and making skills which do not show themselves in a product. This means that you need to observe children as they work.

What do they know?

This is not closely defined but the children should know a range of simple mechanisms (for example, pneumatic devices, catches in umbrellas, conveyor belts, powered devices, rails). They should:

● know about the effect of forces on materials of different shapes and a range of structures which provide support (ribs in an umbrella) and protection (book covers);

● know some working characteristics of materials they have used and the tools used to cut and shape these materials;

● know some combinations of materials and their properties (foodstuffs, for example);

● know hazards associated with particular tools and materials they are using.

● have extended their vocabulary so that they can discuss tools, materials, and technological matters relating to products they have made and disassembled.

What can they do?

They should be able to:

● gather information and use it to generate ideas relevant to the task in hand;

● disassemble some relatively simple products and find out how they work;

● clarify and communicate their design ideas verbally, with drawings of various kinds (for example, sketch, side view) and with models;

● consider an alternative solution as a possible course of action;

● work from their own plans when making a product;

● make realistic suggestions about how to proceed and accept compromise solutions;

● generally avoid difficulties by ordering how they will work and by drawing on their knowledge of the properties of materials;

● choose materials, tools and techniques purposefully;

● use tools with increasing facility, cutting and shaping with sufficient precision for assembling the product;

● apply what they know of safe and considerate practices;

● begin to choose and apply a finish which enhances a product's appearance or feel or serves a function;

● carry out a simple evaluation of a product and, where appropriate, suggest an improvement;

● make improvements to their products.

Religious Education

RE, unlike the subjects of the National Curriculum, has to be planned from a local rather than a national document. Agreed Syllabuses differ in the way they present the programme of study but are remarkably similar in what they expect children to do in RE. It is very likely that your Agreed Syllabus expects children to:

- develop a knowledge and understanding of religious traditions;
- explore fundamental questions arising out of people's experience of life;
- develop their own ideas and values arising partly out of what they learn in RE.

In terms of continuity and progression in RE we should be helping our children to develop a systematic knowledge and understanding of some religions as well as developing their thinking about religious issues and understanding of common themes across religions which will contribute to their understanding of religion in general.

In these Yearbooks, RE is approached in one of two ways. Some topics are 'human experience' topics. These focus on a significant question or issue about life such as *Who is my neighbour*? or *Why do we celebrate?* This second question underpins the topic in this book, where children are encouraged to consider why humans need to celebrate important events in their history, both personally and communally. All religions have an annual calendar of religious festivals and some of these are explored in this chapter. However, while the religious traditions are drawn upon for examples, this chapter is based on the human experience of celebrating .

What should they be able to do?

Year 5s can be introduced to an increasing amount of information about religions. They can begin to understand that religious traditions have a history and, for believers, certain events in that history have special significance. Learning about festivals is popular in primary RE. However, without a conceptual link between festivals, teaching can degenerate into providing children with a mass of information which they cannot process in terms of the key areas of RE.

Key Stage 2 offers a good opportunity to develop children's capacity to think intelligently about religion rather than merely gather disjointed bits of information. The topic in this chapter gives children the opportunity to:

- explore the background to some festivals expressed through traditional stories and events;
- ponder on the questions of why, what and how people celebrate;
- explore the nature of religious identity and commitment through a focus on the way religious believers celebrate important defining moments in the history of their faith.

Bearing this in mind, here is a guide to what most ten-year-olds can be expected to do and understand in relation to the three key areas of RE.

Key area: Knowledge and understanding of religions

Focus two main aspects of the religious festivals included in this topic. First, as the celebrations here include the recalling of past events significant to concerned, children should be introduced to the traditional stories which underpin the festivals. In the Christian tradition, it is the stories of

Easter and Pentecost. In the Jewish tradition the Exodus story is an important part of learning about Pesach (Passover). The Sikh festival of Baisakhi recalls the story of the five faithful believers, the panj pyare, and the founding of the Khalsa by Guru Gobind Singh Ji.

The second aspect is the detail of how the festival is celebrated in both personal and community terms. This will involve appreciation of some of the feelings and experiences of those who take part in the celebrations.

Concept development is an essential component of Religious Education teaching at any level. In this key area the concepts drawn from the festivals which are specific to the religious traditions are resurrection, atonement, Eucharist (or the Lord's Supper or mass), church and holy spirit in Christianity; seder (meaning order, referring to the special Passover meal), hametz (meaning leaven from which the house must be cleaned) messiah and torah from Judaism and, from Sikhism, Khalsa (the community of the pure, baptized Sikhs), singh (title given to a male at amrit samskar, meaning lion), kaur (the female equivalent meaning princess) and amrit samskar (the rite of initiation into the Khalsa).

Sometimes children should explore the meaning of a concept from the study of religion in general rather than any one particular tradition. Such a concept is a 'symbol' and this can be explored very well in learning about these festivals.

Key area: Exploring human experience

Here it is important to help children to explore some significant concepts drawn from human experience. Because the festivals outlined above are so linked to the believers' understanding of their faith, there are two important overriding concepts which can be explored: identity and tradition. There are a variety of other concepts connected with each of the traditions studied, such as humility, sacrifice, compassion, goodness and new life associated with Easter.

In studying Pentecost, human experience concepts such as presence, change and new beginning can usefully be explored: in Pesach, concepts such as tradition, identity, community and freedom are central; for Baisakhi, important concepts are identity, purity, initiation, faith, and courage.

As well as exploring the festivals in terms of these concepts, the children can be encouraged to think about and respond to a variety of relevant questions such as *What is worth celebrating? Is it important to remember? What is worth remembering? Is it important to belong?* While these questions are important in themselves, they also form a sound basis from which the children can explore the content of the first key area.

Key area: Responding to religion and human experience

Responding to questions plays an essential role in this area. The children should be encouraged to respond personally to the types of questions outlined in the second key area. Teach them to answer such questions with statements like *I think …* or *I believe …*. This helps them to appreciate that people can respond to important questions in their own way and to develop positive attitudes such as respect for another person's point of view. Encourage the children to respect the lifestyles and concerns of people who are different from them. Such positive attitudes are essential if they are to understand fully the concepts identified in the first two key areas.

Some children may begin to be able to make connections between their own feelings about what is important in their life and how others celebrate what is important in theirs. Also, by exploring and responding to personal questions such as *In what do I believe?, To whom do I belong?, Who sets examples for me?, Who is my community?* we can enable the children to learn effectively from their encounters with the different faiths.

Most Year 5 children should be able to express their responses to what they have learned using various media and be able to take an increasingly positive part in discussions and to write at length.

Practical ideas

With all the following activities it is important to remember that you may have Jewish, Sikh and Muslim children in the class as well as Christians and you should encourage them to make a major contribution to the topic if they want to do so.

Making a start
Introducing the theme

Show the children a selection of souvenirs and mementoes that have special meaning for you, for example, something from school days, a wedding photo, your wedding ring, your degree certificate. You could, on the other hand, ask the children to bring in photos or souvenirs which help them remember something or someone special. Discuss with the children the kind of memories that are good and those that are bad. *How do memories make us feel? Sad or happy?* Make a list on a flip chart or board of things we remember that are happy (for example, birthdays) and those we remember that are sad (such as losing something or someone who has died). The class could compile a class book with writing and illustrations of happy and sad memories.

Introducing new key areas
Pesach (Passover)

● You will need a seder plate, a box of matzos, a Haggadah (a book used to retell the Exodus story). Wrap each artefact and pass them round the group asking the children to feel each one and try to describe it. When the objects have been passed around everyone, ask the children to guess what each one is. Ask different children to unwrap each one and show them to the rest of the group. Ask if anyone knows what these objects are for.

● Explain to the children that each spring Jewish people use the objects in a special 'seder' (meaning order) meal to remember a very important time in their history. It was a time when they were slaves and had no freedom. Discuss what freedom might mean and why it is important.

Read the story

Try and get hold of a shortened version of the Exodus story, or alternatively tell your own summary. It is found in Exodus: slavery of the Jews (Exodus 1 v2–22), plagues (Exodus 12 v1–42), crossing the Red Sea (Exodus 14 v21–31).

Follow up the story

Initiate a discussion using questions such as *Why do you think the Jewish people still want to remember this story? Why is it important to them? What do you think it helps them not to forget?* If possible, allow the children to taste some of the seder foods and ask them to guess which bits of the story the food reminds Jews of. For example, the matzos, dry unleavened bread, remind them of the haste with which the Jews left Egypt, horseradish of the bitter taste of slavery, and salt water of the tears of the slaves.

Prepare for Pesach

Discuss with the children occasions when we prepare for something special, for example, birthdays, holidays, school trips. *What do we do? How do we feel? How might Jewish people feel as they prepare for Pesach?* Show the children the matzos again and explain that Jewish people clean their homes before Pesach and get rid of 'hametz' (food which contains grain). Discuss why this might be so. Discuss the idea that it can represent, just as bread rises, being 'puffed up with pride'. Look in the classroom for hametz – perhaps in lunchboxes?

Make a class Haggadah

The Haggadah is the book that contains the story and is used during the seder meal. Jewish children often have a children's illustrated version. Make your own with illustrations and text from the story.

Celebrate a seder meal

Use your Haggadah and artefacts to simulate a seder meal. You might like to look up more details in any Jewish textbook. You can get good examples, including children's Haggadah's artefacts, from The Jewish Education Bureau (see page 160).

Make seder plates

Use large paper plates and have the children draw or paint in the symbolic foods and display them in the classroom.

Invite a Jewish visitor

If you do not know anyone who would be suitable, contact your local RE adviser or centre for advice.

Easter
Remembering Jesus

Introduce Easter by using the same technique with artefacts as used in the Pesach example above. This time you will need a chalice, paten, bread roll, or altar breads, bottle of wine (full or empty!). When the artefacts have been passed around and unwrapped ask the children if anyone knows what they are and who uses them. Remind the children (they may have already studied forms of Christian worship, see the Yearbook for Year 4, for example) that these objects help Christians remember Jesus, especially in church on a Sunday. Explain also that this special meal recalls the first Easter when Jesus died and, according to Christian belief, rose again.

Read the Easter story

Don't get carried away, deal with the story in three sections: first the last supper, then Good Friday and finally Easter day. Please note that there are many aspects and dimensions to Easter and you can't deal with them all.

When discussing the stories, explore what Christians remember about Jesus, look for things like love, kindness, helpfulness, peace.

Explore Easter symbols

Provide the class with artefacts including a crucifix, plain cross, bread and wine, an Easter candle. Discuss the contrasts implied in the artefacts, such as sadness and joy, good and evil, light and dark. Get the children to trace the Easter story by sequencing the artefacts, and perhaps to draw each and write a short text to explain how the artefact symbolizes each aspect of the story.

Easter and baptism

Ask the children what they know about baptism, maybe get them to bring in certificates and so on if they have been baptized. (Baptism is covered in the Yearbook for Year 2.) Look at a Paschal (Easter candle) and a baptism candle. Explain how the baptism candle is lit from the Paschal candle. Discuss the importance of this. *In what way is this another way of remembering Jesus?*

Baisakhi

Learn about the Sikh gurus

Look at pictures of the ten gurus (good examples can be bought from artefact suppliers, particularly Gohil Emporium, see page 160). Talk about Guru Nanak in terms of his message that all humans are equal and should not be divided by race, wealth or religion. You can find accessible versions of the story of his 'call' in *Leaders of Religion: Guru Nanak* by Dilwyn Hunt (Oliver and Boyd). Ask the children what people in different religions might think of Guru Nanak's message. Talk about Guru Gobind Singh (the tenth guru), in particular. It was he who founded the 'Khalsa' (the pure ones) in 1699 during the month of Baisakhi. This happened at a time when the Sikhs were suffering persecution and discrimination because of their beliefs.

Tell the story of Baisakhi

The story of Baisakhi remembers the 'panj pyare' (the faithful ones) who were willing to lay down their lives for the faith. It remembers the founding of the Khalsa and the symbols of membership: the five Ks. Read the story which can be found in *Teaching RE: Festival 5–11* published by CEM (see page 160).

The meaning of the five Ks

Divide the class into groups to look at the five K's and explore their symbolic meaning. Ask the children if they wear anything special as a sign that they belong to a group or community. (You can buy packs of the five Ks from Gohil Emporium, see Resources, on page 160.)

Symbolism in the Sikh flag

The 'khanda', the two-edged sword symbol on the Nishan Sahib, the Sikh flag, is an interesting one to explore. The double-edged sword is a symbol for divine knowledge, its sharp edges cleave truth from falsehood. The circle around the khanda is called the 'chakar' and it symbolizes God as eternal; a circle has no beginning or end. The other two swords, 'kirpans', symbolize the twin concepts of 'meeri' and 'peeri', which remind Sikhs that obligations to society, especially in 'sewa' (service) are as important as remembering God through prayer. The Guru Granth Sahib (the Sikh holy book) says that there can be no worship without good deeds.

The amrit ceremony

Sikhs who commit themselves to the Sikh code of discipline which includes not eating meat, smoking or drinking and staying faithful in sexual matters, are initiated into the Khalsa in a ceremony called 'amrit samskar'. The ceremony can take place at any time but, for obvious reasons, Baisakhi is a popular time. It usually takes place in the gurdwara and you can find full details about what happens in the CEM book mentioned above, *The Sikh World*, Daljit Singh and Angela Smith (MacDonald Young Books) and other reference books on world religions. Explore with the children any ceremonies of initiation that they have experienced, for example, the Brownie promise, first communion. Explain that Khalsa Sikhs adopt the name 'singh' (lion) if male and 'kaur' (princess) if female. Look at the children's names and find out their meanings.

Celebrate Baisakhi

Show a video of Baisakhi celebrations, for example *Believe It or Not, Video 2* which includes a programme on Sikhism and Baisakhi (available from RMEP, see page 160). Explore the meaning of the food eaten at the ceremony, and get the children to design Baisakhi cards and write descriptions of the celebration. *Why is it important for Sikhs to remember the events of the first Baisakhi?*

Hear about the Khalsa

Invite a Sikh visitor to tell you about the Khalsa. Contact your local RE adviser or an RE centre for advice.

Ideas bank

This section contains some other festivals which can be explored under the theme of celebrating a faith by remembering.

Christian Pentecost

The 'birth' of the church. Primary RE does not commonly deal with this festival but it offers an opportunity to extend this theme as well as exploring some vivid symbolism. Begin by telling or reading the story from Acts, Chapter 2. Explain that you are going to read a story from the Bible which is important for Christians because it helps them remember the birthday of the church. Tell them that this happened after the death of Jesus. Show some pictures of churches, talk about what the word 'church' means (the body of Christ, the whole community of Christians). This is not an easy story but it is worth the challenge of exploring the symbols.

Pentecost symbols

When you have read the story, show the children some examples of symbols; they can come from everyday life or you could use some of the Easter symbols. Explain that there are a number of symbols in the story and ask for responses. *What do you think the symbols such as fire and wind stand for? What do you think the holy spirit might be?*

Take an example of one symbol, perhaps water as the children should be familiar with baptism, and explain how a symbol works; for example, water sustains life and washes us clean. *Can you think of any other uses of water? Can you see how it can 'stand for' the holy spirit?* For example, as water washes us clean and helps things grow, it is responsible for change. *How were the disciples changed in the story?* Show them pictures of confirmation and Pentecostal worship which illustrate people 'receiving the spirit'. Discuss how the holy spirit might change a person who is baptized or confirmed. Then get the children to explore the Christian symbols of the spirit. These are many but can include the dove, wind, fire, breath, water. A useful source for reference is *Teaching RE: Pentecost 5–11* (CEM, see page 160) or *Christianity Topic Book 2* by Margaret Cooling (RMEP, see page 160). Make a display of the symbols, and ask the children to write a simple, explanatory text.

Symbols in a church

It is worth visiting a local church to see the symbols in context. They can be found in stained glass (the yellow) or on church banners and altar cloths.

The Salvation Army

● Look at the flag for the Salvation Army which has the inscription 'blood and fire'. (Borrow a real flag if you can.) It is full of symbolism. The dark blue of the flag stands for God the Father, the dark red for the blood of Christ, the gold star for the holy spirit. Within the badge there are the symbols of the crown, which stands for life after death; the rays of the sun, which stands for Jesus as light of the world; S, for salvation; and the sword (of truth), which represents the word of God, the Bible. Get the children to draw the flag and explain the symbols, and to find out about the origins of the Salvation Army. (It was founded in 1878 by William Booth.)

● Invite a Salvation Army officer to visit the school and show his/her uniform and talk about their caring work. Encourage the children to ask questions such as: *How is your work influenced by the Holy Spirit? What does the Holy Spirit mean to you?*

Milad al-Nabi

Although Muslims don't believe that Islam began with Muhammad – for it is an eternal religion ('din') – many do celebrate the birthday of the prophet because it was through Muhammad that God revealed the most perfect revelation contained in the Qur'an. Aspects of Muslim belief which could be explored are: the line of prophets of Islam beginning with Adam and including Moses and Jesus: the Arabic Qur'an and the importance for Muslims of not changing it or translating it; the five pillars of Islam: 'Shahada' (declaration of faith), 'Salah' (prayer), 'Sawm' (fasting during Ramadan), 'Zakat' (almsgiving), 'Hajj' (pilgrimage to Makkah).

Learning about Ramadan

Alternatively, the children could learn about

Ramadan. Concentrate on remembering the revelation of the Qur'an to the prophet Muhammad which is particularly remembered during the latter part of Ramadan, and remembering those who are poor and needy through fasting.

Invite a Muslim visitor

Ask a Muslim to talk about what Ramadan means to Muslims. Consult your local RE adviser or centre.

Resources

Artefacts, pictures and other resources are available from: Articles of Faith, Resource House, Kay Street, Bury, Lancashire BL9 6BU, Tel 0161 763 6232 (mail order); CEM, Royal Buildings, Victoria Street, Derby DE1 1GW, Tel 01332 296655; Clear Vision Trust, 16/20 Turner Street, Manchester M4 1DZ, Tel 0161 839 9579; Folens Publishers, Albert House, Apex Business Centre, Dunstable LU5 4RL, Tel 01582 472788; Gohil Emporium, 381 Stratford Road, Birmingham B11 4JZ, Tel 0121 771 3048 (mail order); The Jewish Education Bureau, 8 Westcombe Avenue, Leeds LS8 2BS, Tel 0870 7300532; The National Society RE Centre, 0171 932 1190; RMEP Tel 01603 615995; Westhill RE Centre, Westhill College, Selly Oak, Birmingham B29 6LL, Tel 0121 415 2258 (mail order).

Assessment

When you have finished this topic you will have a pretty good idea whether the children have enjoyed it. You should also be able to judge by the outcomes how much they have learned. Evaluation can take the following form.

What do they know?

There is a great deal of information which the children could have picked up. Being selective, it is possible to suggest that from this topic most children should know:
- the names of different festivals of remembering;
- the stories related to each festival;
- some of the ways in which the festivals are celebrated.

What can they do?

You can expect children in a typical Year 5 class to respond at different levels. In this topic, for example, you can expect all or most of the class to be able to:
- talk about the festivals studied and use some correct vocabulary;
- talk about some reasons why people want to remember things and celebrate them;
- handle artefacts appropriately and with sensitivity;
- express their ideas in verbal, written or visual form.

You can expect some children to:
- explain what a symbol is;
- talk about and explain some of the symbols encountered in this topic;
- explain why it is important to celebrate key events in the life of communities.

What have they experienced?

The children should have:
- listened to stories associated with festivals;
- researched aspects of religious festivals;
- handled religious artefacts associated with festivals;
- talked to a religious believer about the importance of his/her faith.

How have they made their knowledge public?

The children should have made a public display of their knowledge through discussion, writing and illustrations. They should have handled artefacts with due sensitivity and spoken to and listened to others, both classmates and visitors, in a respectful way.